JOURNEYS WITH OPEN EYES
Seeking Empathy with Strangers
by
Hugh P Roberts
ISBN: 978-0-9955729-9-7

Published by

i2i Publishing. Manchester.
www.i2ipublishing.co.uk

Contents:
Journeys with open eyes
Seeking Empathy with strangers

The Author

Hugh Roberts has spent over forty years in planning, design and development consultancy for new towns and urban, industrial and regional infrastructure. He has lived as well as worked in all six continents, working for a wide range of clients and with project colleagues of every nationality, character and humour. He is a graduate of the Universities of Oxford and Wales and his first book *'An Urban Profile of the Middle East'* was first published in 1979, then re-published in 2016.

He lives in London with his wife Sylvie. They have two adult children Mark and Shân, and one granddaughter to date, Lola.

Dedications

In the brave new world of crowd funding, covering part of the publication costs of new books, dedication pages have necessarily become a bit lengthier. The following championed my cause on the strength of a promise of one or more copies of the book once published. They were also provided with regular bulletins on funding progress (whether they wanted them or not) spiced up with the first half of various anecdotes or stories of which they can now finally read the outcome. So not quite sponsorship for a marathon, because subscribers get a book out of it (though it felt like a marathon to me occasionally).

But there is also a good cause involved with any surplus to my production costs. This will be the charity *Action for Happiness* whose patron is the Dalai Lama. I could not think of any better cause for an enterprise involved with travelling the globe, working at what I love in terms of the challenges of urban development and learning new things along the way, regardless of age. It was indeed an Action of Happiness.

Almost all of those listed are relations or good friends, leaving me in no doubt that advance sales are a loyalty call rather than conviction about brilliant writing. How could it be the latter when they have not yet read the book so have necessarily taken so much on faith? No different to picking up a book in the bookshop of course, but just as for the old ways of choosing what to read, I hope they will not be disappointed.

Falah Al Salman
Qutaiba Al Shaheen
Arta Azizi
Simon Babes
Rose Balingall
Graham Ball
Marie-Christine Banvillet
Rob Barnes
Judy Barrows
Merce & Andres Bassedas
Geoff & Madeleine Bell
Marco Bianconi
Jayne & Michael Blackwood
Rob & Nancy Blackwood
Chris Braithwaite
Fiona & Peter Butler
Marie Camille
Andrew & Louise Campbell
Paul Castle
Mariejo Chaudet
Michael Charalambous
Youssef Choucair
Lee Constantine
Ken Conway
Anne-Marie Costain
Josette & Pierre Constantini
Michelle Cottrell
Richard Crappsley
David Croom
Eric & Sophie de Branche
Rob de Jong
Roger & Penelope Dring
Andrew & Fiona Drake
Peter & Katy Dunscombe
Mary Durkin
Andrew Edkins
Jocelyn & Mark Edmonstone
Edgar Einhorn
Peter & Jenny Erlanger
Andreas Faust
Ricardo Fayet
Sylvia Findlay
Carles Fressinier
Henri Fressinier
Roger Gilmore
Neil & Olivia Goldman
Franki Gray
Kate & Klaus Groenholm
Kathleen Harris
Rob Harris
Shahram Hemmati
Jon Herbert
Charlie & Charlotta Horrell
Jo House
Monika Jakubowska
Emily Jarrett
Martina Juvara
Vasudevan Kadalayil

Andy Kirk
Angela Koch
Eve & Ted Lanigan
Nigel Lewis
Joanna Lloyd-Davies
Andrew & Kim Macleod
Peter Marsden
Will & Flick Mather
Finbar McKeogh
Nick McKeogh
Patrick & Shan McKeogh
David Mears
Paul Mews
Laura Micalizzi
Gwyn & Pat Morgan
Edgar Mourad
Faiz Nassiri
Richard & Rafaells Nicholas
Lib & Craig Nicholl
Nuriyah Noori
Colin & Sue Norman
Anthony & Cate Orr
Jeremy & Amanda Payne
Sue Payne
Lance Pierson
Mike & Marie-Pierre Polya
John & Louise Pounder
Tim Prager
David Quarmby
John & Nina Redmond
Duncan & Marilyn Reid
Liz & Vern Reid
Mark Roberts
Jordi Roca
Nuri Roca
Phillip Roos
Ann Rosenberg
Tim Scarbrough
Rachel Smyth
Yaritza & Stephane Sojo-Foucaud
Vanessa & David Southern
Phil Staveley
Ian Stephenson
Peter Stone
Jennifer & Sean Tai
Margaret & Rene Tayar
David & Julie Treacher
Phillip & Natalie van Overberghe
Guy Vincent
Martin Wedderburn
Michael West
Megan Wheeler
Jarl & Kirsten Whist
Pat & Brian Williams
Jonathan Wright
John & Rita Yadoo

There are of course others. Lionel Ross who saw the potential in my title and its contents, and his long-suffering illustrator Dino Caruana, whose patience with the cover design was equal and more to my uncertainty. Lionel is that rare being of whom a few others may still exist; a publisher with genuine interest in, and commitment to each of his authors and their work. He and I have seen eye to eye on every aspect of this effort, so his publishing house is aptly named.

Ricardo Fayet at Reedsy gave sage advice and network contacts all through the process, Scott Pack at Unbound grounded my excesses with a sober literary review, and Justine Solomons at Byte the Book was ever enthusiastic as befitted her force of nature personality. Guy Vincent in Australia, Lee Constantine, formerly of New York and subsequently Bali (he got that bit right) and Ylva Monsen in Norway shepherded my uncertainty over digital marketing and sales via Publishizer.

My immediate family - Sylvie at home with me; Mark and Laura; Shân and Patrick and their little daughter Lola, all also here in London, have tolerated a lot, as I transitioned during the writing from full-time employment to semi-retirement (now feeling like anything but). Writing this book and Sylvie's quiet advice and unflagging support helped me through the unexpected process of finding a new reason to get the brain going each day. This is now steadily being replaced by a series of pro-bono and paid consultancy commissions in UK and overseas. No one should ever stop work, but Sylvie's wise counsel to just slow it down a bit is my new objective. She is also credited with some of the most insightful photos taken while travelling, of which there are several examples in this book.

Lastly, there are the multiple characters in this book, both named and un-named all over the world, after more than fifty years in some cases, and only last week in others. My subject matter is humanity in all its forms and seeking the good in all of them. The ultimate dedication goes to the huge majority of the human race whose follies and stupidities, selfishness, cruelty and self-seeking will always be outdone by their positive nature, noble intentions and ultimate good works. They still make it a beautiful world.

Hugh Roberts
Fulham, London. March 2017

Preface: What on earth am I doing here and why?

"It is only with the heart that one can see rightly; what is essential is invisible to the eye."
Antoine de St Exupéry, The Little Prince 1943

I suppose I see places, towns and cities in particular, a bit differently to most people. As a Geographer and Town Planner, I am immediately drawn to how places work and sometimes why they don't. There is always an explanation for either state. However, it is sometimes quite hard to find, because things grow up in a particular way over centuries, then they suddenly change for one particular reason. This might be a new transport system or direction of new growth which becomes the new determinant of overall function whether good or bad. The saddest factors when a place is declining in fortunes are invariably economic, when a town's reason for being there dies, such as changes in agricultural practice, the end of coal mining or shipbuilding, and these days, climate change and susceptibility to drought or floods.

I have lived and worked in all six continents, planning for new towns, industry and urban infrastructure throughout five decades and meeting many wonderful and a few less appealing people on the way. My work has been as much social as technical, requiring at least a quest for, if not a guarantee to find, empathy with the people and places encountered.

It is always difficult to tell the inhabitants of a place why things may not be working or how they could be improved. They have lived with the problems far longer and have strong opinions based on lots of day to day evidence. Who is this newcomer and what are these theories of function and form he brings to tell us any better than we already know?

Harder still is the blank canvas, where a new community is to be built, or rather the superimposition of new land uses on old ones, because in our overcrowded world, there is never really a blank canvas. But lots of people treat new communities as if they were blank canvases, as if the climate, physical features, relative positions of other settlements, places of employment and most influential of all, value systems with which the new inhabitants will inhabit were not critical to success or failure.

The abiding appeal of geography and planning is that every urban situation is completely unique and there is never a justification for 'one size fits all'; we should only do ' bespoke'. Trouble is, and what gets planners a bad name sometimes, is that we do often apply a 'one size fits all' mentality even when not intending to, because bespoke is too complex or long-winded a solution and its implementation too expensive in a cash and time-strapped world.

But this book is not only about the theories of planning, and what makes places work or not. There is a bit of that in most chapters but it is more about what makes *people* work, together, apart or not at all, and only from my totally subjective viewpoint. I focus on individual relations in whatever part of the world I was working, though I sometimes stray into generalisations about societies as a whole just to be controversial and stimulate a response which might range from quiet agreement to its usually more vocal opposite. The result is an eclectic mix of journeys with open eyes that have taught me a lot about the world, almost all of it positive and therefore uplifting. See how you feel when you have read through to the end.

In the course of my journeys, I have been in all sorts of situations both good and bad, from inspiring to downright dangerous and I have learned something from them all. Many times, I have asked myself, 'How on earth did you get yourself into this predicament? More to the point, how are you going to get out of it? '

The predicaments vary enormously, but a lack of familiarity with an environment is always a risk. You stand out like a sore thumb and your persona probably lights up in the crowd to the beady eye of those intent on mischief. To pick one situation at random, that is how my nightmare in Delhi started after losing my passport and mobile phone to a professional pick-pocket routine. I would have admired the choreographed professionalism of it all, if it had not caused me such bureaucratic grief.

Getting off the train from Chandigarh, the eager porters were grabbing bags from the luggage racks to lift them down to the platform. Chasing anxiously after them, my attention was focused away from my little backpack where resided most of my precious possessions suitably zipped up as I thought. All except my wallet that is – that was down my underpants and hopefully thus a no-go area. The bags were safely returned to us on the platform, so after the compulsory tipping, we relaxed into a taxi for the journey to our hotel. Only on check-in at hotel reception did the critical disappearances from my backpack reveal themselves – passport and mobile phone gone! Absence of identity documentation, together with their all-important entry and exit visas, without which you are almost literally non-existent, together with the absence of a means to communicate about it by phone, are not a good combination in India.

With a tightly defined itinerary abandoned, the next day was re-scheduled for queuing at the British High

Commission for a temporary (cheap cream cardboard) passport, then the Indian Interior Immigration department for new Entry and Exit visas. While the former offered limited tea and sympathy and a wait of merely an hour, the latter did not. Indian Immigration departments are not for the fainthearted or those of an impatient disposition. I had eight long hours in which to savour aspects of the many human frailties on show.

I may not have liked it much at the time, but the experience taught me so much about human nature, now stored in my memory for future use. There was after all little else to do during the interminable and otherwise mindless waiting times, other than to watch, listen and learn from my fellow sufferers and those in charge, as we all endured the process of identity re-instatement. Of course, the objective was keeping India safe from illicit entry and exit and the terrorism that doubtless lurked beneath its surface, all lost if bureaucratic vigilance was not being observed. Vigilance was minutely observed as only the Indian Civil Service knows how.

Name anywhere I have lived or worked throughout the world and there has been time enough for a bizarre situation – life threatening sometimes, mildly dangerous more often, but almost always revelatory. Let me list a few.

- Left on a sand spit in the middle of the Pacific Ocean with the tide coming in, while our boatman disappeared over the horizon *'in search of a better island for our picnic!'*.

- In the middle of the 1970's Rhodesian Bush War, left at passport control on the South Africa border by my gun-running mercenary driver, hoping he would remember to come back and pick me up.

- Lost on my first cross-country solo flight over the English Midlands with a line squall obliterating all visibility and no radio contact to seek help or direction.

- Two months before the revolution against the Shah of Iran, questioned in Isfahan Airport by the Iranian secret police about having someone else's airline ticket.

- Walking through dry desert bush in west Australia and coming one pace from treading on a deadly poisonous Tiger snake.

- Stuck in Kuwait's Al Wufrah Desert with wheels in soft sand in mid-August at over 50 degrees Centigrade.

- *"Helping the Peruvian police with their enquiries"* just off the Lake Titicaca overnight ferry from Bolivia after an attempted murder in the next-door cabin

- Just 18 months after the 1968 'Prague Spring' in Czechoslovakia, retracing steps through a minefield at the German/ Czech border crossing having been refused entry by Russian soldiers.

- Regardless of being British, receiving call-up papers from the New York State draft board for the US military; *'Status 1A'* = Boot Camp then straight to Viet Nam.

- Invited by its patron into a La Paz brothel, asking some of the girls what they were doing with their lives, and being assured they, their boyfriends and husbands were all happy they were their families' main money earners. And would I like to go upstairs with one of them?

These delicate predicaments help me now, in some cases many years later, to remember a particular journey bringing one of its unique features vividly to life again. A lot of self-survival instinct was in play, providing a vivid backdrop to a place and its people. But building lasting impressions takes more time. Deeper feelings about people and places are constructed from experience that reveals itself more gently; the kindness or otherwise of strangers, familiar or unfamiliar reactions to an unexpected situation, and the humour - always the humour - with which people cope with everyday life, from the tragic to mundane by way of the downright farcical.

That is what this book is really about; wondrous impressions of the world through lots of long journeys, learning something from each particularly about empathy with strangers, and either finding it to warm the heart, or not finding it, disappointingly but often more insightfully about what makes people tick. We glean as much from negatives as positives; learning from mistakes perhaps. And much of what we are, evolves from what we are not.

The enduring appeal of empathy is that there are no rules about when, where or how you will find it. I had my passport and mobile phone stolen in India, so almost literally lost my bureaucratic identity. But my eight hours with the Indian Immigration officials was comparatively relaxed and friendly - from their point of view that is, contrasting with many of the stressed-out supplicants in front of them, such as myself. This probably owed something to there being a cricket match on the wall-mounted TV, and India were winning.

Context is everything. It revealed more about Indian culture than the foreigners in front of them. Officials rarely raise their voices or lose their calm exterior despite many provocations. The victims of loss of identity understandably revealed much more of themselves under stress, and the stories I heard about how people had lost their passports put my Delhi based experience into focus. There had been violent muggings, people left stranded hundreds of miles from the capital, requiring them to beg, borrow or steal their way to Immigration in Delhi. For them no amount of a calm bureaucrat's demeanour would ever be sufficient compensation for their misfortune, and they were not going to let off lightly anyone deemed responsible by association for their situation. This was a fascinating exercise in human psychology at work during which I no choice but to study and learn while I endured the same delay. I ended up feeling enriched by the experience of the loss of my passport. Strange world!

Chapters are arranged geographically, though not to imply similarity between national or cultural neighbours. Understanding and empathy is more elusive than that. Most explore aspects of my work as a Planner within major development projects in each country over more than forty years, providing a mix of social and anthropological observation about people and communities for whom I had been commissioned to implement new towns, industrial complexes and/or urban infrastructure generally. But the projects are the backdrop, not the main feature of the book, which looks principally at the people I met and managed to connect with, or otherwise

There are a couple of exceptions. One chapter deals with learning to fly - a mental as well as physical journey covering a lot of ground fast, testing one's ability to operate in a strange environment, spurred by others on the same learning journey. Another chapter Island Postcards looks at the geographical individuality of offshore places, chosen from all over the world to compare them with nearby 'main lands'. There is a special 'otherness' about islands and they share insular characteristics regardless of location. Being microcosms of the human state, they were nice to catalogue in a collective way on their own.

The book probes human behaviour, governed as much by moods as by the physical or social environments I wrote about at the start of this preface. Enriching my life experience as a visitor as well as a planner, has owed a lot to good fortune. But it has also been testimony that a smile or laughter will likely get you through strange situations or out of trouble, more often than not. There is always more to be gained through sugar than vinegar.

Despite so many mishaps - no, because of them! – and because of my fascination in the work I have done over more than forty years, the world remains for me a beautiful place and its people worthy of it. Empathy found? I think so, but not always as expected!

Chapter 1 Journeys through a Child's Eyes

"The greatest secrets are always hidden in the most unlikely places."
Roald Dahl: Charlie and the Chocolate Factory 1964

In a small Welsh country town like Haverfordwest six and seven year olds born in the 1950's usually walked home from school; unusual today, normal back then. The walk was about a mile and a half, the first part through town along Bridge Street passing Toms' Toyshop window with its range of model cars and planes to save pocket money towards or wish for at Christmas. The second half was through Cartlett, past Mr Ellis's grocery emporium (Telephone: Haverfordwest 7) where, with enough pennies, we might buy a sherbet fountain, then up the hill, over the New Road railway bridge. If we were lucky, the 4.30 to Milford Haven would be leaving the station and enveloping the bridge with steam. After watching it out of sight over the river and round the curve to Merlin's Bridge, we could go home, smelling sweetly of coal dust.

The last half-mile passed houses and bungalows set in their neat little gardens with names like The Lindens (unimaginative) St. Saëns (a French composer, very posh), or Crud y Gwynt (Cradle the wind, 'ah the romance of Welsh!'). Suburbia Welsh style, described as *'tidy'* in the soft lilting Pembrokeshire vernacular. This last part of the journey offered two contrasts. On Tuesday and Friday market days, we might catch up with Old Stevo with his horse and cart. If you were quick, you could jump up behind and ride on the large white sack of grain for the last part of the journey. The cart had rusty red peeling paint and wooden wheels as tall as the cart itself, already by the late 1950's a relic of a bye-gone age. Old Stevo seemed not to mind our intrusion but he never spoke to us and we had to jump on and off as the horse plodded homeward. People said he lived at a small place called Old Ovens but we never went there. Nearly sixty years later on Google Earth, I can only make out a small cluster of ruined buildings in trees, a field away down an overgrown track off the Rhos Road. The place must have died with Stevo a few years later. He did not seem to have to drive the horse; it knew the way on its own. The two of them seemed to live in perfect harmony – Stevo went down to town twice a week to get grain for the horse and the horse pulled the cart back home. I doubt much farming took place at Old Ovens.

The second possibility walking home was confrontation with our two neighbourhood bullies, JD and his older, more menacing friend NJ. At first, they just offered mild harassment, but one winter, after NJ hit Jayne my big sister, with a snowball containing a stone, things got a bit worse. It still only amounted to harsh words and a bit of pushing around, but with Shân, my next-door neighbour and school contemporary, 1950's gender stereotypes were no barrier; she would give as good as me in the oral reply stakes usually around what our Dads would do to them if JD and NJ *'carried on'*. One day JD was on his own so we invited him home to see my new train set. Then, with the added courage of walking down my own driveway, I bashed him - just once and not really very hard – more of a shove really. Away from the familiar ground outside his own front gate, he ran home crying. While we got a severe talking to, the bullying stopped after that. Even in little country towns, you have to deal with some threats on your own.

Cars in the 1950's seemed heavier and slower than later on, especially my Dad's Vauxhall Wyvern. Roads were often tortuously slow, with tractors and trailers on our country roads and diesel spewing underpowered lorries on the bigger national highways, few of which had adequate passing places. We went once to London, in 1957 I think, for my Mum to see a back specialist. It took most of three days to get there with two nights in hotels on the way – Brecon the first night because Dad could only get off work late afternoon, then Pangbourne the second night after crossing the old Aust ferry out of Wales to England – no Severn Estuary Bridge before 1965 never mind its successor more recently - to follow the A4 across Wiltshire before the assault on London up the Great West Road on the third day. What a revelation of urbanisation to a small country boy!

The battle between parochialism and metropolitanism, is pretty much universal to all cultures – country boys and girls mistrust city slickers and the latter see us as hayseeds, with straw in our hair and not much else between the ears. How wrong we both are! A lovely local story captures the contrasts. A lorry driver from Llangwm (regarded by we metropolitans from nearby Haverfordwest as hayseeds under the above definition) was asked to take bedding straw and hay from a local farm to London for the pre-Christmas Smithfield show, because the cattle would naturally be stressed if they did not have their own grass to eat and sleep on at night. Setting off up the A40 and arriving in Carmarthen thirty miles up the road, Ianto (for that was his name) marvelled at the big buildings and asked if he had reached London. *"No,"* came the reply, *"A48, over by there!"*. Same thing happened in Swansea the next big town, where the A48 eastwards was more or less politely pointed out. Ianto repeated his wide-eyed enquiry in Cardiff then again onwards through Gloucester and smaller English country towns until at last, he reached the edge of the great metropolis. On being told he was nearly there, he replied with relief *'Oh great, where do you want the hay?"*

You will only be amused by this if you were brought up deep in the country or have learned to love it since. Its gentle humour still gets to me. That animals would be stressed without their own grass to eat and hay to sleep on is entirely plausible. It is probably better than the punch line, which reveals that we are all more or less on a voyage of discovery.

All that parochialism started changing for me in September 1959. At the grand age of eight 'going on nine', I prepared to undertake my first train journey alone, away to boarding school – well alone apart from my big sister of nearly thirteen who would be on the same train but a separate carriage slowly filling up with girls, going further than me to her own school, with the insouciant air of the well-travelled sophisticate. I was proud to be *'on my own'* for the first time, dressed in stiff, new, grey woollen uniform, and with strict instructions not to talk to strangers on the way, to get off at the right station and introduce myself properly at the other end!

'My parents', as I was soon to learn to refer to them at school, relented and drove us the first one hundred miles to Cardiff. It was the biggest noisiest station I had ever seen. Steam trains were everywhere, with their bitter tang of coal dust in the air like on that New Road Bridge, a smell that comes back to me over nearly six decades later. I could not wait for the train to start, but the fact that we were boarding one of those new-fangled diesels apparently without an engine, did not bother me much. At least I would not have to slide back the door to an old-fashioned compartment of eight seats and invariably seven older passengers, all of them weird, to sit in silence waiting for someone to cough, get out a revolting sandwich or, horror of horrors, offer a boiled sweet with an unctuous smile. Just say, "*no thank you*," were my Mum's instructions.

These were the stiff upper-lipped 1950's, so tears were held back on both sides when it came time to part. As the train crawled out of Cardiff, some of life's harsher realities crowded in. Being on my own might not be so much fun with much to learn and no one trusted to turn to. I often reflect now that much of people's stress is born from the unfamiliar, not knowing what to expect and worse still, how to react to it. Happy is the person who welcomes uncertainty with open arms, but are they truly at ease with life, or even themselves? Not at aged eight going on nine.

The train gained speed slowly, crossing each set of points with that comforting and timpanic clickety-click, a sound to become so familiar in future years. It still sends me to sleep even now. We progressed up the line through Newport and Pontypool Road (*'why not the place itself?'* I thought) towards Hereford. Boys slightly older than me, wearing the same or slightly different uniforms boarded the train after saying farewell to similarly tear-suppressed mothers. The new arrivals did not acknowledge me, nor I them. I was new so that was understandable, but they did not talk to each other either, which initially seemed strange. Later experience taught me that this was the adjustment period from home to school. We all needed time to adjust, and no one was quite ready to dive back into school life so soon after saying goodbye to that long lost Indian summer of 1959.

It was all change from Hereford, after the Chester and Shrewsbury train joined ours, together with a noisy lot evidently back in raucous school mode, and ready to embarrass everyone with their fooling around. One larger than life character of maybe eleven or twelve, later my occasional nemesis for a couple of years, before his merciful departure aged thirteen, took control of the whole open plan compartment for the last twenty miles, throwing boiled sweets deliberately at, rather than to, his friends, and looking theatrically hurt when they protested because he had pinged them on the forehead, when he was *only trying to be give them a sweet'*.

More interesting were the reactions of these so-called 'friends'. One or two suffered the indignity of being pinged for the benefit of recognition and getting a free sweet, behaving like faithful lapdogs for the purposes of this cheap street theatre. Others affected indifference until pinged then ate the sweet anyway. Only one threw the sweet back - but unfortunately missed, offering me another life lesson – there is rarely justice when you need it, timing and context being everything.

This taught me something about how to read such a situation. I had little sympathy with the sweet thrower's fawning toadies always waiting for the next free gift regardless of the indignity. Those who ignored the sweet thrower and took life as it came, would not be pushed around and they seemed like the ones to get to know. But most interesting of all was the budding bully himself. He had apparently brought a complete bag of unopened boiled sweets with him onto the train, avoiding the temptation and pleasure of eating any beforehand, preferring the gratification of other people's reactions to his throwing performance. He probably also pulled wings off flies.

No sweet was thrown at me. Despite the grey and green uniform identifying us all, I was obviously beneath contempt as a new boy, and an implied invitation to join 'his' fun was not on the agenda. Thank goodness, I thought; I won't have to decide on toadyism, letting things be or serious defiance. Now I know that types like this exist everywhere – always pursuing their own agenda, pleased to raise a bit of hell and usually best avoided. I have not always been successful, but this was an early experience of reading a situation – empathy by any definition, and the rapid necessity to acquire it.

My sister had long since retreated to a compartment full of similarly certifiable girls, putting her totally out of bounds to me. After her dutiful but sympathetically discreet check that I knew the right place to get off, I found myself on the platform of the little village halt of Colwall, under the looming Malvern Hills away to the east in the gathering dusk. A bit like someone from a motorised Charles Dickens' novel, Mr Banford the kindly caretaker was there to meet me, to drive me in the school's ageing grey Land Rover the couple of miles to The Downs School, my destination each term for the next four and a half years. As the only new boy off the Cardiff train, it seemed the rest of the crowd had to walk or catch a bus. Children were expected to develop their independence back then.

For the new boys, there was a cream tea (with light blue Bakelite teacups rattling in their saucers that I can hear to this day), a luxury sadly not repeated again until the end of term, thirteen weeks later, before Christmas. There was a bedtime story in dressing gowns, followed by bed in a small dormitory next to five others. Clad in thick Winceyette pyjamas under 1950's Witney blankets, this was the first private time to shed a quiet tear for whom and what we had left behind at home, and a future not yet revealed. Later in life, Mum told me she also shed a quiet tear that night too.

Lots of theories abound these days, that sending children off to boarding school at eight or nine is to risk psychological damage which may only come out in later life. It is claimed that to be pulled from the warm embrace of a loving family and placed in a community where displays of love are actively discouraged, is to present a child with a lasting sense of rejection.

Most people seemed to cope happily enough, secure in the knowledge that parents were only a letter (compulsory on Sunday afternoons) or a weekend visit away. It is true that I saw a few examples of boys (sadly no girls at my schools in the 1950's and '60's) who should not have been there. They usually displayed a lack of self-confidence in who and what they were rather than the opposite, and a consequent inability to cope with the harsher aspects of an institutional way of life. One or two of these lost souls were close friends I recall, as their 'otherness' was sometimes appealing. I was fairly conventional myself, but always curious about how others might see the world differently to the common herd. The herd thundered on regardless.

The worst examples of this condition of 'otherness' were occasional needling or bating of those who seemed not to fit in. Those who could not control their emotions and lashed out verbally or physically at any provocation became the most usual focus for torment. Open confrontation was rare, subtle wheedling to induce a temper tantrum much more common. When someone lost control (it was usually the same culprits doing the bating and victims succumbing to it) it was seen as the best of spectator sports. We were fascinated by the destructive power of bad temper as chairs were thrown and desks upended in a classroom, or beds upended in the dormitory.

Yet, over nine years between 1959 and 1968, I do not recall ever witnessing overt physical violence. At The Downs, neither boxing nor any martial arts were taught nor encouraged in a school founded by the Cadbury family, well known for their Quaker pacifist values, including sometimes heroic lifesaving deeds in war. Later at public school in Malvern, there was a boxing competition for which my housemaster enrolled me without asking me first, but I broke my collar bone playing rugby the week before the boxing lessons were due to start. That thwarted him successfully; I think he reckoned I broke the bone on purpose, but the next year, boxing was off the syllabus altogether. The softer '60's were taking hold.

However mental bullying was much more common and like all schools anywhere, learning how to cope was vital. I believe that doing so away from regular parental influence is an advantage in the long run. Even if they are closer to hand, parents can do so little for you as you work through the mental stress alone. Telling them of the torment is its own barrier. So, a boarding education is as good an environment as any for this painful rite of passage, and with sympathetic friends or even unexpected allies revealing themselves in support, it may be more effective than most. Bullying requires both culprits and victims, and what I have observed over many years since school, is that both bullies and bullied are culprits and victims in equal measure. A strange psychology seems to work among the worst victims of bullying which invites their condition; a defiant individualism attracting the attention of those seeking to make them conform. They do not know how to let the provocation bounce off, either with humour or confrontation. Mild resistance would usually be enough, resigned acquiescence never. Watching the bully in these circumstances was equally fascinating; he could not help himself as he sought new victims for the process to be repeated until stronger authority intervened. Almost all bullies are cowards and they play to a gallery.

It does now seem odd that aged nine during my first term away, I spent the next thirteen weeks until Christmas 1959 with only three visits from Mum and Dad. These included a half term in which they stayed in a nearby hotel. I was allowed out to see them after the Saturday afternoon rugby match and then for breakfast and lunch on Sunday - after morning service of course. With minor relaxations as time went on, that became a norm for the next nine years until leaving Malvern in 1968; it never seemed unusual.

Freedoms from school to go home mid-term have now changed significantly, but this separation from parents was not odd in the 1960's. People were generally happy within the framework of their friendships. If you came from a loving home, it certainly made for extra pleasure to go home for Christmas or Easter holidays or the long summer break. Journeys home at the end of term were a special joy, as you slowly transitioned from the institutional to the personal realm. I was usually the last green cap off the train by Haverfordwest, only two stops from there to the end of the line at Milford Haven. The last few miles through Whitland, Clunderwen and Clarbeston Road were always the most delicious, rehearsing stories from school term experience as much as thirteen weeks long. With so much to talk about that was just yours to relate, not something already shared, there was a sense of growing up in your own space as well as that of supportive parents looking on from occasional distance. For kids from unhappy homes, it was doubtless very different, but at least they had an alternate frame of reference on life for much of the time. That much would have been consolation.

Eight to nine months of separation annually from the rest of one's family avoided the over familiarity which sometimes blights relationships between parents and children growing up. Holidays away from home, usually in the spring or summer were not therefore accompanied by a foreboding of enforced incarceration at the hands of domineering adults; for me at least, there was a sense of the younger and older generations getting on with each other but from their own space.

Family holidays were necessarily long car journey affairs living as we did a good distance from the main accesses to continental Europe. Pembrokeshire offered all the seaside opportunities imaginable but my Mum, in particular, insisted on our getting exposure to foreign countries and cultures, including France, Germany and Italy as well as the easier to reach Ireland, both north and south.

The enforced automotive enclosure necessary to get anywhere from where we lived provided endless opportunities for conversation on all and any topics imaginable, the objectives of which were to listen and learn, but also to play successive rounds of 'scoring points without winning'. This required each player to expose all the others to the silliest of schoolroom jokes, the riskier or more lavatorial the better, just short of the point of being told off, or to catch each other out with inconsistencies in what had been said previously on a former topic. The rules were made up as we went along, subjects ranging from simple 'I Spy' through 'Simon Says' to what to say to Germans on the beach in Italy after they had lost the World Cup final in 1966. I recall my Dad reading a phrase book in Dutch as we drove into Amsterdam, so he would know to ask where were the toilets. We wept with laughter trying to pronounce unpronounceable phrases, translating them all plaintively as, "where's the lavee?" in a cod version of a Welsh accent; definitely not adult humour, but our way of dealing with a mildly new and strange environment.

My Mum had a convertible Morris Minor in the early 1960's and it brought smiles to peoples' faces when racier models might have invited envy. It seemed especially popular in Ireland, perhaps because it was dark green and Jayne and I would defy parental advice by riding on the open hood with our backs against the suitcase rack on the boot lid. We became adept at getting the roof up and down, especially in Ireland as rain showers were frequent but pretty benign – hence that lovely Irish phrase *'soft weather'* meaning light drizzle as if it were *'not really raining at all'*. No seat belts, no radio and a maximum of sixty mph downhill with a following wind, this was basic motoring, but it was carefree and that little car kept going for well over two hundred miles on each fill of the six-gallon capacity petrol tank.

It is worth reflecting what those innocent family travels in tiny cars and far off days, brought to a growing child. Living half the year away from a happy home, fairly remote from the mainstream of current affairs, the filter of parental guidance brought through travel was critical to forming judgments. What responsibility this puts on parents - not to dump their prejudices on their children, but rather to leave them curious and with their own enquiring mind. The best epitaph on a gravestone I once saw was, *"Interesting, but also interested"*.

Being a small boy with sometimes obtuse thought processes, the strangest things occurred to me as differences between home and abroad. In France, this took the form of fascination with the local makes of cars and lorries. Just off the Cambrian Airways Viscount into the tiny terminal at Le Bourget in 1961, I remember staring at the taxi queue with all its incomprehensible conversation and strange French cars coming and going – Panhards, Simcas, Peugeots and Citroens. I had never seen their like in distant Pembrokeshire, deeply conservative in its preference for British makes. Like most small boys at the time, I could identify pretty well every British make, but these were French! I recall thinking that failure to recognize car types might be nearly as serious as not being able to speak the language. How could I possibly relate to things here – no language and no car recognition! It was all very strange; unsettling but fascinating.

Apart from post and telephone boxes, familiarly shaped but painted green, Ireland had taken up in the 1920's what seemed like the remains of the British number plate allocation, all the 'I's' and 'Z's' presumably disdained in Britain in case they were mistaken for 1's and 2's. I used to know all the county registration plates in Wales and quite a few across England; 'DE' for Pembrokeshire so 626 ADE for Mum's Morris Minor. So, you knew where people were from, especially in Ireland where there were fewer permutations to choose from. All change now of course, no one knows or seems to care where cars or their occupants are from.

In Germany and Italy, the contrasts in motorway design intrigued me. German autobahns were straight and usually flat, carving recent command economy new lines across the landscape, thus affording scope for unimaginable speeds for the cars that could do them. Italian drivers seemed just as fast, but their autostradas were sinuous, caressing the mountainsides and crossing deep ravines on gracefully engineered long bridges. Dad suggested to mild admonition from Mum, that Italian engineers were more romantic than the Germans, imagining themselves to be stroking the curves of a woman's body. I thought a lot about that aged fourteen – as you would. Does landscape help shape personality? British and French roads meanwhile were still in the pre-motorway stage with our old 'Trunk' or A roads or their Routes Nationales, both offering a scary middle passing lane on the straighter sections, for those prepared to play chicken with traffic doing the same in the opposite direction. The few stretches of motorway such as the M4 immediately west of London or the M50 connecting Welsh steel plate with Birmingham car making, were lingered over for their fast, smooth rides, rather negating their purpose for speedy travel.

I remember the food, especially in France and Italy as a revelation compared with school food or even most restaurants in Britain. Neither France nor Italy appeared better off than us, but we in Britain seemed to be living with colourless fare when compared with the wonderful things that could be done with their recipes. Cured ham and saucissons, Mediterranean fish, crème brulee, meringues vacherins, mushroom omelettes, and… petits pois! I recall one evening being asked by a pompous headwaiter, "*Parlez vous Francais, monsieur?*" and replying "*Oui, un petit pois*". For once, I hated the fact that everyone thought I had made a joke, but I kept quiet rather than admitting my mistake.

I recall in France and the Belgian Ardennes, my Dad slowly reliving military memories ahead of his part in the British retreat to Dunkerque in 1940, and his vivid imagining of far worse, as he described what it must have been like for his own father's generation before his untimely death in 1916. It was hard to get Dad to speak of his war, going backwards through France, then forwards again through North Africa, Italy and Austria. But confronted with the physical evidence of where he had been, his reticence was gradually replaced with vivid descriptions even of the most mundane aspects of life in a field regiment of the Royal Artillery. I recall thinking that he had so much more experience of life – and death – than me, but his sense of the ridiculous reflected army life as vividly as the shorter sharper periods when things were life threatening. It made it all seem more bearable, but how could I know?

Going back to school after such family holidays provided lots to talk about and compare with others. People seemed less inclined in those days to want to trump your story or better your experience with their own up to age thirteen at any rate. We listened and learned as well as broadcast our own stories. Perhaps we have become more blasé about travels and the impressions they offer. The world is getting smaller.

Sex was a slowly dawning surprise in an all-male institution. Again, as for violent bullying, I was not subject to, nor witnessed others making homosexual advances over nine years of boarding school. There was from the age of thirteen, plenty of stern lecturing about such matters, but also a homophobic horror of the imagined acts and implications. We needed little official sanction to be repelled. Now we are more socially tolerant and accepting of homosexuality, it would be interesting to know how co-educational boarding schools cope with the different implications between youthful heterosexual and homosexual relations as they develop. They are probably both discouraged vigorously between teenagers, but I suspect that like the freewheeling late 1960's, most teens would now regard a heterosexual relationship as a badge of honour, while the homosexual variety would be a far more complicated challenge to school authority.

We were so physically removed from the company of girls that they became exotic creatures apart from our real world; an unattainable mirage. Many of us had sisters of course, to remind us that girls were only (merely?) human. But, on the whole, they became exotic objects of wistful longing such that any contact with them via chance encounters walking on the Malvern Hills or the occasional shy exchange of letters, were plotted and worried over for days previously. Anxious anticipation of these encounters remains a vivid memory even fifty years later. If empathy is a way of understanding what others are thinking in a given situation, pursuit of the opposite sex is where most young people acquire it fastest.

I recall with bitterness having written to one girl I knew of at one of the Malvern schools, seeking a Sunday afternoon tryst or a much riskier midnight equivalent, only to have my letter presented to me a week later by my housemaster, it having been passed to her school's headmistress first. I knew something of the reputation of this girl as a party lover, (which of course is why I was writing), but I had not bargained with her shopping me to the authorities and seeking much-needed credit with her school hierarchy for previous misdemeanours. The housemaster was wise enough to leave the exposure of this action as the sole sanction against my intended meetings. They never happened.

I viewed certain women with greater care after that, but there were always two target-rich opportunities for meeting girls on a less casual and passing basis. The first was the regular choir practices for 4-part harmony Oratorios such as Elgar's Dream of Gerontius, performed with Malvern Girls' College in the town's Priory Abbey in

1966 and Handel's Messiah the following year. These attracted far more volunteers than anything generated from natural musical talent. Those possessing less than perfect pitch kept quiet while they stared dreamily at the sopranos and altos.

The second was richer still – joint school plays! There were two with which to get involved – Jean Anouilh's Becket in 1966 and Dylan Thomas's Under Milk Wood in '67 with girls from the neighbouring Ellerslie, now subsumed into Malvern's co-educational boarding system. Boys and girls together in the same school! How things must have changed, but in 1967, Ellerslie like the other five girls' schools in Malvern was off limits to us - except for the School Play!

Teaching demure English maidens how to speak like Welsh fishwives was a particular pleasure. Despite being able to produce the best (by 1967 for some reason, pretty much the only) Welsh accent in school, I only had a small walk-on part (as *Fourth Drowned "Alfred Pomeroy Jones, Sea Captain"*). But I was also appointed Stage Manager. If you want the run of a play without the overall responsibility for its production, stage management is your thing, especially when there are lots of scene changes and props for each actor. Under Milk Wood ticked all those boxes. It gave me freedom to roam the Winter Gardens stage, back-of-house, lighting, sound effects and props departments at will, including, by accident or choice, the dressing-rooms. Despite the segregation, there were encouragingly large numbers of girls in the cast and their screaming sense of fun was intoxicating compared with the studied cool of most of the male actors. At last! Here was real exposure to actual people of the female persuasion. I have all their end of the play signatures together with treasured hugs and kisses written either genuinely or ingenuously in my copy of the play to this day.

By 1967/8 with testosterone running rampant round our teenage anatomies, egged on by the then permissive society in full flow out in the real world, the same housemaster who had roasted me for making inappropriate advances to a not-so-innocent object of desire the previous year, had to yield to our indignant demands that we could hold an end of term Saturday night party for some of the girls we now knew from Under Milk Wood. We blacked out the Prefects' Common Room windows, found candles and coloured light bulbs (red naturally) and planned the music with military precision – Beach Boys, Beatles and Byrds - all the B's - to afford the right romantic atmosphere for anticipated furtive gropings in the semi-dark. It all seemed pretty tame by the eleven-pm curfew time, but was analysed and 'post-mortem'ed' over endlessly during those final contented days of term.

The boarding life certainly taught early age independence of spirit and a capacity to cope from age nine onwards with such things as changing trains on busy railway stations and not talking to strangers. This does now seem odd in the era of helicopter parenting; not so much the separation from parents but rather the freedom to be out in the public domain at such a young age. Life has changed so much and not always for the better, though I feel that as parents we have been much closer to our children, a fact shyly acknowledged by ours in their older age.

Mum and Dad's crucial choice of first boarding school had much to do with my happy memories of boyhood aged nine to thirteen; it was far more Swallows and Amazons than Tom Brown's Schooldays, though it did include daily cold showers and freezing open-windowed dormitories even in January – especially in 1963 when there was snow on the ground for over six weeks. I am lucky not to be looking back on worse. Teenage years in Malvern brought many of the attendant hang-ups and self-doubt, not to mention the acne of puberty – both mental and sebaceous. But there were also happy and often hilarious times, of the sort that National Service might have brought to a previous generation not exposed to life away from home albeit at a less tender age. Taken as a whole, it was a rich experience, and cost the government nothing. Thanks Dad!

These first impressionable journeys to, from and during school days – the first away from home alone – set the scene for the others to follow. Maybe though, it is the one journey that is still going on - the one about growing up, learning from everything you see on the way and moving on a little wiser. You never stop learning, but maybe you never stop 'growing up' either, and more important, acquiring the empathy with new situations which makes each so meaningful. It is that journey in life that you travel maybe some of the way with others but mostly on your own, and you must make of it what you will. That is not depressing – being alone is very different from being lonely, and empathy with your surroundings can be your close companion. So, this first great impression of the life beyond a cosy family was just the curtain raiser for what was to follow.

Author aged 10 at school

Mum, Jayne and I, in Paris in 1961 (why did I have to wear school uniform?) With George Gamblin married to Mum's school friend Barbara from North Wales. Dad must have been the photographer. By the time this photo was taken, I had identified the car on the Champs Elysées as a Peugeot 403. I was to encounter many of these ageing models fifteen years later in Algeria.

Chapter 2 Summer of '69, the Great American Road Trip

Kiwanis Summer Camp Bunk 4 hiking chant for their campout night, Catskill Mountains
Massachusetts June 1969

1. "I don't know wot you been told, but Bunk 4 is as good as gold!
Sound Off: One, two!
Take it on down: Three, Four! (repeat all the way to 16)

2. We got Counsellors One, two three!
They ain't pretty like you and me!
Sound Off etc.

3. We got Nature Boy and he's ok, he chases bugs all the livelong day
Sound Off etc.

4. We got Dieter from Germany, he ain't no Nazi, but he's mean to me!
Sound off etc.

5. We got Hugh, he's from En-ger-land. Speaks kind of posh but got no rock band!
Sound off, Take it on Down" etc.

The Preseli Mountains of north Pembrokeshire are the last point of Britain overflown by airplanes heading for the United States or Canada. From there, on a clear summer evening, you can follow their jet trails when they reach cruising height out of Heathrow over the west of England somewhere; all the way to when they sink into the far west over the Atlantic with the setting sun - white when you first see them, pink shading to a darker red as they disappear over the western horizon on a clear evening. I calculate they are visible for over three hundred miles or fully forty-five minutes at an airspeed of five hundred knots. They change direction over the navigation beacon at Strumble Head west of Fishguard, so Pembrokeshire sets their course – a bigger navigational deal in the 1940's and '50's than in 1969, but still a romantic indicator for my first long distance destination. How could I go anywhere else?

Aged 18, I walked those Preseli hills imagining the destinations of those airline passengers and wishing to be going there with them. Rural life was just too limiting for me; "Got to Get Away", as in Georgie Fame's hit song that year. Hippie songs from Haight Ashbury's summer of love such as Bob Lind's "Bright Elusive Butterfly of Love" beckoned me westwards, but also Glenn Campbell's Wichita Line Man to which I hummed myself to sleep that early summer of imminent liberation. After all, if spaced out hippies and buttoned down telephone linesmen could both sing about finding love either through a butterfly net or a phone wire, there must be something out there worth going to see. I just had to 'go empathize' – US phrase, US spelling!

To earn enough money to travel, I worked my first six months of school's-out freedom in the Pembrokeshire County Council Planning Department. Chock full of intrigue and parochial Welsh humour about who was drinking or sleeping with whom to get planning permission, this was an early introduction to the best and worst of post-school human nature. But by early summer, I was busting to leave and had bought a cheap flight to New York, an open Greyhound ticket for journeys anywhere in the 'States and stashed a princely £50 to tide me over until I found a job. Go west young man!

Those were the days when you collected addresses assiduously to stopover with friends of friends. Students on a budget could not afford hotel prices or more than one night's YMCA, but the reputation of Americans was legendary. 'You'll be ok' said our local MP the renegade Labour politician Desmond Donnelly. He apparently knew the mayor of New York, John Lindsey and a raft of big shot senators like 'Scoop' Jackson, as well as seriously well-connected people like Fran McPheeters who ran the English-Speaking Union, living up in 92nd St near Central Park. Would I ever get to meet such movers and shakers?

My country boy awe at walking down the high-rise canyon of 42nd St, was soon relieved by the sight of a small sidewalk diner. Breakfast! The black dude behind the counter in his skinny jeans and Afro hairdo introduced himself as Marlon. He seemed to be the only person running the place. The menu was far too long, so I asked lamely for 'eggs?' Sizing up an out-of-towner, Marlon asked if I wanted them 'griddled, scrambled, flip side, sunny side up or (in his best cod English accent) 'Easy Ovah'. Easy Ovah would be fine. With Percy Sledge's 'Put a Little Lovin' on me' easing from his elaborate speaker system, he proceeded to perform a well-rehearsed floorshow, in the behind the counter kitchen, lighting the gas ring, cracking eggs, oil in the pan frying and toast on the griddle, all done without missing a beat to Percy's rhythm with every part of his double-jointed anatomy. It was clearly not going to be easy to be both 'British' and as cool as this, but I felt I was going to like this place; the empathy was rising.

I had to get a job. Imagine pitching up in the States these days with merely £50, a visitor's visa and no other means of support. After being iced in solitary to check out terrorist or vagrant tendencies, I would have been back on the plane in short order. So, after shaking Marlon warmly by the hand and promising to be back at lunchtime, (ok li'l brother, y'all stay cool now!") I was off down to the New York State Employment Bureau, where they were hiring for summer camp counsellors. I reckoned a few weeks in the woods imparting my Duke of Edinburgh's Award skills would be just the thing for the kids of the huddled masses from the Lower East Side.

And so it turned out. Interviewed by the earnest Camp Leader – another Marlon, this time white - from the Kiwanis Summer Camp Club in upstate Bash Bish Falls, on the Massachusetts border for kids from the Bowery in New York - starting in 3 days' time! Marlon (already on first name terms with me), explained that lots of the kids would have never seen the countryside before, so they would go pretty wild encountering so much space, but they were usually pretty scared of the dark, in short supply in the high-density tenements of lower New York. He seemed to like what I had done while still at school, so I got hired to run the camp-outs in the woods. I would probably also be a quaint reminder to the kids that some people speak English 'funny'.

Leaving the recently termed 'Big Apple' via Grand Central, on the slow train to Albany was an interesting variant on that first long train journey to school 10 years previously. One or two student types were sitting in the same compartment heading for similar venues and I got chatting about what to expect before the conductor chimed 'next stop Copake and Bash Bish Falls!' like out of a 1940's movie. Bash Bish Falls was a well wooded farming and tourist village beyond the reaches of creeping suburbia and with kindly directions from the ticket inspector, I walked the half mile to the Kiwanis Camp with my rucksack where other counsellors of my age and a little older were assembling ahead of the onslaught of junior campers due in two days' time. Most were like me, there for the first time, just looking for a summer outdoors, earning some money with no living expenses but only one other non-American – Dieter from West Germany. We were assigned as three counsellors each to a bunkhouse with sixteen boys or girls, there being five male and three female bunkhouses – 128 kids in all, so quite a handful. I got to share with the earnest, geeky but endearing nature counsellor Walter Oliwa from South Orange, New Jersey, and Dieter Deputy Sports Counsellor to teach the then strange new sport of 'Saccer'. When the kids arrived two days' later they immediately dubbed us Nazi, Limey and Nature Boy and that we stayed for the next eight weeks through two four week drafts of budding anarchists, troublemakers, Olympic seeming sportsmen and women and down-to-earth charmers in broadly equal numbers.

Most of the kids were no trouble at all and a joy to be with. "Hey Counsellor, I've found nature", was a constant cry as they brought you a new creepie-crawlie to look at. But one or two, like everywhere, let down the rest. Otto was a real standout eleven-year old troublemaker who showed every symptom of not wanting to be there. While a born athlete, Otto was also an Olympic-standard swearer, cussing everyone in the most colourful language and phrasing. 'F... you, you're still in your mother's stomach' he would yell in a fit of quivering rage. It was hard not to laugh, as he would then lash out with feet or fists. It is clearly the right of shockers to shock and not be laughed at, as I quickly learned. Some of the counsellors applied an old-fashioned routine of soap in the mouth 'to wash out your filthy language 'Atto!' while others had him running around the bunkhouse thirty, forty, then fifty times until late into the night. Otto would just never give up. He seemed to relish the challenge of facing us all down. Like so many troubled kids, it was probably quality attention that he really craved. If he had known the word, he would have said that no one was empathising with him. The street vocab. of 'disrespect' - "you are dissing me man!" was still a few years away.

But Otto was also very creative and the other kids would follow his lead if he chose to take it. He was at his best in such circumstances. He composed the marching song for our Bunk 4 campout at the beginning of this chapter and the other boys would join in marching along the Appalachian Trail in the Catskill Mountains like a bunch of trainee marines. They would sing it all day. I hope Otto found a career in music or show business; he would have been a natural if he could find a way to channel life's frustrations positively.

Some of the girls were a different kind of challenge, as at thirteen and fourteen they were more than artfully capable of winding you up by developing real or faked crushes on male counsellors only a few years older than themselves. Nadia followed me everywhere for a few days, saying things like, 'Lucky water!' when after an arduous camping trek, I was washing my face in a stream. She gave up on me after a bit, and fixed her loving gaze on Ronnie Grunberg, the Swimming counsellor, who, despite a thirty-cigarettes a day habit, could do three lengths of the pool under water. My 'English ahhccent' could not compete with that. Maybe it was Ronnie's Red Mustang vintage 1963 which Nadia really fancied. I got to drive it once, with a bunch of counsellors aboard and did a half a mile on the quiet country roads forgetting to drive on the right. No one said a word until a truck came barrelling around the corner, everyone screamed and I beat a retreat sharp right. It was completely by accident, I swear.

The flag-raising ceremony was all American. Each morning we would stand at attention round the flagpole and sing, 'Raise the flag once again at the start of the day,' which I now know to be etched in most American kids' memory. Imagine that in UK! The Scots would want the Saltire, the Welsh the Red Dragon, and even the English might nowadays prefer the Cross of St George to the Union Jack. But the Stars and Stripes is sacred, more akin I suppose to our royal family (well in 1969 at any rate) which of course they had unceremoniously thrown out in 1776.

But guess who's turn it was to hold the flag for the raising ceremony on Independence Day, 4th of July? Correct, the only Counsellor present, still a subject of 'Her Majesty'! And there really were some at the camp who thought I might throw the flag on the ground and stamp on it. I was duly respectful of course, being only a closet rebel (or should that be loyalist?), but it shone a little light on young people whom I had previously thought were pretty anti-establishment, what with all the anti-Vietnam student demos at the time in which several Counsellors had been active participants. Faced with (in my case) a totally fabricated threat from outside, Americans of almost all political stripes, bind together in common cause, belied by, or perhaps because of, their multi-cultural origins. I don't feel that has changed much in 45 years.

That summer of '69, NASA put a man on the moon and we watched it late at night in grainy black and white to whoops of joy from everyone. People could not help to feel proud of and fascinated by what had been achieved. But as in the Thunder Clap Newman song of the year before, there was also a strong undercurrent of revolution in the air, focussed on the morbid fear of call-up papers - for the dreaded Vietnam draft. I remember Barry Flast, our lead Counsellor, and resident heavy rocker, going white one morning as he received his 1A classification by mail from the NY draft board, ("Do you remember Alice's Restaurant?"). It took him two weeks to prove he was a full-time college student and thus eligible for postponement before he relaxed and started playing guitar again. I lost touch with Barry after returning to England so I never knew if he later had to go to 'Nam. He was never cut out for forced army life, but '1A' was first stop boot camp in South Carolina, then the plane to the war zone. I was to relive this fear in person a few months later. Read on!

During that summer, Barry and some of his St Stephen rock group pals from New York were key to the organisation of the now famous Woodstock pop festival of July that year. There were many evenings when the kids had finally (even Otto) gone to bed, when we would sit plotting the way to pay off one of the local sheriffs not to invade the chosen venue for the festival on a drug bust. Right up to only a week before, there remained a lot of uncertainty as to where the so-called Woodstock pop festival would occur, as the organisers were sure the Police would intervene. A dairy farm at Bethel Woods forty miles from Woodstock was finally identified and on the third day of the festival and our precious day off, a few of us jumped into Ronnie's Mustang and headed off across the Hudson River, destination farmer Max Yasgur's venue for the now iconoclastic but inaccurately named Woodstock Pop Festival. The roads got busier and busier as we got close, and we were hours sitting motionless in traffic 'lines' exchanging hippy goodwill with our fellow trippers. While still stationery on Route 178, west of Bethel village but still a mile short of the venue, we were close enough in our open-topped Mustang to hear if not see, Jimi Hendrix. We eventually ran out of time and had to turn around and go home. But did you really need to see Hendrix, when he played Star Spangled Banner like that? The whole traffic line was 'grooving to the vibe, man' with that combination of patriotic and subversive rendering of the famous anthem. So, I now consider myself a Woodstock veteran, though I never actually made it onto the festival site.

My idyllic American summer camp experience drew to a close, by the end of July and it was time to start travelling again and start using that Greyhound ticket. I said good bye to my new-found friends promising faithfully to visit them back in 'Noo Joisey' at the end of my round America tour, and before they went back to 'school' in late September. But first I was determined to go all the way to the west coast, something few of the other Counsellors had done.

Montreal, Ottawa and Toronto lacked the appeal of young people to get to know and people make places, so I pretty soon, headed out west to the Rockies. I bussed through oil and mountain country to Calgary, which certainly fitted the wild west bill but as the Stampede and Rodeo were not due for another few weeks, I cadged a lift with friends of friends up the great highway through Lake Louise and Banff to Jasper. To be in the mountains again! And what mountains – this made Snowdonia look pretty tame and even the Alps seemed modest by comparison to the sheer scale and dimension of North America's massive western mountain spine. Deep turquoise coloured lakes fed by glaciers and heading north via the Athabasca River to the Arctic were framed by vertiginous mountain ranges, pine tree covered on their lower slopes and bare rock above the tree line. This was mid-August, but I could still feel the chill of winter at night when the sun went down. Barbecuing on a bend in the northward flowing Athabasca River, it seemed that night to be coming back the other way.

Vancouver had an atmosphere a bit like home – western seaboard and a sense of removal from bigger metropolitan centres though that is much changed now. The rain certainly reminded me of home. I stayed with a family whose name I have conveniently forgotten over 50 years later. So, common those days; they were riven by angst and generational tensions between parents and kids. There were two boys of around my age, and their parents were convinced they were smoking every mind-altering substance known to man. On each of the three nights I was there, titanic arguments erupted as to how long we could stay out. The next day, I would be quizzed for what had happened, despite it all being pretty innocent, as far as I could recall. But it got uncomfortable when the mother of the boys tried to recruit me to her crusade against what she saw as their inevitable drug-induced downfall.

There are no hard and fast rules about how to handle these situations either with my contemporaries then, or my own kids since. Too much rope and kids go off the rails, too little and there is often an abrupt, sometimes savage, cutting of it with families splitting apart with a welter of excessive pride getting in the way of reconciliation for agonising years to follow. I took quite a lot of stick from certain friends especially in the 'States and later Australia, for never smoking anything stronger than a cigarette (usually other people's), but I would have surely gone AWOL if I had tried stronger mind-altering substances and lost control; or at the other extreme, my parents had imposed on me a stricter regime or too much control. The Big C; get it right for the people and the family that you are. Empathy is everything.

San Francisco was of course the real west coast target. How could it not be, with all that Haight Ashbury stuff, the west coast capital of hippiedom, from only a few years' before? I did the whole trip down most of the west coast on the Greyhound night bus. If you have ever listened to Simon and Garfunkel's lesser-known ballads, you will know how many have to do with journeying, departure and moving on. I suppose that is the lot in the lives of most young people at some time or other. The twenty-hour overnight marathon from Vancouver to SF is a good example, stopping in desolate all-night coach stations in places like Medford Oregon, or Redding north California, with near empty coffee bars and derelict types hanging around, looking for someone to speak to and spare them a dime.

The waiting always seemed interminable for the bus to re-start, with a fresh driver each time, who might or might not entertain his passengers with commentary on the dusk, darkened or dawning countryside through which we travelled. I longed for the seat beside me to be taken by a long-haired maiden on an odyssey like mine, and whose head would fall asleep on my manly shoulder, rocked by the rhythm of the wheels. It did happen a few times later, over thousands of miles of flying or bussing in various countries, but if it is not someone you already know, it turns into a pain quite quickly. You didn't want to move too much and embarrass her as she might later become the girl of your dreams – a decision in abeyance while you did intimate things like smelling her fragrant hair or listening to her soft snoring. I recall now some of the factors which made it less the fantasy and more a reality after listening to Garfunkel's 'Homeward Bound' for the nth time.

At last! San Francisco and the golden west coast so much the target of our grey British schoolboy imaginations through the mid 60's. For once, considering how often SF gets fog, the weather was luminous crossing the Oakland Bay Bridge, so it was magical to be arriving there on a late August morning. 'Be sure to wear some flowers in your hair' went the words of Scott Mackenzie's plangent song. Yet only 2 years after its heyday for all of the 'beautiful people' in the summer of '67, Haight Ashbury, was looking pretty tired and run down.

Remembering my first impressions of American music as an unlikely mixture of Bob Lind and Glenn Campbell, I was as much a 'Bullitt' fan as I was a proto hippy. Bullitt, as all movie buffs will recall, is the iconic car chase movie from the mid '60's, when crash and bang car wrecks took on a wholly new dimension via about 25 minutes of uninterrupted mayhem through the up and down streets of SF. And Steve McQueen held just as much appeal to me as Scott McKenzie with his dreamy lyrics. Steve McQueen seemed to get the really cool girls (Jacqueline Bisset, I recall) rather than the hazy/lazy/laid back and get laid sort of hippie Flower Children like Mama Cass. So, though I was there to look with fascination at the hippie culture, it was probably more look but don't touch.

That became quite obvious when I crashed for a few nights with a couple of dreamy girls, friends of friends from the Summer Camp who had made it to the west coast. All very nice, and I went around for dinner with them one evening to an Indian friend's house. That is Indian as from India, not the name still then used for native Americans. The conversation got around to the evils of imperialism of which the British were deemed to be the arch bad guys, while of course the US was less prone to such behaviour. As I am wont to do when cornered, I pointed out that the US was not lily-white on this topic, the occupation of the west of their continent, then later in the 19th century the Philippines, Cuba and Puerto Rico to their debit as pretty-good examples of annexing other places.

Sensing an argument advantage and not knowing when to stop, I then made a big error suggesting that Britain had also left at least two good things in India – the railways and the English language. Trouble was, I was dealing with the south Asian equivalent of Cato, Inspector Clouseau's Chinese sidekick and judo instructor, trained to attack without mercy when least expected. I think mind-altering drugs may have had something to do with his frame of reference, but he went bananas and grabbed the bread knife threatening me across the table as if I were still dressed in a redcoat and pith helmet. The girls went bananas in turn (I have learned that Americans are more prone than Brits to turning dramas into crises.) One of them hustled me out fast, while the other stayed behind to calm down the anti-imperialist Cato as best she could.

We two went back to her place where commenced a long psycho-analysis of behaviour patterns as they vary between different cultures. It never occurred to me it might have been a put-up job to get each of us paired off, and I eventually went off to sleep still surprised at the injustices of the world. What a walking innocent! I should have just kissed her and told her she had nice eyes. But she was a hippie chick and I liked the cool ones.

I was running short on money, so ignoring the siren call of southern California, with the Beach Boys singing all through school days about Surfin' USA and 'If only they could all be Californian girls', I flew the Friendly Skies of

United to New Orleans (NO) and the 'duip sayouth' of Mobile Alabama where there were more friends of friends offering hospitality, 'Mint Julep' style!

New Orleans itself was so laid back. Louisiana with its French origins is much less uptight about drinking laws than most US states so walking the length of Canal Street I ventured into one or two of the bars. I felt I was going back in time. Jazz and Blues were taking a back seat in popular culture back then, with the Beatles, Rolling Stones and many copycat bands taking over. The British invasion of American musical consciousness was at its height! But jazz - the devil's music! - is perennial, as I have come to appreciate since, with its own style and method of communicating musical annotation as much by ear as on paper as many jazz artists cannot read music. Pop culture comes and goes and I doubt many of us could name more than the few truly iconic groups and artists from the subsequent decades to the '60's. Even my own kids who grew up in the 1990's will admit this.

Louis Armstrong has come to epitomise New Orleans and has now got his own centre there. In 1967 he had recorded 'Wonderful World' specifically as a slightly cheesy antidote to the noisier beats of late 60's bands. It was a wonderful backdrop to walking through New Orleans in that warm September sunshine – God's music more than the devil it seemed, so hardly true jazz but who was counting?

It was sometimes difficult in the US to eat local and authentic cheap food. Already by 1969 the creeping domination by nationwide fast-food outlets was well established. on most high streets. Big Macs, Colonel Sanders' KF chicken and Ben & Jerry's ice cream all seemed to be better quality then than now, but they were the same wherever you went. New Orleans was different. There,

there was gumbo! Gumbo has west African roots but also French and French Canadian (Cajun) re-interpretations with its bases of onion, bell pepper and celery, but with fish bouillabaisse, chicken or sausage depending on what was available.

There were also delicious steaks served from open air barbecues in some of the street restaurants off Bourbon Street. I recall once being asked, with extravagant attention to detail, how did I like my steak; "y'all can have it creeemated', weeall dern, medium rare, blue or walkin' cow! "

New Orleans retains its historical authenticity like few other parts of the US; shame about the floods and continued racial tensions but they will always have their jazz and their gumbo.

Mobile Alabama has never been part of any main tourist trail, which is why I was pleased to go there. Yet another 'friends of friends' family from the back country behind Mobile seemed pleased enough to see me, I was a curiosity from the 'old countree' as far as they were concerned. Pretty soon we got onto familiar issues which dogged such relationships between southerners and others – from the north or overseas in those days – 'segegrashun' and 'integrashun'' as they pronounced it. These were still hot topics only a few years after the Little Rock Arkansas demos and riots and the bussing of black kids to formerly whites-only schools etc.

They turned out to be good ole' boys and girls from the best southern tradition, welcoming to a fault but ready to have a gentle go at my presumed northern/foreign and therefore probably 'liberal' attitudes. Only in the US is the word liberal still loaded with such assumed left-wing affiliation – akin to communism for many deep conservatives. In Europe, liberal, especially in Germany, often means right-wing, but pointing that out in 'ole Alabamy' was not likely to win friends or influence people. Only time was going to resolve some of the deep-seated issues we talked about, but there was humour on both sides and things never got so tense as to have to take my leave early.

It was a different matter a few hundred miles north in Birmingham, where a similar if more humourless version of the same issues came up. My host on this occasion was another conservative family but without the essential humour gene, the father of whom picked me up from the Greyhound bus station with an audible sigh of relief at having got out of there without getting mugged or lynched. Even as he drove me to his safe white suburban home, he proudly showed off the handgun in the glove compartment of the car, backing it up with the 'intenshun' not to hesitate to use it if anyone tried stopping his car at night. When we got home, he opened what looked like a coat closet in the hall to reveal a whole arsenal of rifles and handguns ready and loaded, he claimed, in case anyone came visiting with 'hostaile intayunt'. I sometimes did double takes to understand what I was hearing, suppressing a smile at the use of such quaint old English. It was as if these southerners were visiting from the 'old countree', not me.

I was struck throughout Alabama, by how much more Anglo-Saxon people were than elsewhere in the US (a quaint term for a Celt to use, but Scots, Irish and Welsh were certainly included in this Stateside definition). Compared with the more cosmopolitan north, where immigration has been so much more diverse and continuous through the last 150 years, Alabama seemed culturally frozen in time with potentially armed camps of whites and blacks staring at each other uncomprehending but distrustful across invisible but very real fault lines through society. How much of this has really changed over more than 50 years?

Ever northward now, Knoxville Tennessee was a smaller but equally musical version of the more famous Nashville. I had the afternoon there before catching an evening bus north and overnight through Roanoke Virginia to Washington DC. It seemed a laid-back sort of place with cars cruising the strips at that oh- so-slow speed which the drivers loved - "look at me an' mah wheels!" they seemed to say. But when you're in transit, no town seems worth lingering in as there are places to go, and you live in dread of missing the connection. Nice music though, coming out the doors of the downtown bars.

Heading east on Interstate Highway 40 towards the Blue Ridge Mountains, which separate Tennessee from Virginia, I saw some of the most beautiful scenery on my whole North American circuit, and in the best back-to-the-setting-sun dusk. Little wonder they were called the Blue Ridges. They went on and on and north and south, sightline horizon after horizon until it was quite dark. For once the bus driver was not assailing us with his down-home philosophy, but letting his passengers soak up the scenery as we climbed sedately through the leaf turning early evening. All seemed so right with the world. You could see from where Bing Crosby got his horizontal - stance singing about 'the Blue Ridge Mountains of Virginia on the trail of the lonesome pine' while Bob Hope played the fool in the background.

Passing though Jonesboro just before sun set, it struck me as the quintessential American small town with its clapboard houses, board walks and (in those days) confederate flags now apparently replaced with the stars and stripes. Maybe time does heal. I thought about Jones;

who he was and what part of Wales might he have been from? My hometown? And did he know Daniel Boone and Davy Crockett - kings of the wild frontier - also sons from nearby this most historic of settlements. I had a warm glow leaving the south. Maybe I did not understand their politics but where they had come from resonated with me differently than more cosmopolitan places further north. Comes from being a country boy I suppose.

Roanoke is the big town in southern Virginia, but it was the middle of the night, so just a pit stop not doing it justice, then more soporific driving on through the night to the national capital reached in the early morning of the next day and another night spent for the price of a bus ticket. Moving on, forever moving on – Simon and Garfunkel would have been proud of me.

Washington DC, the capital of the 'Yew Ess of Ay' was a very different proposition on the northern border of the sleepy south. I arrived there suitably enough on a fresh new September morning right on time at the Greyhound downtown bus terminal. It was in Washington that I took full advantage of the best of the contacts offered from home in Wales. Desmond Donnelly knew the then famous, and later legendary, Henry 'Scoop' Jackson, the influential Democrat senator, and member of several high-powered Congress committees controlling millions of dollars of public expenditure, and a full-time scourge of Republicans. Despite his awesome reputation and range of responsibilities, he agreed to meet me for thirty minutes - an eighteen-year old student from a foreign country! He then arranged for me to listen in on parts of sessions of both the Senate and House of Representatives, followed by a conducted tour with one of his interns, of the White House public rooms! No matter that the debates were on numbingly tedious subjects – (pork belly price fluctuations

I recall), or that there were hordes of tourists also going around the President's official residence. I felt like a million dollars and kept the official passes with which I had been issued, for many years afterwards.

It takes so little to make young people feel valued. That day I was on top of the world because a great man had taken time to talk to me. I am no great man like Scoop Jackson (RIP, he died in 2013) but I have learned from him always to take time out for people starting out on their careers in life, to listen to them and hear of their aspirations. The listening is the really good part. No good just seeing people to show what wonderful opinions you have or great deeds you have done. You can immediately tell when people are not only interesting, but interested. They remain in your memory forever.

I was struck in Washington with how many young men, a little older than me, I kept seeing with one or more limbs missing. The result of anti-personnel mines in Vietnam. By '69 this was one of the most effective ways the Viet Cong could hit back at their enemy. The victims seemed to be employed in public sector jobs throughout the capital – one way the government deployed to pay them back for their sacrifice. It is a bigger deal since after Afghanistan and Iraq, so hats off to the latest Invictus games' initiative for affording motivation, recognition and respect to wounded veterans.

By now I knew what I enjoyed most on this as in subsequent journeys alone – not the sites and scenery, but the people and especially young people my own age. I was now back within touching distance of my pals from Summer Camp, many of whom had come from South Orange, Noo Joisey. So onward into the tender care of my best mate at the Kiwanis camp from 6 long weeks ago, Larry Devinsky. Larry was a final year High School student and the archetypal nice Jewish boy, desperately trying to be the cool rebel without a real cause, but without much success, being far too bourgeois and respectful of his parents. I went to stay and my first night at his parent's house was 21st September - Yom Kippur in that year. They were all so welcoming and we duly celebrated the religious holiday while Larry squirmed with embarrassment as his parents and little sisters made such a fuss of me with their welcome. No problems at all me being a gentile and all that; we were all mensch together.

Next day, I accompanied Larry to his High School history and politics class and sat at the back trying to keep a low profile and just listen and learn. But the teacher was not letting me off lightly. She chose a debate revolving around the US relationship with the British over 200 years. It was scary to be on the spot like that and participate in a debate, but as with kids anywhere, humour was always bubbling below the surface, so there were few of the tensions from the south. Humour is the universal lubricant for empathy.

That flavour did not change in the bright yellow bus on the way home, with all Larry's mates wanting to imitate my 'English ahhccent'. One of the girls said I sounded like Paul McCartney. Whaaaat? Could she not recognise a Liverpool accent? We hung out at a coffee bar stopover with a nice crowd - South Orange then being a real crossroads of different cultures – Jewish, Italian, Hispanic and increasingly Black families, all relatively well-off middle class but not obscenely prosperous.

Larry was stressed out about me 'dating' anyone other than a Jewish girl, not that I had enough time to 'date' anyone at all. He said that because I was with him, I could not cross the divide and start chatting up the 'Eyetalian' or Hispanic girls. "Why not?" I asked, immediately peeved at who might now be off limits. "Because their guys would cut you and more to the point, my life would not be worth living at High School. It would cause a turf war!" he said.

"But I am a Wasp," I whined.

"Doesn't matter, you're with me," and that was the end of the subject. What tribalism! But then I suppose in those days we had nothing like this at home. Wasps were things you avoided getting stung by, swatting or letting out the window if feeling kind. "Quite," said Larry in his best English ahhccent, "swatting's too good for you!"

I was drawing near to my homecoming, but just time to scoot across the Big Apple to New Haven Connecticut, and Yale University where a good mate from my school in England, Don Fearey, an ex-American exchange scholar, was just starting his Freshman year. New Haven was bathed in the gold and red colours of early Fall, and I found Wrexham Tower built by Eli Yale, the University's founder, born in my parents' hometown in North Wales. Don was totally unfazed by this stunning piece of cultural history as he contemplated his future as one of America's gilded youth. Then quickly back to New York to see Barry Flast of Woodstock fame again, living in Chinatown and still free of the clutches of the New York draft board and the US Army, before he was off to the University of Maryland for his second year of studies.

Then homeward bound at last via JFK and Shannon, with about $5 and 50 cents in my pocket and my student rail card to get me from Heathrow to Haverfordwest via Reading and Cardiff Central redolent of journeys from school just a few years previously. It all seemed so much smaller now than Grand Central in New York.

What places and wonderful people I had met 'Stateside! In 1969, there was still a bright optimism about the US and a fundamental pride in things American, even among those protesting 'human rights' and peace against their government's policy in Vietnam. Well established in the era of rampant consumerism with only the beginnings of protest against it, they had never yet lost a war and with men on the moon, everything seemed possible for the future. Compare 1969 with now when there is so much more disillusion and even fear for the future. But from later visits, I still perceive Americans to be a broadly welcoming, big hearted and open people despite a lot of negative European media coverage. It seems just now they need to keep open to the world and resist turning in on themselves - as sadly they did in the 1930's.

There was an intriguing postscript to this great American road trip. I had been in Oxford for about a month by October 1969, when I received out of the blue, a New York Draft Board call up card – 1A – equating to going straight to boot camp in South Carolina for 6 weeks, then the plane to Vietnam! How could this be? – I am British! I harrumphed. The summer camp had, as part of my wages, paid my nominal $9 state tax and having no social security number, I was immediately suspect as a draft dodger.

I was immediately afforded instant celebrity status among my new-found fresher student friends, but they were not much help about how to extricate myself. Practicalities were rarely Oxford students' strong point, then as now. I rang my Dad at home in Wales and told him what had happened – veteran himself of six years of war only twenty-five years previously, so accorded deep respect by me on such matters.

There was a long silence on the line, then he asked quietly "Don't you think you should go?"

Another long silence this time from me. "Are you kidding?" I said in my best American accent, "I am British!"

A third long silence, then in his worst American accent, "Only kidding, never did like that General Clarke in Italy, all piss and wind, and he never got off the pot at Anzio." I would never have gone anyway, but I could have hugged him at that moment. His opinion counted for a lot; he had been through so much more than me in life and if he said no, that was it. What if he had chosen to say yes?

Now my student friends were full of how to reply and with typical youthful hubris, I wrote back that 'as a British subject, I would not be attending the Board, and if there was more trouble we would be sending a gun boat up the Hudson River and this time, unlike at Boston Harbour previously, it would not be stacked with tea.'

Ho, ho, what jolly student japes! But I thought long and hard about the Barry Flasts of this world, probably less cut out for a military life than me. They would not have let him avoid the draft like some subsequently famous people in Oxford such as Bill Clinton were doing at that time. When he finished in the University of Maryland, in 1971, Barry probably went to Vietnam, and if he survived, who knows how it would have changed him? I never did get to hear from him again, but his rock star talent reverberates in my memory. Rock on Barry!

"Hey Counsellor, I've found nature

Bunk 4 Campout expedition, Catskill Mts. Massachusetts June '69. Walter and Dieter look uneasy about taking this unruly mob into the woods. Otto is the fourth from the left in the middle row. The only one not looking at the camera

American sense of humour in evidence on 4 July 1969. The only subject of 'Her Majesty' present that day was required to perform the flag-raising ceremony. To everyone's surprise I avoided dropping it as a gesture of pre-revolutionary loyalty

Chapter 3 Learning to fly

This is the only part of this travelogue with its feet off the ground. Flying as a passenger is different to keeping an aircraft straight and level, properly trimmed. Remember the 1940s' song sung by the Andrews Sisters. Straighten up and fly right!

I had toyed with the idea of flying after the influence of the RAF section of the Combined Cadet Force in school. The CCF plays a lesser role now, but used to combine a recruitment role for the forces with some of the best reasons never to go near the forces for those who were disinclined. There were a lot like that in the peace loving 1960's. Some of the training was vaguely serious and some of it risible. For example, the school's RAF section had an ancient glider which it kept in a shed on the main playing fields, together with an enormous, rope-thick elastic band thingee with which, via help of large numbers of willing dupes, it was supposed to be projected skywards. The poor sap sitting exposed in the open-air pilot's seat was probably in more danger of the elastic rope snapping and rebounding to coil itself round his open legs and sensitive parts than he was being rendered airborne. And, if he was sent skywards, what then? Did he have the remote knowledge, not to mention airspeed, to get the thing back on the ground again without killing himself? Small wonder there were few volunteers to sit in it while we 'junior aircraftmen' marched off heaving the rope. What a farce!

Most CCF training was a mixture of the numbingly boring and the ridiculous to point of hilarity, unless you were a complete nerd and believed in all the stuff being taught. To that extent, it was probably 'National Service Lite', given that an unluckier previous generation including my elder cousins, had to tolerate an entirely more invasive version of military training in their young lives. They in turn were better off than my Dad's generation who were called up to six years of World War 2 and his father, killed in the Great War before that. We were fortunate in the '60's, by which time CCF training had become a Thursday afternoon routine, a change from the games field and evening lessons. I never forget how privileged is our generation.

There was still a serious aspect to it all, including visits to live RAF stations such as Pershore from where we were flown in the hold (metal seating, no cushions) of an ancient Beverley to Finningley in Yorkshire, a live V Bomber station with Vulcans and Valiants. Taking turns, we sat in the restricted visibility cockpit of a Vulcan and heard how merely four years before, during the 1962 Cuba missile crisis, aircrew not much older than us had sat in these same positions, fuelled, nuclear-armed and ready to go off and bomb the Soviet Union. How many might have penetrated the Russians' technically superior missile defences, no one knows, but the RAF had its duty to do, and would doubtless have delivered its 'buckets of sunshine' not only to the Russian population but to themselves and the rest of us in the Mutual Assured Destruction which stood for cold war strategy at the time. No wonder so many of us were sceptical about the whole thing.

The Air Experience flying was far easier to relate to and arranged during away days from school. Sitting in the back of the RAF's Chipmunk basic trainer at Filton Airfield outside Bristol, I had my first experience of aerobatics and all at once, it proved scary, sick-making, exhilarating and motivational to learn to do it all for myself. I was hooked for learning to fly – one day.

The opportunity came at University where the Fresher's Fair had a stand for the University Air Squadron (UAS). There, amazingly, they were offering to teach you to fly, in exchange for a commitment to regular training days, a two-week spring or summer training camp, occasional wearing of an uncomfortable blue serge uniform as a Cadet Pilot, and some essential desk-based theory on engines, navigation, principles of flight and, oddly, survival techniques in the event of being shot down in enemy territory. In a Chipmunk? Were they crazy?

There was also, of course, a hidden motive that they wanted you eventually to join the RAF, the first of the services only a few years previously, to insist that all future officers would be graduate qualified. Responding at interview, to that crucial last question about career intentions with a vague 'thinking about the RAF' seemed to pass that test, and after some fitness, aptitude and eye sight checks, I became a proud member of Oxford's UAS, from whom the RAF had drawn some of its most famous pilots of several wars. Perhaps like more profound and time committing military experiences gained by others, the OUAS gave me three years of pure challenge, satisfaction, fear and hilarity in approximately equal measures - too often in close proximity to each other - and some lifelong mates among fellow students.

The training was rigorous and comprehensive and despite the aircraft being fairly tame in performance terms, (stall speed at 45; take off speed 50 knots; max speed in a dive 140 knots etc. but ...fully aerobatic!), there was a modest but steady drop-out rate. The training manual in a characteristically uncompromising and Wing Commander Biggles' manner stated, 'if an aircraft is capable of aerobatic flight, the RAF will fly it that way.' Tally Ho!

I am sure the instructors who were all full time serving RAF officers on three-year postings, regarded some of us with our long hair and laid back attitudes as a bunch of wasters incapable of finding our way through a barn door, never mind flying solo from A to B. But they were probably instructed themselves to focus on future recruitment, so kept their council on our suitability as 'officer material' underneath our hirsute fuzz. In fact, we got on with most of them very well. I came to like pilots; apart from the familiar twin-handed gesture of how they could shoot down the Red Baron, they were largely an undemonstrative lot, steady pairs of hands to rely on in a crisis. I wanted to be like them and achieve what they had achieved.

Looking back through my treasured RAF log book, I note it took me a total of forty-six practice landings on the forgiving grass runway at RAF Bicester, and 11¼ hours with my instructor Flight Lt John Curnow, before being allowed to go off solo for that first glorious fifteen minutes on my own – on 24 April 1970 in Chipmunk call sign Whisky Zulu 872. What a huge glow of confidence it gave me. I told no-one about it for a few days while I savoured the sense of becoming something else from what I had been before – a pilot! I could fly a plane!

The RAF never stops training, however competent the pilot, and there were plenty more challenges to come, including practiced engine failures and forced landings, loops, stall turns and barrel rolls, formation flying, and most sobering of all, instrument flying to do controlled descents through cloud, under ground-control instruction. This requires huge mental concentration and an almost physical act of faith in both instruments and someone else's guiding voice, until allowed to look up and (hopefully) locate the runway less than half a mile ahead though the mist and land.

But for me possibly the lasting memory of those days, learning to fly was the solo cross country, which required landing away and refuelling before returning home via a different dog-legged route. The first attempt at this, noted dispassionately in the log book as 'Aborted Navex' could have ended disastrously. North from Bicester, I was supposed to track across the M1, usually an easy feature to spot from the recommended 5,000 feet cruise height, before going on to Nottingham and RAF Newton for the land away, home of the East Midlands Universities Air Squadron. Trouble was that the Met forecast proved very wrong almost immediately after take-off, with a series of line squalls forcing me down to about 2,000 feet. Immediately under the cloud base, with hailstones hammering on the cockpit canopy, it was practically impossible to hear any radio instructions, while even my own outgoing messages were being disrupted by the background noise. Maybe, due to atmospherics, they were not being heard at all. Radio signals provide the means for ground controllers to identify your direction from base and thus, knowing your destination in advance, advice on a continuation course or a reciprocal for returning home. But there is no way to calculate accurately your distance away, which can vary hugely, according to airspeed, itself a factor of head wind and thus speed over the ground.

But with no on board radar and not hearing, nor for all I knew, being heard, I was rapidly lost and unable to get a controller's steer to carry on or return home. Nor was the M1 appearing where it should have been as clearly the ground speed was proving much slower with higher head winds than expected. The worst aspect of such a situation is, unlike in a car, not being able to stop, get your bearings by spotting features on the ground and on a map, and work out which direction to go in. You have to keep flying the damned plane, straight and level, oil temps and pressures ok, trim ok, airspeed constant and looking out for other aircraft. That last one was a fat lot of good, with zero visibility upwards or, for that matter, sideways much of the time, as I strove to keep below the lowering cloud base without wanting to drop below the statutory 1,000-foot limit.

The next five minutes were some of the longest I remember while I cast around below for a feature to recognise from the 1:200,000 navigation map in my transparent knee pocket. This was a scale, deemed by the Ministry of Defence, to provide sufficient detail for ground feature recognition without so much clutter as to confuse or distract the pilot from flying his plane.

Then two things happened almost at once. My instructor John Curnow was on a training flight with my best mate and fellow student Graham Baxter, some distance away to the south. Being higher than our home-base ground controller, he had heard my calls for assistance, and in a break in the hailstones, I heard his reply to me on my frequency. Not that he could help much, not having direction-finding equipment on his own aircraft to know where I was. But hearing a friendly voice made a huge difference to suppressing a growing sense of panic and just then and only some 250 feet below, looming out of the rainy mist were the network of radio masts at Daventry. In the early '70's these covered a wider area than is the case now and were marked in purple on my map as a major hazard to low flyers - to be avoided! They are visible from the M1, so I was approximately on track but very late with the much higher head winds. On reporting my new-found position, my instructor told me to abort the cross country and together we worked out a reciprocal track to get back to Bicester, almost as if he was in the plane with me.

The return home was much swifter now, running with the strong north easterly winds and the instructor and Graham (doubtless sniggering at my predicament) formatted on me for the last 10 miles, offering psychological reassurance, in case I was losing my bottle for the necessary solo landing. It all ended without further mishap and, all considered, was a fairly common set of unfavourable circumstances. But it taught me that you can take nothing for granted when flying a plane, and I was very glad of the training and confidence not to panic and try a forced landing in a field for which, not surprisingly perhaps, we had received plenty of practice. But to do that live onto a sopping wet unseen surface when it might be too late to abort? Not to be undertaken lightly! I was glad to be back on the ground with Whisky Zulu 872 still in one piece – and me with it.

It must have been bad weather in that early summer of '71, because my logbook relates that I did not then re-attempt the cross-country 'land away' for another 3 weeks. But this time it worked ok, and it is all there in black and white in aircraft call sign Whisky Papa 919, 'Navex Land Away RAF Newton', returning via Northampton and the Daventry aerials network', this time at a safe height.

A more amusing event occurred following a kind invitation at the annual OUAS Christmas cocktail party, to which all Commanding Officers of nearby air bases were invited. The CO of the USAF base at RAF Upper Heyford, 10 miles north of Bicester was there, dressed appropriately enough for the Oxford winter in what appeared to be tropical kit with the usual multi-coloured array of war ribbons favoured by American servicemen. He invited us to fly over in a pair of Chipmunks to do circuits and bumps (take off and land circuits) on their runways. The Americans trained their ground controllers on live airfields (the RAF started with simulators), and their standard aircraft at Heyford in those days was the supersonic swing wing F111, which would do a circuit of the airfield in less than three minutes. Our Chipmunks took nine minutes, "so you guys can give our rookie controllers a bit more time to manage four aircraft in the circuit at once!" he beamed. We would also get practice landing on 7,000 feet of concrete runway instead of one of the last grass runways left in RAF operation at Bicester (now a listed feature by English Heritage).

NATO aircraft used UHF while we remained in the steam age with ancient VHF sets, but the Americans said they would dig out an ancient crystal set from their radio shack spares cupboard and all was set. We flew over one cold crisp afternoon in January and duly called up for permission to land. No reply. Repeat request – No reply. Standard procedure with no radio contact and demonstrating a desire to land goes back to the 1920's, and requires a slow flypast of the tower waggling your wings. A pistol firing a green Verey light is the standard reply and you land. In short, this procedure relied on that oldest of RAF technology, known to all pilots as the 'Mark 1 Eyeball'.

Not so this time, and this invasion of their airspace was now proving too much for the USAF. We watched with initially detached interest but growing concern as two pilots sprinted for their planes on the apron for a fast scramble. Taking off on reheat, they were already overtaking us down wind while still on the deck. We were duly buzzed and sent packing, buffeted in the slipstream of aircraft doing five times our speed.

On returning to base, our popular CO, Squadron Leader George England no less - for that was his name - was duly miffed with the Americans' behaviour and rang Upper Heyford to enquire what was going on, given the 5-star airforce-general's previous kind invitation and subsequent arrangements. Embarrassment and apologies all round from the Yanks; they had booked us in for the wrong day and no one knew how to make a VHF radio set work twenty years after they had stopped using them. From then on, we knew exactly how to penetrate American air defences – half flap down on a Chipmunk reduces stalling speed to 45 knots, at which velocity defending aircraft and air to air missiles cannot track the intruder. A German student pilot demonstrated this a few years later when he landed his Cessna 150 in Red Square Moscow – and doubtless spent a few months in the Gulag for his trouble.

Some of the most memorable stuff in the OUAS had nothing to do with flying at all, except to reflect the devil-may-care attitude of those who like to fly. There was mess rugby after dining-in nights during which I witnessed an instructor getting his arm broken, something I rarely saw happen on the rugby field in over twenty years of playing the real thing. Pilot training of the informal peer pressure kind, particularly on wet days waiting for the weather to clear, included trying to circle the mess without touching the floor. Essential initiative tests for escaping Warsaw Pact minefields as part of our escape training, this required inventiveness of an advanced form. Amazing ingenuity was required – injury-defying leaps between armchairs, upended waste bins as stepping stones and so on.

Hanging from the picture rail was a common device and on one occasion which I sadly never witnessed in person, a trainee pilot officer was suspended over the sacred photograph of the Dambusters 617 squadron including several ex-Oxford UAS students, when the CO walked in. The unexpected weight proved too much for the picture rail, which slowly peeled away from the wall together with a shower of broken plaster and said sacred photo of our heroic predecessors. A deathly silence followed while the CO contemplated the unfortunate junior officer lying among broken picture glass and formerly decorative cornices, before commenting wryly that it was a pity that junior PO's could not learn to fly. He then turned on his heel and left the room. Later the only sanction was the redecoration cost on the victim's mess bill towards which the whole squadron chipped in with a contribution each. Silent ridicule of the perpetrator had proved enough; perhaps the RAF encouraged initiative even of the frivolous destructive kind.

I took up civilian flying for a period after leaving University, and here too, I had character building experience, care of Flying Clubs, from Biggin Hill, Birmingham International, Cardiff to Haverfordwest, Southampton to Jersey, all around Weston-super-Mare and even, the Witwatersrand in South Africa, just tooling about in small planes. There is an unwritten code of decent if not always correct behaviour between pilots; have fun but don't push the envelope. As they used to say in the RAF - there are old pilots and there are bold pilots, but not old and bold pilots. Not a bad axiom for life in general.

But civilian flying proved to be a bit tame compared with the RAF. In the latter, you always had the impression you were in a state of continuous training; for safety primarily, but also staying aware, up to speed and perhaps escalating training if war was to threaten. We were in the RAF Voluntary Reserve after all.

I suppose if I had made a career of the airforce this would have progressed to faster aircraft and manoeuvrability in flight, navigation and transport techniques, evasion and interception and, of course, use of weapons. Flying as a hobby was different in that it was usually a means to an end - getting from A to B above the madding crowd, though with the liability of having to return soon to avoid horrendous additional hire charges, having shown off suitably to your friends. Lovers of aerobatics are a rarer breed of showmen, while those who join flying clubs to race cross country and carry out dawn raids on neighbouring clubs, should have been in the RAF circa 1941.

However various civilian flying experiences come fondly to memory - taking friends from Cardiff to Haverfordwest in a 4-seater P28 for lunch at my parents was one such. Seeing from the air, the all too familiar road west and passing along it in a fraction of the time taken to travel it earthbound, was a revelation, but Haverfordwest 'International' airport was a bigger surprise. The flight plan was arranged from Rhoose airport outside Cardiff, so they were expecting me and the 27 left runway had recently been retarmacked - all good. However, cleared to land and just before turning finals, the controller suddenly offered me the option to land on the much shorter 19 almost southbound runway. This was much shorter and did not seem to have a very good surface, so after momentary speculation why he was spreading confusion at the last minute, I declined.

When we had taxied to and shut down at the Portakabin doing service as the control 'tower', departure lounge and customs facility all in one, I asked the controller and sole occupant of this, less than teeming airport, why he had given me the option of two runways. He said that the Council would not re-tarmac Runway 19 unless there was more reason to land aircraft there - not a reason to convince me to oblige him. We got talking about frequency of movements and he boasted that there were now regular flights to France. 'Regular' turned out to be once a week, but the passenger manifests were lobsters and crab destined for the French restaurant trade. I asked about customs clearance and he changed his baseball cap for one with scrambled egg round the peak proudly stating 'that would be me! before picking up his microphone to give the next arrival clearance to land – on whichever runway he chose. Quite a busy place Haverfordwest International!

Another trip saw me cross the English Channel to Guernsey with a pilot friend from Birmingham proud possessor of his own aircraft. This included a brief stop at Bournemouth to refuel, which seemed like excessive caution with a single-engine plane claiming four hours' duration in normal flight conditions for a two-hour flight. But once airborne again and out of sight of land, the fuel gauge should merely have been labelled 'never enough' as far as I was concerned.

On the return journey and out of sight of either England or France, I had one of those St Exupéry moments. He was the French pilot/author/philosopher who wrote 'Le Petit Prince' for children (of all ages to 90+) but also the evocative 'Wind, Sand and Stars' for fellow pilots, after flying the mails in primitive planes down the west coast of Africa in the '1920's and 30's. Alone at night with the desert to his left and the Atlantic Ocean to his right, his vulnerability was a constant source of worry in a single-engine plane with few landing places in emergency. But he coped with it by looking heavenwards to remind himself how small and infinitesimal he was in a great universe. Why should God choose to bestow misfortune on such a small speck in the wilderness? Sadly, though he had time to write another book at the beginning of WWII called

'Flight over Arras'. He died later in the war during a mysterious trans-Mediterranean flight in his Lockheed Lightning. Returning from Guernsey I could not quite replicate the romanticism of the North African Rif and the crashing rollers of the Atlantic swell, but our single-engine status and the prospect of its failure gave pause for some philosophical reflection on life and death. Landing back at Birmingham brought me back to reality.

But civilian flying seemed tame by standards of the ever-vigilant RAF. Their sheer enthusiasm for things winged and mechanical seemed infectious, while by contrast, maintaining the regulatory five hours a year to keep the civilian license seemed like an unnecessary vanity. I gave it up and moved to other stuff.

I sometimes daydream while on one of the interminable international flights, that the pilots are suddenly taken sick with food poisoning requiring me to volunteer shyly to fly and land the plane. After a tense ground-controlled descent and a landing that did not wreck the airframe and nobody died like in one of those cheesy American disaster movies, I would be thanked by the stretcher-borne pilots on their way to hospital, garlanded with flowers, and beautiful air hostesses would fall at my feet with gratitude and admiration. Of course, in reality, I would be as incompetent as the next person with all the sophisticated systems they have to contend with these days, but the principles of flight remain what they have always been and I hold that in common with those who made flying their profession.

It was not for me, but I have many happy memories. Straighten up and fly right!

RAF Log book showing first solo flight on April 24th 1970. I told no-one for several days just to savour the feeling myself

Desperately trying to look cool having parked a Piper Cherokee, Johannesburg South Africa July '73

Chapter 4 MMBA – 'Miles and Miles of Bloody Australia'

Lest in the city I forget true mateship after all,
My water-bag and billy yet are hanging on the wall;
And I, to save my soul again, would tramp to sunsets grand
With sad-eyed mates across the plain in Never-Never Land.
Never Never Land by Henry Lawson, Australian poet 1867-1922.

University was great but studying is not everything. The wanderlust captivated me in my second year beckoning me away to new experience. My Oxford Professor was unimpressed by my plan to spend the long vacation in Australia. But his preference that I spend the time reading to improve chances of a good degree could not have been further from my thoughts. Anyway, with a special paper in the syllabus on Australian urbanism, I figured on selecting and doing fieldwork into the bargain. I would never have made a good academic; I learn more from visual and first-hand experience than books.

My best mates planned a trip to Greece on shoe string budgets vaguely in pursuit of some girls to whom we had taken a fancy, so there was some soul-searching that I was going off 12,000 miles to the other end of the earth. I had visions of them all pairing up on some balmy beach in Lesbos while I sweated it out in the great Australian desert, but I went anyway. There were no real regrets as I gained experience to knock their furtive groping into a cocked hat, though it was a hard parting at the time.

There had been an Australian government sponsored undergraduate programme running for years, encouraging soon to be qualified people to emigrate to the southern sun. As with the RAF eighteen months before, I made the right noises about 'thinking of emigrating' and after interview, their offer unfolded as the most generous imaginable. A guaranteed job and accommodation for approximately eight weeks; followed by four more free to travel around their vast country on TAA, Ansett airlines and buses at 50% concessionary fares - all for a £150 return airfare! Not much not to like.

The flight to Sydney was a 26hour marathon on a Qantas charter 707 for about 100 lucky British students, with merely half hour refuelling stopovers in Beirut, Delhi, Singapore and Darwin. In those happy go lucky far off days, pilots kept the cockpit door open the whole flight and let people up on the flight deck, especially for the girls, to admire the skill and complexity of their task. They were applauded for anything other than an airframe destructive landing and the whole trip was treated like a prolonged party.

Arriving in Sydney I still faced a four-hour trip back to Perth the next day, having planned to work for the West Australian Department of Mines Geological Survey, in the wildest parts of the country. This guaranteed access to the remotest spots before coming back to the urban fleshpots for my four weeks of travel. But first there was a full blown civic welcome by the mayor of Sydney with press and TV, straight off the plane. These exchange trips had become an established if tiny part of traditional national culture, started in the early 1950's by Sir Robert Menzies, Australia's longest serving PM with strong affiliations to the 'old country'. The 'hands across the sea' stuff was unexpected and quite emotional by the mayor who clearly had an eye to future advancement in the ruling Liberal Party. All this was set to end abruptly in 1972, when, the new Australian Labour PM Gough Whitlam, decided he did not want to pay to encourage more whingeing POMs to come to his land of opportunity. I got there just in time.

I flew on to Perth the next day right into another welcome reception for the five of us wise enough to choose the west, including more expressions of loyal partnership with the 'mother country'. I thought that expression to be long dead with the empire, but I had reckoned without the strong ties of far-flung places. I should have known better coming from Pembrokeshire. But as the mayor waxed lyrical about the 'toyes that boind', I spotted an 'okker' among the welcoming party, with similarly raised eyebrows to my own and his arm in a sling. "Rugby injury," I asked out of the side of my mouth, to which he replied "How the fxxx did you know? Everyone plays Ozzie Rools in this state!" Vernon George Reid and his quaintly named wife – Lizabeth Anne became from that point on, lifelong friends. To this day well over 40 years later, we have exchanged travelling children, career support and mutual national abuse in approximately equal measure – Australian matemanship at its best.

I stayed in the quadrangled and ivy-covered St George's College at the University of West Australia, sharing a room with a bloke from Bunbury in the south of the state where he said the world's best wine came from. At the time this was a disputable statement, but possibly more true now than then. I kept my counsel. On our first night in College, we visitors were applauded in traditional welcoming fashion as we sat down to dinner in the College's great hall. I had thought this old-world style had long gone; I was starting to like Australia.

The Department of Mines and its Geological Survey section were much more down to earth – literally speaking - as befits the sector and its people rapidly re-forming a new Australian spirit of outback frontiersmanship; more straight-talking types here. The minerals boom has gone from strength to strength as Australia has become the iron ore, coal, nickel and copper source of choice for the voracious maws of rapidly industrialising China and south east Asia. But even in the '70's, it was an industry of impressive scale, dwarfing anything similar nearer home.

I was soon instructed to pack a bag for a trip to the far north, teaming up with a geologist - Bob Leitch another Brit - going into the field to relieve one of his colleagues, Angus Davidson, on a remote site 900 miles north of Perth. The Survey were conducting water resource research across the de Grey River 100 miles east of Pt Hedland. Issued with a canvas-sided long wheel based Land Rover, tents, bed rolls and sleeping bags, we set off on a three day 900-mile road trip north to the De Grey, taking the direct inland route north via Meekatharra, Mt Newman and Marble Bar, practically the only settlements after the first two hundred miles north of Perth where the tarmac ran out.

Seventy miles before breakfast on the first day, saw us stopping at Walebing's roadside diner for a typical Australian outback breakfast of T Bone Steak, 3 eggs, hash browns and a gallon of coffee. This would lay me low for the rest of the day nowadays, but at age 20, I now felt like a million dollars as we got back on the road. A few miles further north, the tarmac ran out and it was on to graded dirt roads for the next two days and seven hundred miles. Vegetation got progressively sparser as we drove north and the farms, each already defined in square miles of territory, finally ran out giving way to open scrubland.

This part of the great Australian desert is pretty flat and featureless, but roads still needed frequent rolling by a big yellow grader to iron out the ribs. You could see the grader for miles ahead or behind as it dragged up so much dust.

Not a good thing to be caught behind, with the cab of a Land Rover being anything but dust tight. But without the grader, ribs get worse and worse across the soft sand surface, with wheels developing regular traction frequency. If you drove between 30 and 45 mph, you got shaken to bits, while above those speeds you seemed to ride over the ridges. Sometimes the sand got so soft and fine that the ridges suddenly disappeared and there was no purchase on the road as you fought for grip. Not a good idea with one of those massive livestock or pipe-work truck trains barrelling towards you from the opposite direction – over seventy tonnes of speeding destruction, if you found yourself in the way. You could see them for miles ahead as they kicked up huge dust clouds in their wake, giving plenty of warning of approach. You learned all this pretty quickly if you wanted a comfortable ride and the techniques for staying out of trouble rapidly became second nature.

Boredom is another enemy of such long featureless travel and you start to anticipate the next stop in an hour, then forty minutes, then twenty and so on. This was late June, so mid-winter in the southern hemisphere, not too hot during the day but freezing cold at night as cloud cover was non-existent in the aridly dry atmosphere. You could spot changes in ground features miles ahead, slight undulations in the gradient and subtle shifts of vegetation density as the rare occasional watercourses or underground water approached the surface, sustaining patches of green. I did not see rain for three weeks, but apparently brief precipitation revives the wild flowers into stunning profusion, colour and variety, often with roots across the surface to catch moisture. Lenses of crystallised minerals were also common, drying out differentially in the sun like a giant petri dish and tracing patterns across the flat, sandless creeks. Somehow the terrain never seemed utterly empty.

It was relatively slow going in the Land Rover, so we only covered 350 miles to reach Meekatharra at the end of the first day. I started to appreciate that the human environment was changing as subtly as the physical one. The Meekatharra Hotel is a classic 19th century stopover, which it would be unthinkable not to visit, given its splendid ornate exterior, and the miles of empty distance to get there and before the next remote water hole. People from towns such as Perth were as much strangers to this milieu as I was, as a foreigner; in fact, there were as many Brits and other nationalities in this wilderness as Aussies. The prevailing contrast, as in all remote places I have subsequently found, is not between those of different nationalities but between the metropolitans and the hardy outbackers. Fellowship among outbackers was invariably based on how few of them there were, combined with a deep mistrust for incomers which tipped over into open contempt if they were found to be 'metropolitans' with airs and graces come to laud it over them. Best you can do in these circumstances is to make clear your own outback status ('Pembrokeshire in Wales's far west' provided a colourful identity once there was time to explain) and a shared level of disrespect for city slickers. But you are still an incomer and wherever you are in the world, you have to earn your place, a stimulating challenge to which it is important not to be seen trying too hard.

Though this was mid-winter, it was sunny and clear, in fact a beautiful dry mid 20's temperature, so in the Meekatharra Hotel, beers were being consumed steadily but without interruption. But drunkenness was not common among long distance drivers, as the average Oz beer at the time was not strong, and the drinkers sweated much of it away long before it addled the brain, or slept it off before hitting the road again. There is a self-reliance code in the outback, which I came to respect. Beer is a social lubricant to help normally taciturn males to talk to each other or strangers and even on rare occasions the womenfolk; there did seem to be quite a gender separation in these deeply conservative establishments – not many 'Sheilas' to be seen.

The outback Australian way is to find a place at the bar being careful not to get between a drinker and his beer and to place your money on the counter. Without asking, you get a filled glass, typically a 'midi', with no rush for the seasoned drinker, and the barman takes the value of the drink leaving the rest. When your glass is empty, he fills it again, usually from a telescopic hose dispensing the amber liquid - taking more money. You can signal for refills and your shout for a round for your mates, in which case the barman takes more from your stash up to the whole value. There is a lot of trust. Once your money has gone there's no more beer. It's that simple so that the important process of drinking is uninterrupted by needless orders, or that painful eye contact moment in crowded big city pubs where micro seconds of timing are necessary to get your order in before the next bloke. This is also a safety valve in a macho environment; jumping the queue is not a good idea.

The atmosphere stayed pretty friendly, provided no one behaved like a city drongo; an abiding contempt being retained for people trying to be something they are not. This is an especial Australian talent but it is particularly marked among people with ample time to scrutinise everyone around them when there are so few. Remote areas are goldfish bowls with everyone discreetly watching everyone else. In the era before daytime television and its internet successor – still twenty-five years in the future in the early '70's - it was practically the only entertainment.

This time however, the animation of diverse company after the lonely miles of travelling was to be fleeting, as we decided on an early night. A short drive just out of town, we rolled out sleeping bags and bed rolls under the stars, a suitable distance from the road, thus avoiding passing insomniacs who might run us down. I am sure this casual attitude to such sleeping arrangements is now banned on health and safety grounds; what about snakes, scorpions and red-back spiders lying in wait? At the time, it just seemed entirely natural, so I never gave it another thought and in the cold clear air, sleeping was no problem. Up early in the cold of a winter morning and back on the road again before breakfast at a refuelling stop for the Land Rover with its 100-litre expanded fuel tank, I felt more alive than ever.

Bob was good company and we had many and varied conversations, but geologists are also a breed who know and presumably like working in remote areas, so silences were also comfortable. I got to thinking of my Uni friends swanning on the Greek beaches with lots of nubile young women who they would be trying to charm with their puerile banter. With a twinge of jealousy, I nevertheless concluded that they were not getting the better of it as my experience was spectacularly more out of the ordinary. I recall there was a song that June by a now practically un-remembered artist Lobo, called 'Me and you and a dog named Boo'. Its plangent tones and melancholy words fitting my mood together with memories of the USA of two years previously, as it told of two vagrants crossing the south of the US in an old car, 'luvvin and a livin' off the land'. In reality, it had little in common with my expenses paid road trip, but the romance and sadness of the words got me into a typical reflective Celtic mood while dreaming of Greek beaches.

As we pounded northwards, the vegetation got sparser. Slowly the southern winter sun rose over the dry parched landscape. We only managed a further three hundred miles that day, all now on graded dust roads and plenty of degraded surfaces to negotiate. As dusk gathered on that second day we were closing in on Mt Newman, even then, as now, one of the largest iron-ore sources in the world and centre of a huge extraction industry on an awesome scale. So flat was the landform, that the lights of Newman township were visible fifty miles out, seeming like a beckoning oasis of human contact for the long time before built features became visible.

Days of the week tend to count for little in much of the mining industry, as shift work tends to operate a seven days on/seven days off routine, with little else to do while working. But it was now Friday night, and Bob quietly suggested we pay a visit to the enormous prefabricated pub, which stood for social contact in Newman's male dominated and macho environment. As we entered the industrially scaled drinking establishment, the wall of sound that hit us was almost physical and wholly deafening. Five hundred men were looking to get themselves well tanked at the end of another long shift before sleep, or maybe, in those pre-Health and Safety regulation days, suitably prepared for a night shift. This was not a place for intricate conversation. No cash on the bar and the refill system here; eye contact with the barman was essential to get your beers in, but woe-betide anyone thought to be pushing in, this was not wise.

Oddly several drinkers had dogs with them – where did they keep them when on shift? You could immediately correlate human behaviour of the dog owner from his choice of mutt. Scope for disagreements between the dogs in this noisy, drink spilling, smoky atmosphere was infinite and quickly escalated to the owners. Perceived slights were infinitely more common than the real thing, especially with dogs nosing around the masters and each other. We saw several disagreements break out with shouting and posturing, a few boiling over into short sharp violence. It tended not to last long, as the protagonists were wearily pulled apart by their mates who had doubtless seen it all before. Strangely while the dogs often started the razzle with some tetchy moves between each other, they tended not to get involved in the real fighting. It seemed enough that they had caused the aggravation in the first place. Calculating hounds, but a wonderful master class in the complete absence of empathy to a student of social anthropology. Quite an atmosphere; and definitely one not to linger in.

There was a big outdoor barbecue facility where man food – steak, eggs, mountains of fries with a minimum of greens, then ice cream – was being dispensed in huge quantities. So, we chowed with those of a marginally more discerning nature who realised food was an essential ingredient for alcoholic absorption and basic nutrition, before plunging back inside for another briefer session of beers, and hitting the road out of town. Twenty miles further north we stopped by the roadside once more to sleep out under the stars again, the sleeping bags and bed rolls warding off the desert night cold. Now well used to the routine, I stayed awake briefly staring up at the clearest starlit sky, with its unfamiliar southern hemisphere star scape. I got to reflecting on what a strange world it was, how I came to be here watching stupid disputes between miners in such a remote place, but how small and inconsequential we all were before dreamless sleep took over. What it was to be young!

Now into our third day and road surfaces notwithstanding, we were getting bored with endless driving and determined to reach the De Grey River by nightfall and the prospect of at least a caravan bed and a warm canvas bucket shower promised as a start to the next three weeks of bush life. Still with another hefty three hundred miles via Nullagine and Marble Bar to go, two of Australia's most remote communities, we could only average forty-five mph, given the uncertainty of road surfacing. But now we were seasoned drivers able to anticipate the rolling loss of traction of the trusty Land Rover as it encountered the softer sand at the foot of the regular dry riverbed crossings. So, while it was slow, it was steady progress as we headed out of the iron-rich Hamersley Range through the northern Pilbara region towards the distant north west coast.

Marble Bar is another classic frontier town said to be the hottest place in Australia during the summer, though others probably dispute this honour. Who would argue? Even in late June and mid-winter, it was warm enough at midday as we took the obligatory cold drinks in the Ironclad Hotel. Its zinc-topped bar is a throwback to the 19th century and the first discovery of the iron rich ores of the area.

We were now in smelling distance of the Indian Ocean and our destination near Goldsworthy on the de Grey River, fifty miles down off the Hamersleys and just short of the river's estuary. We could see the ocean in the far distance as we descended the sun scorched hills and slowly the vegetation got thicker approaching the lower river basin. Over nine hundred miles and three days hard driving north from Perth, we had at last reached the

Department of Mines' latest geological survey site to look for regular ground water supplies underneath the surface river basin.

Consistent and plentiful water supplies to support the mining activity are as much a challenge as locating the minerals themselves – more so in the Pilbara as iron ore was there in profusion while water was not. This part of the north coast of West Australia has a winter season, while the atmosphere is more stable, that is drier than the occasionally stormy summer. So, the de Grey River was only really a watercourse in name. Wide swathes of its multiple lowland channels near the coast were nothing more than seas of the finest grained sand. As we had discovered on the dust roads north, these were the toughest of terrain to traverse in lowest ratio four-wheel drive. But under the surface there was an abundant aquifer fed water table, often over three hundred metres down but all the sweeter and more consistent for its depth below the surface - if only it could be found and brought to the surface.

There to greet us were Angus Davidson the geologist whom Bob would be relieving after three months in the bush, and two teams of drillers operating a series of diesel drills, sinking deep boreholes to ascertain depth and quality of the deep-water table. The drillers were a motley collection of seasoned survey men and casual roughnecks earning big money compensating the extremity of the remote location. They were overseen by a foreman – known to all as Boss John - who conveyed the weary air of a man who had dealt with all that life could throw at him. Almost all the drillers in those far-off pre-Health and Safety days had lost a finger or two. The casings round the shafts and drill bits had to be guided into position by hand while they dangled from a crane as each length was attached, sunk and the next one was suspended over its partly buried neighbour before being attached and sunk in turn. Astonishingly, most of the drillers chose not even to wear gloves. Boss John explained that the average was one lost finger per six man months, and he sported no less than three shortened fingers severed at upper or lower knuckle on his right hand and two on the left. These were badges of honour.

They all revered Angus who had won their respect as a quietly competent geologist (universally known as 'golliwogs' to the drillers) who had a nose as well as his academic training for where to find the water. Despite his affluent background in Peppermint Grove, one of Perth's smartest suburbs, Angus was all the drillers hope for and respected in their golliwog, knowing where to drill, respectful and rarely raising his voice to laud it over them, thus observing a strict adherence to the outback code. Angus knew his trade and they would have followed him anywhere.

So, at first, they all eyed Bob and me - the replacement crew - with baleful disdain. They wanted Angus to stay on "instead of these two fxxxing POMs the Depaartment has sent us." But Angus was due to go back to Perth to get married no less, so there was no argument.

There were two very big men nicknamed 'Lurch' a New Zealander, and 'Ivan the Terrible', who was Croat. Lurch's Dad had been in the 8th Army in North Africa, while Ivan the T was equally proud of having been a young fighter with Mikhailovic's partisans supporting the Germans against Tito in the savage Balkan wars of 30 years previously. Ivan had left Yugoslavia to come to Australia to start a new life, while Lurch was just passing through, suffering the specialised abuse focused on all Kiwis by the neighbourly Australians. Ivan and Lurch did not get on, or so it seemed. Every morning, they would go off into the bush and beat the daylights out of each other for twenty minutes before starting work. On our first day, we saw a dust cloud about fifty metres away and Boss John explained it was, "Nothing much, just Lurch and Ivan the T having their little local disagreement." They would come back into camp apparently tolerating each other and work all day without trouble – both scared of the authority of Boss John who let them take it out on each other, but could probably have taken them both on at the same time.

Drillers, like seamen, are a superstitious lot and would not share their caravan campsite living quarters with the golliwogs. So, Angus lived in glorious isolation in two caravans about two miles from them, nearby one of the few patches of open water, one as sleeping quarters and the other his field office. We set up our tents, safe in the knowledge that in winter the open water was not infested with mosquitoes. It was an idyllic spot just off the north coast highway, which runs away northwards to Broome in the Kimberleys and eventually Darwin. The drillers meanwhile had a caravan park of their own and would invite us over for beers and we would invite them back, but we never bunked or ate most of our meals together. This was a traditional – almost naval – arrangement with lots of insubordinate banter, but under Angus and Boss John, it was a happy crew – Lurch and Ivan the Terrible excepted.

Not surprisingly the banter during the working day was never ending, and with Bob's and my arrival, the opportunity to take the piss out of the POMs became too much to resist, especially when they discovered what had not occurred to us, that our Land Rover had been built in England and not like the others, under license in Australia. Crossing those river basin sand seas became an ordeal for us, and the source of endless strife and amusement, as it was reckoned that no Land Rover had the right low ratio to work its way through the slick almost liquid surface. Determined not to be out done, Bob and I would set off, sometimes in reverse when lower ratio traction could be achieved, but like Angus's vehicle, ours invariably failed, to ribald comments about 'shit British engineering etc. etc.' They would leave us there in the middle of the 'river' for half an hour before firing up their huge balloon-tyred tractor, which came floundering across the sand surface to tow us out amidst much catcalling and further abuse.

These diversions seem now almost puerile, but they were the essential glue that bonded the de Grey River team together. The daily routine was fairly repetitive, if sometimes mildly hazardous, so every opportunity for diversions at someone's expense was seized on gleefully. Men in the 1970's, especially those doing tough manual labour, were never tactile, but they replaced this mildly homophobic froideur, with perpetual jokes that often got quite intimate. The ability to take part in, go along with or accept being the butt of the practical jokes was part of the bonding or its opposite, the means of winkling out those who could not play by the rules. This may seem strange in an apparently more caring 21st century society where men are expected to show their emotions and even hug each other as part of a more openly expressive style of relationship. But this remains surface behaviour and teams are still built out of recognising the ability to cope with adversity, whether to go out of the cave to kill mammoths, fight wars shoulder to shoulder or merely work together in potentially hazardous circumstances with a degree of trust and reliance, physically and mentally. The silly games may have been just that, but I suspect they had and still have, a deeper purpose. Will I be able to rely on this person in a crisis or not? Let me test the water and see! We are all under examination in this way much of the time and it pays dividends to understand it...

In Australia, this tradition goes deep. The history of occupation of the vastness of the continent by so few Europeans (displacing more but still not numerous indigenous groups) has built a huge belief in and respect for self-reliance. When there is no one else around, you fix the horse's hoof or the car's puncture 'on yer own mite!' This is a big contrast with ideas of division of labour in socially stratified Europe, for whom the early migrant Australians engendered an abiding contempt, thus creating the tradition of 'matemanship'. There were so few others around in the vast Australian emptiness, that you came to rely on each other like brothers, never ever to let each other down. Proving you were a mate was hard and testing, but once established the bond was for life. Nothing so intense seems to exist in other cultures, but when an Ozzie calls you mate as more than just a passing remark, he usually means it and you better treat the moniker with respect. It is not easily won!

Being super-numerary to main survey activities, I was sent on various lone missions, in particular the one-hundred-mile round trip shopping expeditions to Port Hedland, to collect the mail and buy extra provisions. This was the way to get back into favour with the drillers, because they all had some individual and often furtive requests for a type of tobacco, sickly sugary sweets or the more lurid types of lad's magazines. Shopkeepers in PH did not bat an eyelid when I went through the checkout with these purchases; they knew the score in the outback. I just had to ride the odd looks from the check-out girl.

Once on the way back, on a long featureless strip of road, I was passing the only single bush in sight, when a sheep broke cover and ran straight under the Land Rover's wheels. There were two sickening thumps as it hit – for front and back wheels, - then, there it was twitching on the road behind me, so still alive but horribly mangled. A truck train coming the other way also slowed to a stop, but the driver stayed in his cab, and it was left to me to get out, lift the sand shovel from its place on the left front wing of the Land Rover and finish off the poor mangled sheep with a sharp blow to its head. Satisfied with the right procedures observed, the driver of the truck train ground his gears, set his vehicle in motion again and rolled away westwards. There was no one else about, no farm in sight and not even another bush to be seen. I dragged the dead sheep to the road edge and left it there – to join with every other sort of road kill to be seen on outback roads – in particular kangaroos, who graze on the road edge grasses at night and get dazzled by headlights. Hence the origin of 'Roo Bars on outback vehicles – most drivers were more concerned for the damage to their rigs than the appalling carnage of wild and semi-domesticated animals wreaked by speeding vehicles.

After one long hot day with the drillers, bush showers were a special luxury of the well-organised campsite and Angus was nothing if not well organised. We heated water in a large disused oil drum and filled a canvas bucket with a shower attachment and set it up in a tree. A few duckboards completed the arrangements and as the sun went down I was enjoying a leisurely douche starkers, looking forward to the first beer of the evening. Out of nowhere, a car pulled off the road and three girls got out apparently lost and asking the way onwards, up the highway past Goldsworthy to Broome. None of them seemed especially surprised at the sight of me naked (disappointing me somewhat) but Bob and Angus thought this was hilarious. Having not seen a girl for several weeks, my towel disappeared mysteriously under the caravan. While I danced around like an idiot looking to protect my shredded dignity, the girls stopped for a beer or three and stayed chatting for over an hour as the sun went down. They were charming but practically the only female company we saw in three weeks and soon drove on north on their own quest for adventure. I was suitably clothed by the time they departed.

Any girls of remotely eligible age living in this remote territory seemed long ago to have fled to the big cities. Except that, when we went into Goldsworthy for beers in the only pub, there were plenty of Aborigine girls - and older men for that matter - hanging around, mostly in a state of inebriation that was sad to behold. Worse still – far worse - was the deep contempt with which they were commented upon by the drillers, whose longing for women stopped short of going with a 'Lubra' as they contemptuously described them. I felt it was best to avoid the subject.

It was always delicate going in conversation with the drillers, absorbing their barbs while resisting the temptation to strike back with anything more than harmless banter. This started on the first pub night when Boss John had extracted from me an admission that I was a student at Oxford. "Fxxxin' Ada", he said, "what the fxxx you doing here?" The implied compliment of my answer "having a good time," only lasted a minute before they all started an entirely new line of piss taking, from then on asking Angus to consult 'Professor Calculus' or 'Einstein' what I thought of the water test or surface percussion results. Angus watched with tolerant detachment as if he had gone through the same early on in his relationship. I endured in silence; you have to know how to take it in the outback.

There was one runty little man who was always first with the smartarse comments. He used humour to keep his place among his brawnier mates. He hated all forms of outback creepie-crawlies and was teased mercilessly about it by the others, often suffering livestock put down his sleeping bag. One day there was a twenty-four-hour pump test staged, when having drilled to water table level, we would pump the water out over twenty-four hours to measure its quality and pressure from which to ascertain suitability for extraction. The water spilling out of the top of the borehole had to be piped away at least two-hundred metres into the bush so it did not soak back down to the drill base. Bob and I had to check the drillers had laid the pipe fully two-hundred metres out, and not just cheated by taking it round the back of some bushes.

Walking its length to check, we were side by side when he suddenly hit me in the chest telling me to stop. There, under my hovering foot, was a four foot and venomous tiger snake, with its fangs stuck through the clear polythene pipe having its fill of sweet aquifer water. We backed off and went back to camp, whereupon the runty humourist grabbed a spade and said he was going to kill the 'fxxxin' snike'. Everyone wanted to see this, as Runty headed off, armed to the teeth, singlehandedly to reduce Australia's reptilian population. We all stopped well short of the snake, which was unconcernedly enjoying its drink. "Be my guest," said Boss John lazily, "but remember they move fast, and if you miss …. he'll getcha!" Runty thought about that, circled the snake and took a few futile lunges at it to everyone's growing ridicule, then he backed off completely contenting himself with throwing rocks at the snake until it slithered off into the bush. I was very lucky that day, a tiger snake bite can be fatal; I survived but Runty lost any remaining shreds of dignity he had retained from the last incident.

The time soon came for Angus to depart. He was flying back to Perth to commence marital bliss, and a ceremony was organised to bid him farewell with the, by now customary ribald humour, about the 'lucky broide'. The drillers assembled the largest collection of cold beers they could muster and we were all invited to a 'barbie' at their campsite to celebrate. Lurch looked particularly stressed by this gathering, as he had drawn the shortest straw to make the presentation of a gold watch to Angus – an outrageously expensive present, which had cost them all a fair proportion of their weekly wages. I know, I had picked it up a few days before at Pt Hedland's only jeweller, and Angus was seriously embarrassed to receive it. Lurch made us all cringe with a forced farewell speech to much ribald comment from the rest, to which he threatened to retaliate in normal fashion with fists and boots, but he eventually got through his eulogy to everyone's relief. Underneath their macho exteriors, these were men who knew a good colleague when they saw one. Hearts of gold, and it got me thinking what qualities of leadership it took to motivate men in difficult and remote circumstances. Angus truly had achieved 'matemanship' status.

It was also soon time for me to go, for I had really only accompanied Bob on the long journey north for company, co-driving and general factotum duties. I was due to go back to Perth with a foreman of mines – Dave Blackett - who roamed the north west inspecting the Geological Survey's various exploration sites as an Inspector of mines and boreholes. He had a big Holden Estate - a four-door car, one vehicle of choice for the average outbacker, but not one with four-wheel drive. So, we took the coast road home via Exmouth Gulf, Carnarvon and Geraldton – a journey of over 1,200 miles and potentially four full days. Dave had more experience even than Boss John, so he knew the route out of the north well, in fact he was due to retire from field assignments very soon. But within twenty miles of leaving Port Hedland, a stone kicked up by a passing truck shattered our windscreen into an opaque star pattern - no visibility whatsoever. Undeterred, we picked out all the glass and left it without remorse on the roadside – average outback behaviour.

Closing all the windows and moving off with no windscreen, high pressure would build up in the car so most of the dust from passing vehicles billowed round the vehicle and passed over the roof. Slightly heavier objects, of which our greatest fear was bees, came straight through the open screen however, so we donned goggles and masks to protect our faces and avoided getting close-up behind vehicles whose dust clouds would envelope us. Luckily the 'coast' road – often over fifty miles from the coast but still hugging the lowlands round the edge of the Hamersley Range had more tarmacked stretches, when we could greatly increase speed and eat up the interminable miles southwards.

Late on the first evening with darkness almost complete, we had the inevitable and luckily (for us) non-fatal impact with a large boomer kangaroo. Fully six-foot tall he was grazing by the road side and startled by our headlights, remained frozen to the spot as we saw him too late and hit him at over sixty mph. Again, luckily for us, it was a glancing blow hitting the side of the vehicle and the frontal Roo bars, rather than a full-face impact which could have the animal coming over the hood through the non-existent windscreen and probably killing us both. We stopped and searched but there was no sign of the Roo, who must have run off scared to death and probably already fatally crippled. That was not a pleasant thought, but after twenty minutes fruitless searching we had to give up and move on. Ten miles further on, while I was driving, we had a rear tyre blow out and I just managed to get the car to the road edge where we groped around in the dark to replace the wheel. Dave was a man of few words but remarked that we were lucky not to have a front tyre blow out. "Probably cause us to roll the car," he admitted drily. Great, what next?

The Holden was much faster than the plodding canvas-sided Land Rovers, so we kept going and covered the distance in just over two and a half days, being eager to return to the bright lights of the big city. Getting into Perth on the third day, we looked like the original outbackers. The car was covered in red mud and dust; there was no windscreen, the two ockers inside wore masks and goggles and the whole of the near side was stoved-in where we had hit the Roo. 'Department of Mines' was just visible on the doors, a dead giveaway. The well-behaved suburban traffic gave us a wide berth and there were many ribald comments from the mechanics as we delivered the trashed vehicle back to the vehicle pool.

Post script: I have been back to Australia several times since the 1970's, and have observed several subtle and some more obvious changes since. Those were the days of cartoon and comedian character Barry McKenzie in his chauvinistic prime, utterly unaware of what an ignorant 'okker' with deep prejudices he was – on the contrary rather proud of it and travelling the world on a tide of Australian ignorance and chauvinism. McKenzie's creator Barry Humphries was as aware of the chauvinism as his creation was blissfully ignorant and in Britain we loved his antics in Private Eye.

The lack of political correctness among many Australians in the 1970's was breath-taking but often endearing considering what a pain such behaviour was becoming in UK. On the issue of gender politics, you could sometimes attend barbecues and the men would not talk to the women, but if single, saunter over towards the end and expect to pick up a Sheila to take home. Young Australian women meanwhile seemed much more aware of current world trends, were often very stylishly dressed, and a lot of them had given up on the local males, dreaming of going to 'Yerp', or the 'Stites.' The blokes affected not to care; to show too much concern for what women thought seemed effeminate. Weird or what?

I have also previously alluded to the racism concerning aborigines, whose lives seemed to be so much in contrast to those of comfortable suburban whites. But in the predominantly white big cities, there were hardly any aborigines to be seen other than as small groups sleeping rough and begging. Without sufficient decent employment, they could not afford the urban cost of living and largely unseen by the white majority, prejudices could grow as the malign extension of pure ignorance.

How things have changed! Australia is now more politically correct than the USA. Health and Safety reigns supreme in everything you do. Smoking is not only banned all over the place but often looked upon as a social disease, and the 'indigenous population', as they are often now called, are given at least the token respect they lacked for decades previously. But some of this reaches cringe-worthy proportions, and sometimes tips over into patronising behaviour, probably no one's fault but a fact of life between two societies who have such different values.

Indigenous Australians at their most traditional, have an almost completely non-material culture, where dream time and ancestor worship reigns supreme within their philosophy of life. Few whites understand that. Modern economy land rights have to grapple with completely different value systems as between white farmers, property developers or mining companies on the one hand and indigenous pastoral grazing and roaming rights on the other, claimed to go back thousands of years. These contrasts go straight over the heads of most white Australians who are as materialist as the rest of us in the western world. The clash of cultures could not be greater.

But there was previously an innocence in most people's pre-disposition to others – men for women; whites for Aborigines etc., where the harm was done through negligence or innocent ignorance rather than overt acts of cruelty. How many more crimes of omission than commission there have been in the world! Nowadays, the media has made everyone aware of the (sometimes appalling) wrongs of the past in which, it must be said, we British played a full part during colonial days. However much of the time now given to respecting minority culture seems just a bit like posturing; many indigenous people would say they remain significantly disrespected, despite politics.

The new zeitgeist of token respect was summed up for me perfectly when I attended an AGM of a big company I was working for in the Brisbane conference centre a few years ago. There were nearly eight hundred staff shareholders present and two days of intense reporting of annual performance to go, but we started proceedings with a half hour display from the local Burrumbidgee tribe, described as traditional guardians of the land on which the conference centre had been built. This already stretched my imagination a bit, as they went through a routine which entailed setting fire to dry grasses without use of matches or lighters – rubbing sticks together, like we used to do when kids. To the weird sounds of a didgeridoo, this all worked well enough, but the ensuing smoke set off the fire alarm system, thus causing a procedural crisis in the safety conscious assembly as the default response required complete evacuation of the building. But everyone knew the source of the smoke and fire, which one of the performers was already putting out - in obvious contrast to his traditions - with a modern fire extinguisher. The evacuation was cancelled as we needed to get on with the agenda, though of course there could have been a fire started elsewhere at the same time, so should we not have trooped out? For me, this recent respect for indigenous tradition had come up against the corporate religion of health and safety – and to my surprise had won. What a strange world!

Another oddity in Brisbane was the apparent ignorance about a magical place merely two hours flying time due east, out over the Pacific from the Queensland state capital. My wife Sylvie had accompanied me on this trip (one of the few corporate freebies we ever received together), and we had planned to spend ten days in French speaking Nouvelle Caledonie after the AGM. "What do you want to go there for? Oi've never been!" was the common reaction of many people. The prospect of having to speak "Frinch" was evidently too much for some.

I put these changes down to a loss of innocence, probably my own innocence rather than that of others. But while travel was by no means so common nor so relatively cheap in the early '70's as it is now, there was an openness at that time to hearing about other people's experiences. Lots of prejudice yes, including holding your own with conversational give and take spiced with a good sense of humour. But there was an interest in other humans just because they were standing there. Now, wherever you are in the world, this is often replaced with cynicism, indifference or too often, that habit some people have of needing to trump your story. We are in the midst of a 'Me' culture.

None of this is exclusive to Australia. These are universal trends in an age when our attention spans have been foreshortened, first by Disney, then computer games and now instant multi – modal access to movies, tweets and blogs. There were thirty years between my first and next visits to Australia, so perhaps I noticed this contrast there more acutely than at home where it crept up inexorably so as not to seem so abrupt. The changes have clearly been a fact of all our lives but less noticeable when you grow with them.

Australia is still a wonderful place and I like the 'can do' attitude of so many of its inhabitants. That much at least has not changed – Advance Australia Fair!

Ironclad Hotel, Meekatharra W Australia, June '71

Drilling for ground water, de Grey River Basin, North West Australia July '71

Chapter 5 Among Africa's last white rulers; South Africa and Rhodesia

"Our party must continue to strike fear in the heart of the white man, our real enemy!"
"The only white man you can trust is a dead white man."
Robert Mugabe, PM or President of Zimbabwe since 1980

"For to be free is not merely to cast off one's chains, but to live in a way that respects and enhances the freedom of others."
"If you want to make peace with your enemy, you have to work with your enemy. Then he becomes your partner."

Nelson Mandela 'Long Walk to Freedom' Little, Brown & Co 1994
President of South Africa 1994 to 1999.

There are countries in the world that invite instant judgments about those who choose to visit. Of nowhere was this more truly spoken during its apartheid years than South Africa. The anti-apartheid movement was well organised and focused in its attacks on support for the white-ruled Republic, and with considerable justification. Quite apart from the denial of human rights and the cruelty with which it was implemented, it seemed like a social regime that could never work. This was particularly so within my chosen profession, in spatial planning and the artificial arrangement of urban and rural settlement patterns.

But did this explain people's reluctance to have anything to do with the country and its people? Would it not be a good thing to go see, and form particular opinions rather than the blanket disapproval so much the fashion among the student communities of which I was by 1973, a four-year paid-up member?

By 1973, I had graduated from Oxford and was studying for a Masters in Urban and Regional Planning at the University of Wales in Cardiff. The Welsh capital was a great place to be during Wales' golden rugby era, but the University was also a powerful antidote to Oxford's dreaming spires, the self-righteousness of left-wing anti-establishment and anti-apartheid views matching neatly for me, with the complacency and assumptions of status at England's oldest University.

Vernon Newcombe was my Professor at Cardiff, after he had enjoyed a wide-ranging international career with the UN in New York and across Africa. He was not easily swayed by popular opinion and when I declared an interest in African development, it was he who put the idea into my head of going to South Africa. The Prof argued it was a system that I could both relate to because of its institutional similarities to the UK system, while offering big contrasts where social planning and cultural references were concerned – especially for black (African), Indian and Coloured (mixed race) communities, all of whom were required to develop separately. This racial vocabulary was going to take some getting used to, not to mention the philosophy behind it.

He introduced me to Professor Alan Lipman at Cardiff's School of Architecture and a well-known radical South African exile who was equally keen for me to go. Not for these Profs then, the fashionable political correctness of mere dis-association from matters disapproved of. Get involved was their mantra, so in May 1973, they helped me through their substantial networks to secure a summer vacation, work experience job at the Johannesburg City Council Planning Department in Braamfontein, starting in two-weeks' time. Prof Lipman gave an inkling of his underlying thoughts as I left in early June; "you might not like it," he said, "but try to stay out of trouble!"

After twelve hours, c/o UTA's budget flight from Paris via Gabon, the impact of 'separate racial development' was immediately evident at Johannesburg's Jan Smuts Airport. Passengers were immediately segregated into white and non-white lines, but that did not correlate with better treatment for whites; indeed, some of us were getting longer interrogations than the rest of the passenger complement. As a British student with the usual longish hair of the time, I was viewed suspiciously by the immigration officer, who contrasted me with his own nearly shaven skull. Marginally satisfied with my working status, he overcame his evident prejudices about British students and, with an ill grace and curled lip of disdain, my passport was stamped – 'Permitted to enter the Republic of South Africa' - Welkom!

For my first few days, I stayed in one of the halls of residence at Witwatersrand Uni, a bastion of English rather than Afrikaans academia in Jo'burg. 'Wits' was a focus of liberal if privileged student action against the regime, a reputation that has nuanced subtly since the ANC became the only realistic party of government from the early 1990's. But in the early '70's the Afrikaaner dominated National Party was in charge, and my fellow students were vociferous in their criticism of the regime and eager to hear what was happening on the anti-apartheid scene in London. One quiet individual among the loud anti-government protestations turned out to be the only Afrikaaner present; he pointed out that no matter how much you cared for black community progress and opportunity, it would be a blood bath for the whites come the onset of 'black rule'. The silence greeting this observation attested to its plausibility; the fear factor at work. More than forty years later and twenty since the end of National Party rule in 1994, all those present would now be amazed at the extent to which this prophecy remains largely inaccurate.

At the time, my employer the City Planning Department was also responsible for spatial planning of the so called 'Non-European Affairs Department (NEAD),' so I was well placed, as Prof Newcombe had intended, to take a look at how things were being done under the principles of 'separate development'. We tend to associate apartheid with segregated buses, schools and park benches, but the principle of separate homelands and spatial settlement of people of different races was a far more profound aspect of the apartheid regime, and I would be working close to the heart of its day to day management.

First things first however, I had an interview with the head of department who directed me to Mr. Wessels. This redoubtable individual fully five feet high, seemed to have no first name that anyone knew. He kept his distance from all the architects and planners in the department as keeper of stationery stores. Mr Wessels eyed me balefully through his bottle-base thick glasses and handed me a writing pad and three pencils - 3H; H; and HB. "When you 'ave used them op, bring me the stubs and Ah will issue yew with further pencils as reqwaared," he explained slowly. I could see this place was run on a tight budget but the rest of the department seemed pretty human and there was a lot of amusement and banter out of earshot from, but at Mr. Wessels' expense. He seemed to be a local metaphor for the inflexible stance of Afrikaanerdom.

My first job was sitting at a drawing-board to design street patterns for a new township called El Dorado Park, catering for the influx of thousands of mixed race people migrating north from the Cape in search of employment in Jo'burg's booming mining based economy. It was not long however, before the department received an instruction from the Ministry of Education to go to Soweto, the huge black township south of Jo'burg, to help the Non-European Affairs Department (NEAD) identify suitable sites for new schools. There was always unrest and huge simmering social tension in Soweto, and the City authorities had decided education was the key to solving these problems. Basically right, I thought, but still a bit like putting lipstick on a pig – it was not going to change the fundamentals. But I kept my counsel, remembering the Professor's last piece of advice before leaving Cardiff. I was invited to join the first school sites visit.

I travelled out to Soweto with a chain-smoking fellow planner nearing the end of his career in the department, John Manders, a proud South African member of the UK's Royal Town Planning Institute. We drove into Soweto in his ageing motor and met up with a local official of the NEAD, a small man whose name I have mercifully forgotten. He would accompany us to government property locations deemed suitable for new builds or extensions to existing schools. This official was a representative of separate development in action, and immediately made it clear the new schools programme would be a gross misuse of government funding and said no good would come of it. "For one thing," he pointed out unctuously, "this is a worker's township and families with children are not licensed to be here". John and I exchanged wary looks but said nothing.

What a bleak place Soweto was! Row upon row of small barrack type structures as far as the eye could see, with barely a tree in sight and little sign of shops, public squares or community facilities. Some casual stalls and markets were set up temporarily around the train stations where huge numbers of people disgorged from the overcrowded trains from the goldfields outside Jo'burg. Otherwise shopping facilities seemed very limited. These trains were said to be death traps for anyone looking like they were carrying money; bicycle spokes inserted with a knife into the back alongside the spine did not actually kill (not straight away at any rate), but rendered the victim paralysed and unable to resist, while their pockets were fleeced. Such stories were usually recounted by whites as indications of the barbarous inhabitants who lived in Soweto. I have heard since that the nearby Baragwanath Hospital was a training ground for medics heading into war zones.

The crime rate and violence were signs of people living on the edge, earning barely sufficient wages to keep themselves and their families in the far-away homesteads adequately fed, and preying on their neighbours, as a result. This place was not for the faint-hearted.

We arrived at the first site, a government stores adjacent to an existing primary school. Located in the middle of a Xhosa community area, the property guardian had been selected from a different tribal group, thus applying one of the oldest principles of social control – divide and rule. All government buildings had a guardian, in this case an imposing six-foot four Zulu warrior with high-caste scar marks on his cheeks. He was dressed in a ragged blue uniform, but maintained an imposing dignity thanks to his size and quiet respectful demeanour. But there had been a break-in at the stores site the night before, and several windows had been smashed and chairs and furniture turned over throughout the property.

The diminutive NEAD official went berserk, shouting at the guardian about his neglect of duty. The guard stood rigidly to attention while he endured this public dressing down in front of us embarrassed strangers. It was difficult to know how much he may have been responsible, but the NEAD official had no doubts. Getting carried away with his anger, he grabbed a chair and, placing it in front of the guardian still standing rigidly at attention, he stood on it and slapped the man's face several times. I could not believe it and wanted to disappear, yet remained fascinated to see how quickly the Zulu warrior remembered his warlike ancestry and decided to pile drive the small official into the floor.

He could have done this with one hand, but it never happened; he merely stood there and took this shameful display of public abuse without flinching – a demonstration of self-control I recall vividly. It seemed to sum up so much of what was wrong with race relations in South Africa; complete contempt by so many whites for blacks, and an arrogant assumption that the former could expect absolute obedience from the latter even after a gross display of abuse. In this case, the assumption worked, but again, I kept my thoughts to myself - I was not going to solve anything by open protest. What I was witnessing was mild compared with what had gone before – the massacres of peaceful protestors at Sharpville for example in 1960, and what was to follow when student riots really got going in 1976, at Carltonville and elsewhere,

Bearing witness is at least something, and we duly made a formal report about this appalling lapse of self-control on return to the Council offices. But I am sure nothing will have happened. I wonder where either of the two characters may be now, and if they have met in changed political circumstances, what they would respectively think to say to each other?

Overall, my work duties were turning out to be pretty light, so I was encouraged to take a few days off to travel. First off, I wanted to get to Salisbury – now Harare – capital of the beleaguered state of Rhodesia – now Zimbabwe - which had declared Independence unilaterally from Britain eight years earlier under its white Prime Minister Ian Smith. Britain under the auspices of UN sanctions, was blockading trade to and from the 'rebel' state via its port of choice, Beira in Portuguese controlled Mozambique. It would be fascinating to see how things were progressing – if they would let me in.

To save money, I decided to hitch-hike to Salisbury, getting out on the road north from Jo'burg early on my first day off. I got a few short lifts from commuters heading for Pretoria the legal capital to the north, but from there on, it got harder. I decided humour might be a device to attract people to stop, and found a large piece of cardboard on the roadside on which I wrote, 'London' in big letters. That did the trick for a while and via some longer lifts, I made my way into the deeply traditional northern Transvaal (now Limpopo district of Gauteng Province). I made it to Potgietersrus, (now Mokopane) but by now it was late morning and the road to Pietersburg (now Polokwane) was empty of cars. For some reason truck drivers were not the best prospects for picking up hikers.

Just then an old car with a white family of father, mother and three small kids stopped and offered me a lift. The driver wore a pork pie hat and his best suit, his wife had a hat with cherries on it and a net in front of her face, while the kids in the back were also in Sunday best. English was not their first language and I think they must have been going to a funeral. I recall the kids had runny noses and they stared at me as if I was from another planet. I could relate to that. Their father eyed me in his driver's mirror, and asked in halting English, "Are yew a God-fearing and Christian man?" If I had not been beforehand, I certainly was now, and said so, so he asked me to read passages from his Bible which he handed to me reverently over the back of his seat, so the kids could listen to 'properly spoken English'. "We suggest Exodus", he said not inviting any other choice. I scrabbled around to find the start of Chapter 9, "Then the Lord said unto Moses Go in unto Pharaoh and tell him: Thus saith the Lord God of the Hebrews, Let my People go that they may serve thee".

This section of the Bible is written about the Israelites in Egypt, but I expect my small audience could have regarded it as a suitable text for the Afrikaaner Great Trek northwards out of the British-controlled Cape during the 19th Century. My choice of a yet more modern interpretation might have been the all non-white populations of South Africa under the yolk of apartheid rule; but I did not press the point. If there was any irony in this message, it seemed to fly out the window, and they seemed well pleased repeating the final phrase in ringing tones. I suspect the kids understood only a little of this and cared for less. But I was not comfortable with how things might progress, so suddenly remembered a friend I needed to see in Pietersburg and asked to be dropped off there. They departed northwards with a friendly enough wave, while I paused to think what a different world I now found myself in. Walking into a nearby roadhouse, I was drinking a coke thinking about my next move, when a fit looking middle-aged man with a virtually shaved head, approached me and said, did I want a lift to Salisbury. Salvation at last!

Dirk, I forget his second name, forty years on, said he was a South African volunteer in the Rhodesian Light Infantry (RLI) who were engaged at that time in a vicious war with the 'Terrs' as they were locally known. These disparate groups were otherwise (depending on your politics), known as the African freedom fighters in the bush all around Rhodesia but principally at that time, the north of the country where they could infiltrate from neighbouring Zambia. Dirk was returning from leave and seemed to be well paid. He was driving a brand-new Ford Corsair 2000E, a car of some speed and potency which I recall had recently won the Paris Dakar Rally. He did not offer to open the boot, so I slung my bag in the back seat and we set off for Salisbury, still six hours away - plenty of time to get a very different perspective on an unfamiliar subject.

First came the border crossing at Beit Bridge, where Dirk left me at Immigration to be offered a stamp in my passport or not as I chose, as evidence of having entered Rhodesia. I said yes please, and they visibly warmed to this apparent expression of solidarity with their rebel cause. Crossing into Rhodesia required us to traverse what Kipling had called the 'great, green, greasy' Limpopo River and I could see hippos basking up stream of the bridge, as we entered Matabeleland en route to Fort Victoria (now Masivingo) and Salisbury (now Harare).

Dirk had little time for the Brits and the 'soft' European attitude to African independence movements, and declared his trust in the Ian Smith government to win the war. He referred mysteriously to huge secret funding and weapon imports that were finding no difficulties in breaking the British blockade. South Africa was offering tacit if low key support and the port of Beira blockaded by the Royal Navy was apparently being circumvented via trade through Mozambique's capital and largest port, Lourenco Marques (now Maputo) in the south, where the British had no ships to stop embargo runners.

Dirk delighted in recounting what it was like to fight a bush war. The troops had discarded their normal automatic weapons and equipped themselves with sawn off shotguns, because enemy encounters in thick bush were short and sharp at very close quarters. Firefights were swift, brutal and bloody with the first side to let off a blast of lead shot in a wide ark usually getting the better of the battle. Grenades and mortars were also popular, but most scary of all were the machetes, used in hand to hand fighting to finish off those wounded by gunshot or explosives. He boasted that the Rhodesian army had more black troops than the terrorists, a clear indication for him that the regime had won the hearts and minds of the native populations. I had heard this argument about freedom fighters/terrorists being a minority many times before – in Algeria, Kenya, Malaysia and the Congo, but was never sure whether the interpretation placed on numbers was a fair measure of public opinion. Setting tribal affiliations against each other was a popular control device of colonial rule.

Rhodesia had been under official UN blockade for about seven years by the time I was visiting but it did not seem to be suffering. There were frequent police cars patrolling the roads in the south – in ageing British made Austin Westminsters, built over a decade previously. This country seemed much more Anglo-Saxon than South Africa with its diverse European groups, as well as the multiple black and other ethnic groups. It was an odd feeling to be British like so many of the white settlers yet fundamentally opposed to what they were trying to achieve.

We finally made it into Salisbury and I was dropped at Meikles – the main city centre hotel where friends of friends from Highlands District were going to meet me. They turned out to be quite amenable, but kept themselves to themselves except for a barbecue on Sunday evening. Otherwise I was left to my own devices. I attended the national agricultural show that displayed good quality livestock just like back home, and the massive tobacco harvest that underwrote the farming economy at the time. Mechanical equipment was on show in abundance, indicating that Britain's blockade was failing at the hands of most other European, American and Japanese manufacturers.

As I headed back into Salisbury city centre as evening approached, the bars were full of young shaven headed white and black men together; soldiers on leave from the bush war in the north. No apartheid here in Rhodesia, so the squadies conversed freely around the bars with young black girls seeking their attentions in more ways than one. I looked out for Dirk but there was no sign. Yet when I got back to where I was staying, there was a telephone message from him saying if I wanted a lift back to Jo'burg, he would be glad to take me the next day. Having only really come to look, and with no other reason to stay, I accepted. He picked me up the next day for the seven-hundred-mile journey south.

Once again, the boot of his Corsair remained firmly closed, so I dumped my bag on the back seat, but started wondering about the curious factors around this fortunate encounter of a few days ago, in the northern Transvaal. Dirk had approached me out of the blue; he had admitted he was a South African mercenary in the Rhodesian army; he had separated me from himself and his car, when going through Rhodesian immigration at the Beit Bridge border; I had never seen the inside of the boot of his car; and now only two days after returning from leave, he was heading back to South Africa again. What was going on? But I remembered Alan Lipman and kept my counsel.

We took a different route south through Gwelo and Bulawayo, Rhodesia's second city then as now, and at the border crossing back into South Africa, the same separation routine took place. My suspicions deepened further as I was left in the passport control shed, while Dirk took the car away for inspection, customs clearance or whatever else was required.

Had he been smuggling weapons into Rhodesia? What was he hiding on the way back out? Weapons were the one category of imports that UN sanctions were particularly strict about, but after several years, the bush war was raging as never before. So, the Rhodesians were clearly being supplied from somewhere. Was Dirk using the apparently innocent use of a private car with its foreign passenger as cover for illegal imports? Add to that, were the South African authorities turning a blind eye?

I was not comfortable with asking awkward questions, such as why he was returning to South Africa so soon. If he was half the soldier he claimed to be, normally in charge of a platoon of blood-thirsty troopers in the Bush, he would not have hesitated to get rid of me if he felt his cover was blown. But I kept quiet; after all, who was there to report this to?

A few years later when Rhodesia finally became Zimbabwe, stories about how the regime had been supported started appearing in the Press. Weapons smuggling was the hottest topic. Who knows whether I was the innocent dupe to a quiet and profitable side-line that was making one long distance driver very rich? I will never know.

Back in Jo'burg, I moved out of Wits and in with friends of friends in a student house in the comfortable northern suburb of Melrose. Life was good, indeed hugely privileged, given that we could afford two house servants despite our student or early career incomes. I got talking to the wondrously named Langalibalele, our Xhosa cook and housekeeper. She taught me the pronounced click pronunciations of the Xhosa language and she seemed to have the patience born from having seen everything that life could throw at her yet maintaining a calm and smiling demeanour. She was the only black person I had any real connection with in over three months; so sad. I recall she ironed my shirts and folded them to a military standard of crease definition; some of them were untouched and still in that state when I got home four weeks later. Over the weeks, I lived in Melrose, 'Langa' and I had several interesting conversations about our respective lives and families, but she always avoided politics. When I finally left South Africa in mid-September, she hugged me to her ample bosom with tears in her eyes and bade me come back soon. Sadly, I have never done so.

I accepted an invitation the next long weekend to a private game farm in the eastern Transvaal bordering the Kruger National Park, near White River – just north of Swaziland. This would be living in luxury; the farm was owned by a wealthy Scottish/South African family, headed by a senior director of a well-known international bank. He would not be present but his niece and nephew would be together with mutual friends on their honeymoon from UK. This would be very different to hitching lifts with Bible bashers and bush war mercenaries, but I loved those contrasts!

I was impressed by the quiet understated affluence of the game farm – a series of rondavels (small circular houses with pointed thatched roofs) set in dense bush and covered after many years of verdant growth in rich bougainvillea and frangipani plants. A dignified major domo dressed partly in a leopard skin native costume, was waiting for us on arrival, supported by a discreet group of kitchen servants. We were soon drinking sundowner cocktails on the veranda of the largest of the bush houses. Would I get used to this lifestyle or would my social conscience triumph? I put these awkward questions to the back of my mind.

Next day, armed with a large elephant gun – not for hunting, purely protection against lions or buffalo in case we broke down - we set off in an open-topped Willy's jeep that served as the farm's main bush transport. George – the owner's nephew from Jo'burg - was about my age and seemed well used to bush tracking, though I would have been happier with one of the locals to guide us. We spotted several big-game including rhino and buffalo, well known as the most aggressive and unpredictable of game in the bush, and many kudu and springbok, but no elephants. We went out again that evening, this time in an enclosed car to watch lions feeding on a kudu carcass, which the farm staff had shot.

The next day we were up early to drive out to a waterhole fringed by a magnificent fat trunked baobab tree. We climbed up into the shelter of its foliage to watch zebra and hopefully lion drinking. I remember thinking idly that lions were more than capable of climbing trees, but George did not think this was a big hazard with his gun resting nonchalantly across his knee – looking for all the world like a young Ernest Hemingway. Wisdom or bravado? I did not like to ask.

After two hours and only two big game sightings, we climbed down stiffly and prepared to return to camp. I was driving the jeep and as we moved off slowly it suddenly lurched upwards as the front axle dislodged a hidden but huge dead tree stump. With the bonnet and front of the vehicle pointing skywards, we jumped out and George, looking more serious and less melodramatic than usual, stood watching the nearby bush, alert for lions on the prowl. Closer inspection revealed a broken leaf spring no longer fully supporting the front left wheel. The jeep would be going nowhere without inflicting further damage. We were now stuck in big-game-laden bush with no phone contact other than a crackly walkie-talkie to the farm - no mobile phones in 1973. Big game trackers were suddenly game for big-game. With George watching the edge of the nearby bush cover nervously, we managed to tie the dislodged leaf of metal to the rest of the spring structure with a convenient length of metal wire, and then the whole spring mechanism to the axle. It was not going to hold for long, but proved just sufficient for us to back the jeep off the uprooted stump and limp back to camp, George riding shotgun on the back. The jeep was declared 'out of service' by the farm manager, so that was the end of further safaris! We returned to Jo'burg the next day, but it was not to be the end of the affair.

The relaxed regime as to time in the office continued, and I was even due some paid leave, so I was able to plan another trip – this time to Durban and Cape Town. One of my housemates wanted his car taken to Durban for him to pick up there later, and it turned out to be an ageing but still very serviceable Citroen DS19, a luxury conveyance from the 1960's with innovative suspension affording a very smooth ride.

The drive alone to Durban through eastern Transvaal and Natal province via Standerton, Volksrust and Pietermaritzburg was uneventful. Durban, South Africa's largest Indian Ocean port had a different flavour than the high veldt, and the most conspicuous non-white population here was Indian not African. It was also the home of my friend Manerjee Chowdry, a Uni student at

Cardiff whose Indian family came from Durban. I was welcomed at his family restaurant in the city's Indian quarter, but was bewildered to be placed behind a discreet screen, as the establishment was not permitted to serve other races than Indians. This was a bizarre new twist on apartheid and I expected the curries to be especially hot only to be served to Indians. How wrong I was! it is a European myth that real Indian food is 'hot'; spicy yes but not necessarily such as to blow your head off. I enjoyed the hospitality of civil and welcoming people while quietly enjoying defying the race laws and getting away with it.

I also got lucky staying with friends at Tongaat north of Durban. The local fruit and vegetable company, Tongaat Foods Pty Ltd had a 'bakkie' (small van) needing returning to Cape Town. It would be a three-day drive, but 'would I drive it for them, if they reimbursed me the petrol?' Would I not? This was perfect as it was giving me the opportunity to drive the whole African southern coastline – the famous Garden Route, so called for its amazing variety of flora, for which the country was renowned.

The route took me southwards past Durban and one of the recently declared Bantustan homelands, the Transkei. In the early 1970's, the idea of African homelands was the Republic's answer to the charge of injustice that black Africans were denied the right to settle permanently near their work. The idea of 'homelands' to which they were expected to return after a period of 'temporary' employment in or around the big 'white' run cities of Durban, Jo'burg, Capetown or Pretoria, was really a fig-leaf covering the essentially hollow legal and spatial planning principles of separate development. In reality, the black and white populations were bound together by an economy on which they were both dependent, even if they were forced to maintain separate cultural development and settlement patterns.

The Transkei was a huge area of small towns such as Umtata and Port St Johns, interspersed with large areas of rolling dry grassland only able to support a low intensity cattle-farming economy. The South African government was being wholly unrealistic in believing that anything more than basic subsistence animal husbandry would be possible in the small grazing areas given over to rurally based families with the main breadwinner usually away living in the big cities housed in temporary accommodation afforded by places like Soweto. Small, rondaval-type, circular houses were scattered randomly across the open landscapes with huge long vistas visible from the main road. It was as if separate development depended on a 19th century concept of families and tribal groups subsisting on small scale cattle and sheep husbandry in remote kraals, while the majority of valuable farming land was safeguarded for white landowners.

Largely unremarked by the white population but very much a political inspiration to most black Africans, while he languished in prison on Robben Island off Cape Town, this was also Nelson Mandela's homeland. His extraordinary liberation and 'Long Walk to Freedom' was still seventeen years away and unimaginable to most political observers. I contented myself on my lone drive, eating biltong and listening on the crackly van radio, to the pirate 'Radio LM' from nearby Mozambique, which enjoyed the best pop music broadcasting in the region.

As dusk gathered, road signs seemed fewer and further apart so I had to stop and ask directions of groups of young men hanging out on the roadside. At one point, I gave a lift for about thirty miles to a guy who hesitated to get in a car driven by a white person until he heard my

British accent. Forty years later, when I tell South Africans this, they are astonished that a 'white boy' would take such risks: "you would never do that now, too dangerous!" I am told. It did not seem so dangerous back then, in fact I felt more secure with company than on my own.

The rest of that journey all along the southern edge of Africa was solitary and uneventful except that the Garden Route's floral abundance of spectacular colour and fragrance lived up to expectations. I would occasionally stop on quiet stretches of the road, just to soak up the warming winter sun and the tranquillity of this natural Eden. I could see why the road had been given its evocative name. At times the combination of riotous colour, even in the early southern hemisphere spring of September, combined with the birdsong on quiet stretches of road, allowed me to daydream as if in a private garden. But strangely, with no one to share it, there was an uncharacteristic sense of loneliness. After one night of unexpected hospitality at the University of the Eastern Cape in Grahamstown, and in need of human company, I drove all the way through East London and Port Elizabeth to reach Cape Town in one long day.

A small house just off the beach in Camp's Bay, underneath Table Mountain was my next destination. Once again there was the shared space and spare bed of student accommodation; friends of friends on the never-ending networking of who you know from whom to bum a bed for a few nights. I recall I hardly ever saw the other student inmates, as they were out most of the few days I was there, off doing their own thing at night, except for one or two mutual but brief pub visits. Camp's Bay was then a mini version of the kind of places I had seen in California two years before; laid back, alternative metropolitan to nearby Cape Town and quite hippie in lifestyle – at least as far as anything could be described as hippie in state controlled South Africa. The cold currents up from the nearby Cape of Good Hope did not invite swimming off the nearby beach.

I was running out of leave time so I put an advert in the Cape Town Argus requesting a lift north in the next few days. Seems very old fashioned now but quite a regular routine in the pre-digital age. Two sisters Marion and Erika van de Merwe, phoned me to say they planned to head back to work in Jo'burg after a holiday, and would I share the fuel cost. Next day, they picked me up outside the Cape Town main Post Office in their bright orange VW Beetle. As I inferred from their names, their first language was Afrikaans and they had gloriously accented broken English that, after we had got to know each other better, I started to mimic, while they spoke back to me in a lah-de-dah version of Queen's English. None of the old tensions here between the younger generations of Dutch and English speakers, just kids having fun.

The drive up through the Northern Cape and Vrystaat (Orange Free State) may have sometimes been tedious scenically, but with the banter it was never boring. Once when we stopped in a small supermarket just outside Bloemfontein in the middle of a deeply conservative Afrikaaner area, I went to the counter and asked for something I could not find on the shelves. On hearing English with my British accent, everyone in the shop stopped and stared, as if a black man was trying to board a whites-only bus. But in typical laid-back Camp's Bay fashion, the more assertive Marion went to the cashier and said in Afrikaans words to the effect that, "Ok, he's a rooi nekke" (red neck – term of contempt for the Brits since the Boer War when the soldiers had inadequate protection from the sun) – "but he's with us, so it's ok". Everyone relaxed, but I was reminded again of the tensions under the surface even within the 'whites only' culture. But here was culture blend, not culture clash. The girls could relate to this conservative community as well as the more cosmopolitan Cape Town and not just a foreigner, but a dreaded 'rooi nekke'..!

An unwelcome outcome from the jeep accident in the East Transvaal awaited me on return to Jo'burg. The owner of the game farm we had visited and uncle to my hosts had apparently been furious that the jeep's leaf spring had been broken, only one week before he was due to welcome some big shot Japanese banker associates for whom he had planned some big game watching. The resulting absence of a suitable vehicle to get around the bush had been a severe inconvenience. He was looking for someone to blame. His niece and nephew were clearly scared of him and had rather left me in the lurch by saying that I had been driving, allowing him to conclude it was all my fault for reckless behaviour. Whatever, they said he was looking for me to pay the repair damage and seemed to have said little in my defence or mitigation as to circumstances. Not so nice. The cost amounted to several thousand rand – hundreds of pounds that they must have been aware, I did not have. Their mother, sister to the irate banking grandee, had tried to calm him down, but to no avail.

There was an old wise type in the office whose old-school charm had impressed me previously. I needed advice how to handle this situation and felt he could be trusted with my explaining it all. Identities excluded I told him the whole story, though he probably guessed who had been my hosts; they were well enough known. For insurance, I also telexed my Dad in Wales, and asked him to stand by to wire the money if things got really serious –

one of the most uncomfortable communications of my student years, as I still vividly remember.

The wise man of the office listened sympathetically and told me this sort of behaviour was not uncommon among the hard driving top business people in South Africa; they had not got where they were over several generations by being soft on people who 'crossed them'. But he pointed out various things that might fall in my favour, so I summoned the courage to go and see the grandee in his palatial downtown city office.

Ushered into his august presence by various fawning PAs and flunkeys, I felt I was about to be thrown to the lions, but stood my ground without too much grovelling, and apologised that he had been put to such inconvenience by our use of the jeep and its subsequent breakdown. I explained that it had been a genuine accident that could have happened to anyone. We had not been driving irresponsibly.

This seemed to have little visible effect, but at least he was not ranting about compensation, as my friends had warned. I asked about insurance and whether it would cover the accident and he smiled for the first time, admitting the vehicle did not have insurance as it usually operated off road. I thought it best to say nothing to this, as he would not appreciate a smartarse pointing up his neglect of a basic precaution. We chatted on for a bit with him becoming marginally warmer to my presence, but he concluded the meeting by saying he would have to see where things stood when he finally got the bill for repairs. Not the most successful of outcomes, but at least I was leaving his office on my own two feet, rather than in chains or on a stretcher.

I heard nothing more about the incident and was able with huge relief to telex my Dad that I would not need his money – at least not before fleeing the country. I heard later when back in UK that my friends' mother paid the full costs of repair. When you consider that this sum, while a big amount to me, was probably petty cash to the owner, it does put in context people's attitude to offering hospitality, especially in such a lavish setting. If you own splendid things like a game farm, do you not need to take precautions or at least warn guests that they are absolutely liable for damage they may inadvertently cause? Apparently not in this case! With good cause, I have been cautious of big shot South African business types ever since. They are probably proud of their hard man reputation but it does not pay long term dividends. Elephants never forget; some humans neither.

I left South Africa with a frustrating sense of hardly having met or talked to any non-whites, other than in a service rendering and invariably subservient capacity. A sobering experience in Soweto early on, pleasurable but brief talks with Langalibalele in Melrose, my brief pleasant interlude in a Durban Indian restaurant and thirty miles in the company of a black passenger for the lift in the Eastern Cape, had been my sum total of exposure to non-white people. It sounds bizarre if not disgraceful now, but it would have proved near impossible to do otherwise back then. What a peculiar country, but perhaps a little less strange with some understanding of how it had evolved.

This small understanding was a great deal more than most people in UK were prepared to consider, especially those who fulminated about apartheid knowing virtually nothing about it. The most honest response I got from one friend was, "I would be scared to go to South Africa, because I might quite like it!" Understanding is not excusing however, and on returning to Cardiff that Autumn, I resolved to write my Masters dissertation on planning for separate societies. I did not hold back on how disastrous it was proving, and the examiners seemed to like my efforts, hopefully for academic endeavour, rather than political correctness. You could never be sure amongst academics in the 1970's, but Prof Newcombe must have liked it and that was good enough for me.

As I wrote this chapter forty years later in late 2013, Nelson Mandela's death at his home had just been announced. Madiba, as he is still known affectionately to so many devoted followers, is now a legend of saint-like proportions. He lived through a period when his race was seen by many whites as sub-human. For much of his life, he was treated accordingly. How could anyone who suffered at the hands of the apartheid system over so many years have found the spirit to be so forgiving and reach out to the children of his persecutors and persuade them not to flee the country, but rather to stay and build a multi-racial society? There is undoubtedly crime and corruption replacing much of the pure revolutionary spirit with which the ANC was forged, now that it comprises the country's ruling political monopoly. But freedom from one of the cruellest regimes to have imposed its will on a majority population is now a part of historical context rather than current fact.

What a contrast is South Africa, with sad tormented Rhodesia - now Zimbabwe! Even during the Bush War, Rhodesia prided itself on being so much more open and accepting of black people than its big neighbour to the south, though much of this was probably only skin deep. But now, thirty years into so called majority black rule, a white elite has been replaced and driven off the land and out of the country by a tiny caucus of Mugabe's ruling cadre, who rely on tribal loyalties and naked menace to keep themselves in power. Grabbing every opportunity to blame the country's economic collapse on the old colonial system, Mugabe's approach to independence and majority rule stands in stark contrast with that of his South African neighbour.

My quotes at the start of this chapter capture some of the sense of ironic contrast. Few other examples of the fortunes of two countries can be laid at the door of just two men – the one locked into post-colonial thinking as he clings on to power; the other a man who could forgive and win the hearts of enemies as well as friends in building a largely free country which might – just might – avoid the ruinous fate of so many black African countries to the north. South Africa is a beautiful place and deserves all the luck it can get; Zimbabwe too if it ever gets the chance.

Soweto Township South Africa June '73 contrasting with...

...Johannesburg City Centre from Braamfontein. But Soweto was exacting its revenge. Observe the pollution over the city from coal fires as the only heating and cooking method available in the township 15 miles distant.

Apartheid's 'homeland' policy in action, Eastern Cape South Africa August '73. Scattered rondavels across a sparse landscape were no substitute for viable and sustainable human settlement

Chapter 6 Algeria after the French had gone

"Come, then, comrades, the European game has finally ended; we must find something different. We today can do everything, so long as we do not imitate Europe, so long as we are not obsessed by the desire to catch up with Europe."
Frantz Fanon; "Les damnés de la terre", Ed: Maspéro 1961

By the mid 1970's, I had started my career in planning new towns, seeking opportunities to master plan new communities and industrial complexes on an international scale. Determined to get overseas again, I also wanted to break out of my previous Anglophone comfort zone from countries which used English as a principal if not first language.

My first big opportunity came from my new employer, engineering and development consultancy WS Atkins, who had been commissioned by the Algerian national steel corporation, Societé Nationale de Sidérurgie, SNS - at Annaba on Algeria's north east coast, for engineering design and construction management of a new integrated steel works. This was the ambitious post-colonial era when Algeria like many other recently independent countries, sought economic self-sufficiency in key industries, pursuing post-colonialist thinking of which the quote from Frantz Fanon above is an example. The Annaba steel complex was planned to be large enough to warrant an associated new town at Sidi Ammar to house their workers. This was industrial revolution to follow the civil variety barely a decade after Algerian independence.

On this and a range of other projects I made it my business to join the project team. By the mid 1970's, Atkins had a big expatriate presence there but my visits were only ever going to be short term as few of the engineers running the project were taking the new town scheme seriously. Many of them regarded the idea of a new town with scepticism born of excessive ambition on the part of their SNS client for whom a fully integrated steel complex would be ambition enough. Many of them also singularly failed to understand the ingredients of planning which were as much sociological as they were development by numbers. Key men at the top of Atkins such as Michael Muller and Peter Brown supported our cause however, and a series of quick scoping visits was agreed to, for discussions with the steel works' client about what they were looking for and home again to work up concepts and design elements based on UK deskwork. Few of the Atkins' top management thought that a proper budget would be allocated for building a new town.

I made several visits in the late '70's and early '80's, as Algeria determined to urbanise as well as industrialise rapidly. By the 1990's it became impossibly hazardous for most Europeans to work there, as a vicious civil war erupted between Islamic fundamentalists and the socialist government, themselves the product of the equally vicious freedom struggle against France through the 1950's and early 60's. This represented a toxic cocktail of violence and internecine struggle from which the first to flee were the international funding agencies for new projects, and with them the consultants such as us who had previously planned and engineered the schemes.

Despite the philosophies of Fanon and his literary ally, J-P Sartre, French cultural influence, only thirteen years after independence, was still strong in Algeria, with place names, TV and newspapers still in French, and the local authority département structure only gradually being replaced by a more Arabic Wilayat system. At a human level, there were many Algerians who, despite pride in their independence, were still 'French' when seen by foreigners as regards cultural outlook, dietary habits, style of dress and with a justifiable salute to the former school system for the select few, quality of education. France had conducted its military missions ruthlessly, but its approach to education as elsewhere was similarly rigorous, in particular, in the teaching of good grammatical and idiomatic French. Unlike most equivalent colonial English education, this included logic and composition with which to express technical proposals in writing. Arabisation was still a generation away.

I rapidly caught up and surpassed my painfully acquired schoolboy French, so that I was conversing fairly fluently with clients and working colleagues after just a few days. I much preferred this have-a go-on-the-ground version of acquiring a new language, but I never acquired the standards of those among my clients who had been taught under the tutelage of the French métropole.

There was little Algerian owned private enterprise of any scale in the 1970's, so the country was developing a public-sector command economy model. Contrasts between a metropolitan government and nationalised industrial elite and the rural and semi-urban poor were acute. This was no Chinese style grass roots communism. Teams from other socialist countries in east Europe were helping to 'break the chains of colonialism', so we encountered many Russian, Polish and East German contractors all living in very basic accommodation and already erecting utilitarian medium-rise apartment blocks for future steel workers. The El Hadjar steel complex itself was a typical example of western finance and east European construction standards, between which the twinned firms of SOFRESID, a French industrial design consultancy, and the quintessentially British WS Atkins, were the often hapless, design intermediaries. Atkins had international 'form' in such projects but in this heavy engineering environment, very few seemed to understand the delicate process of master planning a new town.

We fought against the erection of de-humanised five storey walk-up apartment blocks recommending instead a single storey courtyard housing form as the basic living unit with small gardens surrounding each. This was immediately dubbed the 'Bourneville or Welwyn Garden City approach' to Algeria by some of our less sympathetic engineering colleagues, regarded as profligate of land and building materials, and looked unlikely ever to get built. They were right. Sidi Ammar today shows the physical footprint broadly as we had set it out, but with a very different pattern of housing types. The five-storey walk-ups dominate. The only concession to a real Arabic flavour is to be found among the mosques that, like their counterparts throughout the Muslim world, express a dignity of design and integrity of religious culture that would be lost in more secular societies.

If the only built forms in people's lives to display any exceptional quality are also those that represent a traditional religious outlook and way of life, it is little wonder that so many hold fast to religion as a strict but familiar value system in a changing world. In post-colonial Algeria, the people were gradually being forced in one of two directions, a dehumanised socialist modernity or a highly conformist adherence to the pre-colonial past with increasing religious overtones. Neither of these tolerated European-style individual expression of will, so no wonder perhaps, that so many freer thinkers emigrated to better opportunities in northern Europe, especially France. Thereby hangs an entirely different issue that confronts us today, but my canvas for this chapter remains resolutely among Algerian versions of its source.

There was a dour demeanour to our clients; steeped in post-colonial socialist dialectic, understandable after the horrors of the eight-year war, they were probably resentful of French and British professionals living well on overseas contract terms including rentals of the many French style villas left over from the colonial occupants of the past. There was a peculiar lack of humour among so many of our Algerian hosts for whom the pursuit of a socialist and secularist development model did not invite much fraternization with their advisers, designers and project managers.

However, Algeria was not all serious civic issues, heavy engineering and left-wing political dialectic, despite the large helpings of all three. There was a lighter side to these overseas trips, including the weekend when SOFRESID challenged Atkins to a rugby match on a football pitch at Ben M'hidi just outside Annaba – inaccurately but inevitably billed as France vs. Angleterre. Algeria is now a force within African football, but in the mid '70's, sports fields were few and far between and those that existed were basic; none more so than the home of 'Sporting Ben M'hidi', clearly by the 1970's a relic of a French colonial past. To keep wild goats out, a low wall had been built round the pitch, but more recently it had been proving useful for keeping sheep in. Football as a serious expression of national and local endeavour was still decades in the future. Rugby remains, as in the 1970's, largely unknown in Algeria despite many Maghrebian players nowadays at club level across the south of France.

The SOFRESID team had preceded Atkins into Algeria a few years back and were well established as an expat community with all the trappings of a social club, sports kit and good organisation known the world over, where contrasting life styles with those of the locals, do not stop the visitors from enjoying themselves. They had persuaded the shepherd to move his flock elsewhere for the afternoon, and our first task for both teams was to walk in a long line down the ground, taking off the larger stones and removing the copious sheep droppings, showing few signs of fertilizing the near grassless pitch.

Atkins were a few players short, but in the spirit of international cooperation, SOFRESID leant us a player to make us up to 13 each though we stuck with Union rules. This involved longer scrums, and scrums even in those pre-health and safety days, invariably collapse, less than inviting given the frequency of the sheep turds we had missed. I volunteered for duty in the three-quarter line.

A fair crowd had turned up to watch. There was a photogenic group of stylishly dressed French wives and girlfriends in designer jeans and shades – 'WAGs' 70's style – while the French players themselves sported bright blue, matching a suitably nationalist SOFRESID corporate strip. Atkins had found us some red and white hooped shirts, a lucky choice as most of us seemed to be Welsh not English. Rugby was unheard of in Algeria at the time, so a second group of curious onlookers also arrived from the nearby village to sit silently along the walls. When they realised this was an international match France vs. 'Angleterre', they soon got behind the Brits; anybody opposing France got their vote. But the WAGs were a noisy and colourful counter group enjoying at last brief freedom to release their French pride normally suppressed under corporate guidelines in this uneasy post-colonial era.

The game was played in the best of spirits; I think SOFRESID won by a narrow margin, everyone having avoided being knee-capped by the stony ground. Nobody wanted to see the inside of the local hospital. The French victory made them all the more hospitable afterwards and a great party ensued back at their social club in town, this being the era when alcohol was still freely available to Europeans, a situation now much changed.

I managed to persuade the client authorities and Atkins' local project management, that to understand the true culture of Algeria with which to recommend the right social and architectural form for the new town, I should be allowed to travel around the country to absorb flavours of Algerian urbanism. For me, this meant heading south, away from the coast across the steep Atlas and Aurès mountain chains and into the Sahara. We would never have seriously considered recommending desert architecture in a coastal context, but who could come to Algeria and not see the real desert? No wonder those engineers questioned the professional focus of the average Planner.

I was told I could only go south accompanied by a driver as routes were poorly signposted and the desert was not somewhere to break down alone and with little experience of the harsh conditions. I was introduced to Hamed, a young taxi driver recently recruited to the SNS' Administration. He jumped at the chance to revert to his former profession for the one thousand km trip south, to proudly show off his country to 'un Anglais'. Again, there was little point in a geography or history lesson about 'Grande Bretagne'. Very early one morning, we set off in an ageing company issue Renault 4 Estate, on a round trip through Constantine, Batna, and Biskra, then past the ancient Roman ruins of Timgad, before entering the Sahara proper with the ultimate destination of the Touggourt oasis.

Heading south along the surprisingly good mountain roads, the natural and man-made vegetation became progressively drier and sparser. The towns and villages consequently grew poorer though the larger settlements retained French influences announced several kilometres either side of town with long rows of Platanes, the light barked shade trees planted in the colonial era to invite shade and invoke southern France. Many of these have been cut down since, perceived as symbols of colonial domination; a case of cutting off one's nose to spite one's shaded face. We also encountered ex-French military fortifications – sinister little strongpoint towers in line of each other's sight kilometre by kilometre through the Gorge du Roufi in the Aurès region, where resistance to French rule was born in 1954.

Hamed spoke good French and was matter of fact about this recent history, giving me his, or perhaps his parents, carefully objective impressions of the war of independence, only ended some thirteen years before, while he was still very young. Later I learned that among Algerians, there was a deep split between the freedom fighters and those who had supported France – said by many (who was counting?) to have been the majority. Certainly, like Rhodesia visited during its own independence war only a couple of years previously, it was true that the colonial army was mainly made up of local troops fighting the independence movement, in Algeria's case the FLN – the Front de Liberation Nationale. What ironies the end of colonialism generated, ahead of independence or rather the reality of pursuit of new dependencies.

It had been a bitter and savage conflict, sometimes descending into mass murder with both sides committing terrible atrocities on each other in their struggle to engender fear and loathing in the opposition. Even now, more than fifty years after independence, many French cities where migrants from Algeria have moved, suffer from the bitter split between the 'harkis' and the ultra-nationalists as it rages on. If you were mobilised to support France in the war, you will have had good cause to leave Algeria afterwards, rarely if ever, to risk returning home. If you fought for independence, you were probably not welcome in France or you kept a low profile about your wartime exploits, but you might have emigrated to Europe later for its better employment prospects. This aspect of the peculiar love hate relationship between the two countries and outlooks has blurred in recent years with Algeria struggling to offer sufficient employment opportunities for a fast-growing young and broadly well-educated population. It is not surprising that a subsequent struggle between Socialists and Islamic fundamentalists developed rapidly in the 1990's, spreading to France among the emigrants and making life uncomfortable if not lethal for those who had previously been heroes of the anti-colonial war.

The scenery got more and more spectacular as we drove south. The towns and villages seemed desperately poor often with little visible economic activity. Occasional flashes of bright flowering shrubs along the road signified a ruined ex-French farmstead with wild bougainvillea left to grow uninterrupted for years since the places had become deserted. We drove up to one that had evidence of blast damage to one of its outer walls and Arabic graffiti warning the locals to stay away. The desolation was all the more acute, given the national housing shortage for the growing urban population, but few would risk occupying ex-French homes from only half a generation previously - they were forbidden fruit. While understanding how the Algerians shunned these abandoned expressions of colonial rule, I could also see why the French settlers had clung on in isolated desperation through eight years of war in an area potentially rich for crops and livestock, given the right husbandry. After the Great War, during the 1920's and '30's, the French colonial administrators had actively encouraged landless farmers from Provence as well as Italy and Spain to come to Algeria, be granted land to farm and settle a European population. All now shattered dreams grown over with wild flowers.

The hydrocarbons industry was responsible for the roads being well maintained as we entered the real desert. Near to our next destination of El Oued was Hassi Massaoud where Algeria's main source of gas production was located. In early 1960, President de Gaulle had celebrated the exploding of France's first nuclear bomb in the deep south of the country and tried to retain the Sahara for France, while offering to give the FLN the northern littoral regions. The Algerians said no, open space having as much psychological pull for them as for the French before them. Slowly, dry and rocky semi-desert gave way to undulating sand dunes straight from a Beau Geste Foreign Legion film, Antoine de St Exupery's flights across the desert in Wind Sand and Stars, or a Tintin adventure – Crab with the Golden Claws (inexplicably 'Coke en Stock' in the French edition) perhaps?

After many more kilometres of the sandy desert constantly encroaching across the tarmac, Hamed pulled off into a large date plantation within an oasis nourished by brackish standing water from a small lake. I recall the quietness underneath the shade of the big old date palms, despite the presence of small children from the nearby village, climbing the trees to harvest the fruit. They stared at us as if arrivals from another planet, but gave us huge sticky clumps of the fruit, so different in quantity and presentation to our exotically packaged 'Deglets Nours' from childhood Christmases at home. At first I thought this a great luxury, but soon grew tired of their sticky cloying sweetness, not helped by the myriad flies wanting to join the sugar rush at every opportunity. We grow tired of surfeits.

El Oued was the first real desert town and very different to the Mediterranean styles of the north. Here everything was finished in whitewash and stucco low-rise, single-storey buildings with flat roofs for sleeping out during the cool of the summer night. Although modern street patterns crossed the town, the density of housing in the old quarters enabled shade to act as protection against the fierce heat. The single hotel run by the national tourist agency provided accommodation for the few visitors. It was basic; rooms with a simple bed, chair and table, sand encroaching through poorly sealed window frames and sparse fittings and decorations in the reception lobby, all befitting the Spartan approach to socialist vacationing. Hamed went off to stay with unspecified relations in town; perhaps SNS would not pay for his accommodation. There were few other guests – some lean and ascetic French agriculturalists, archaeologists and the like, reading obscure manuals and reference books as they ate their solitary meals.

After supper, I walked out through the back of the hotel straight into sandy desert and with a star scape uninterrupted by any light pollution or cloud cover, I had a marvellous sense of the vastness not only of the earth's open spaces but the heavens above. It was cold in the clear night air, but I lay on my back on the still warm sand and stared for the best part of an hour upwards into the diamond-studded blackness, or rather deepest dark blueness, watching the occasional shooting star or man-made satellite, and hoping to hear the drone of St Exupéry's single-engined mail plane seeking an emergency landing among the dunes. But he was long gone from reality and history if not from my imagination.

As we left El Oued the next day, I noticed a strange single-storey building on the edge of town decked with colourful flags and streamers, and most bizarrely of all, girls dressed in bright veils and long flowing djelabas sitting outside. This was so far removed from normal experience of puritanical Algerian urban life that I asked Hamed what they were doing. At first self-consciously embarrassed, he slowly became as matter of fact about this as about his accounts of the independence war. "That is a bordello," he said finally, "pour les filles tombées". Such a Victorian phrase, how had these girls 'fallen'?

He described the doleful pattern of failed marriages with husbands rejecting young wives and perhaps emigrating to the big cities or abroad. The girls' families all too often offered no protection after such social disgrace, so that the only 'safe' place for them to live was the local 'shelter', funded informally by prostitution services that they were required to offer in return. He also admitted that girls could be expelled from their families for the apparently minor departure from strict social codes – merely talking to boys in the street. With the nearby gas fields of Hassi Messaoud, there was plenty of male demand for such services, but a further tragic twist was that family members would also feel themselves free to use the bordello's services. This feature of a male-dominated culture, untouched in remote districts by Algeria's socialist revolution, made me ponder how far things had to evolve before any true sense of liberation arrived for women unfortunate to fall foul of traditional social mores. I watched in the car mirror as a girl who must have been no more than twelve stared after us, thinking how far removed was her future life from my sister, or daughters of my own, as yet unborn.

Our next and most southerly destination was Touggourt, before the sun got too hot. Now deep in Saharan desert sand, the road often disappeared beneath encroaching barkhans, the croissant–shaped dunes that march endlessly with the wind across the desert plains. Touggourt was even more the product of M'zab architecture, the long-established design and building style south of the Atlas chain that through past centuries, had kept the worst of the desert heat and dust out of urban spaces. I left Hamed to catch up with some friends at a coffee stall (he seemed to have friends everywhere) and walked into the old quarters of town, probably tracing unsuspected circles through the narrow, sanded streets and walkways. This was a true desert town, and these were the real urban areas I had come to see. The silence as I moved away from main thoroughfares was often total. Even footfalls were deadened by the soft sand and the walkways were so narrow I could touch the house walls on either side. I would come around a corner to find some children playing but they scurried inside the courtyard houses and closed the outer door on the approach of a stranger.

The relationship of a traditional Arab town to its wider community is quite different to ours in the west. Family life dominates and the public domain is really only for meeting, segregated strictly by gender, between friends at market or coffee shop. The design of residential building frontages denotes enclosure as courtyard houses turn their faces away from the outward gaze. This is slowly changing as the modern infrastructure of roads, water supply, power and telecoms encroaches along widened streets. But my fascination with this traditional urban form stayed with me for years and has been a watchword in trying through my master planning work to re-promote traditional urbanization throughout the Middle East. It has been a long struggle.

From Touggourt back to Annaba is nearly five hundred km, so we faced a long return journey. By mid-morning, Hamed and I were in our rattling ancient Renault 4, heading north along the dune spread tarmac. Now eager for the lure of home, his young wife and family, Hamed put his foot down on the long straight stretches of road. These old Renaults were amazing. Taking any amount of punishment, they just kept going. Fantastically uncomfortable, they had the compensation of really simple mechanics. The gear stick ran through the dashboard into the engine compartment where the straightest forward and back movement offered the choice of 4 gears forward and one back, the last of these always best for getting slow traction out of the dunes. How different to the hi-tech four-wheel drive vehicles of today, but they kept going despite brutal abuse.

It was gathering dusk as we approached the lights of Constantine in the distance, Algeria's third largest city, perched high on a hill overlooking its deep gorge crossing. Suddenly, a tiny gazelle was blinded by our headlights in the middle of the road. Though Hamed braked and swerved, we hit it a glancing blow as it tried to leap away. There was a sickening bump before we came to a stop, with the small animal lying there, apparently dead. Hamed was touchingly upset, given his previous matter of fact attitude to human tragedy. He put the gazelle in the boot to carry home, with no real idea of what else to do with it. We had travelled on a few kilometres when there was a banging and scraping from the back of the car. The gazelle had clearly only been stunned and wounded and now suddenly awake, it wanted to escape. It seemed to have broken its leg, so we could hardly put it out on the road again to be caught and eaten by the crows. We tied it as gently as possible behind the back seat and continued on our way.

Hamed was in a quandary about what to do, concerned that the police might take a dim view of exporting a wild animal from the desert. We stopped in the next village for him to phone a family relation in Constantine, and he came back beaming with relief. We could take the gazelle to his Uncle Mahmoud's house where the family would look after it. Or maybe eat it, I thought ruefully, as I could not see it surviving a broken leg, but I kept that to myself.

We drove into Constantine and eventually found Hamed's uncle's modern but modest French style villa in one of the suburbs. Just so did I get my first glimpse of Algerian family life in the rare circumstance of not being the main subject of interest to the assembled children. Hamed was welcomed with open arms by his amply-bosomed Aunty, while I was greeted formally in polite and strongly accented French. Of course, we had to stay for a meal, as it was by now getting dark and the roads were busy with late afternoon traffic. There were six children in the house and they all clustered around the little gazelle for whom a cardboard box had been found, lined with straw by the youngest present. They gazed in wonder at this little wild creature staring back at them with beautiful frightened eyes, then at me, the foreign co-bearer of this magical gift from their Uncle Hamed.

We eventually sat down to an enormous meal of mechoui and rice – the delicious lamb kofta of the Atlas Mountains. Wine was brought out for the honoured western guest – Cuvée du Président – Algeria's finest, but no one else drank it. What is the polite response? To respect their hospitality, or their Muslim teetotalism? There is no right answer, so I self-consciously took a few sips and pushed it aside. By the time we were finished, Hamed and I were in no mood to hit the road again that evening for the one hundred and fifty km final leg to Annaba on mountain roads. His uncle insisted we stay the night and, as the honoured guest, the children were turfed out from their bedroom and I got to sleep in a double bed alone. My embarrassment soon gave way to dreamless sleep.

The next morning after a brief coffee and among fond farewells for a good journey, we left Constantine for Annaba. The gazelle had survived the night and was being fed milk by the youngest children, but I doubt it will have survived long and perhaps graced a fine mechoui at some later date, suitably disguised so the children knew nothing of what they had eaten.

Back in Annaba with loads of information but mainly first hand impressions of another Algeria which most expats would not have seen, I looked askance at the type of modern housing the authorities were building for this rapidly urbanising industrial community. If the new workers within the steel complex were migrants from the south, Constantine, or country towns such as Biskra and Batna, would they really be content with a two-bed walk-up flat in a five storey east European style concrete block? No way, but I felt like King Canute in the waves represented by the pace of urban growth. The need for housing was enormous and nothing but nothing stands in way of progress. Looking now at what the authorities have built at Sid Ammar near the El Hadjar steel works, I am merely saddened about the de-humanised environment we planners failed to stop the builders from creating. Yet, people gained jobs, modern appliances and cars, so are they any less happy than when living in remote rural communities where there was so little employment and scarcely anything seems to happen all day? Industrial wage slavery vs. rural boredom – a common choice the world over since Britain started it three centuries ago, but usually with the same outcome. And who am I, to pontificate about lifestyles and preserving the best of traditional architecture, when this is usually only an option for the rich or privileged, while it is unattainable to the mass of population?

I subsequently visited several other parts of Algeria for other project assignments and found it a bewitchingly beautiful place despite its sad and brutal recent history. The best of these assignments was the Algiers City Region Water Supply Master Plan in 1981, a World Bank conception of regional significance to bring secure water supplies to domestic, industrial and agricultural needs of the capital city's wider hinterland over a thirty-year time frame. My job on this high profile multi-discipline project was to forecast what scale of population growth could be expected and where would the people settle. The water engineers would then get to work and model the demands matching them to supply from mountain sources to the east in the Kabylie region and south towards the Atlas chain.

We were about twenty planners and engineers on this project mostly from UK, arriving in Algiers in early 1981 equipped with the obligatory fleet of Renault 4's and 6's which Atkins had stored at Marseille docks for several years since the end of the Annaba project. They all had British registration plates, though with right-wheel drive, and we were careful before venturing into the Kabylie region to put GB stickers on the back of each car. This was a fine hypocrisy given the British talent for ex-colonialism but it pleased us to be a bit different. There were at the time a lot of French professionals – engineers, medics and the like all over Algeria on national service exchange programmes. By and large they were welcomed cautiously by local communities, though memories were long and the people wary. Brits were just a curiosity and we frankly enjoyed it.

The water engineers had to pore over meteorological data and geological maps making occasional forays into the countryside to look at borehole data, some of which I understood more than most others except the specialists, after my Australian adventures recounted previously. I had a small team studying demographic data and we were obliged to visit every town and village across a two hundred km by one hundred km area around the capital. We also recruited a team of house-to-house surveyors to ascertain people's typical usage of water, and means of storing it during inevitable shortages. We advertised at the University and a huge range of young students turned up looking for casual pocket money, most of them girls. This was important because few housewives in a conservative society would open the door to, or answer questions from a man. The girls were enthusiastic members of the team, staying long hours to work on their collected data after the appointed time for finishing their surveys. Despite the march of progressive socialism, there were few opportunities for girls to have independence, so the opportunity to be doing something legitimate and chaperoned such that their brothers or fathers would not be concerned, was too good to miss. Their inventiveness in getting people to answer our questionnaires became a model of how to implement a social survey in a fast developing but traditional society.

However, the highlight for me in this project was the opportunity to travel widely around the region in our ubiquitous Renault 4s, usually alone to keep costs to a minimum, but equipped with excellent Michelin roadmaps which I have kept to this day now scruffy and dog-eared from frequent reference. The project was carried out from February to May, the early spring in the mountainous and beautiful Kabylie region to the east of Algiers. At that time, the use of artificial fertilisers and pesticides was still rare in Algeria, so the mountain pastures were a mass of colourful wild flowers the quality and profusion of which I had not seen in Britain since I was small. These carpets of springtime joy are at last returning to European landscapes as limits are placed on use of chemicals that kill wild flora. But in 1981, it was a wonderful pleasure to drive through scented fields of every colour imaginable of flowers, both recognizable and previously unseen.

The villages and small towns seemed desperately poor with most of the population – or the men at any rate – apparently unemployed with time on their hands to sit and stare at the unusual antics of a foreigner in an oddly registered car, driving round and round trying to assess sites with development potential and future population growth.

I remember these days with poignant pleasure as well because my father had died only weeks before and I felt his loss deeply. Having gone away to school so young and travelled widely first with him then without, he had given me this love and curiosity for new experience. Nor had he been a stranger to this landscape. Thirty-eight years before, he had landed in Algiers with the 6th Armoured Division of British 1st Army sent to wrap up Vichy French forces in Algeria and attack the German held stronghold of Tunisia. All my previous travels abroad had been documented by copious letters home, but with my mother in mourning and taking Dad's sudden death so hard, I had no heart for long missives to describe my own aching loss. But the wild flowers were a balm to the soul, and I would drive miles thinking sadly I could never share it with him, though he had probably seen the same vistas of natural beauty in those long-ago days of Spring 1943.

We were a big party of expats and we frequently linked up with others of various nationalities. A good deal of fun was had by all, as is usual with all expat groups abroad. Food was relatively cheap and plentiful to foreigners who could afford it, and wine and beer was still freely available. Nowadays it is largely for export and many vineyards in North Africa have been dug up. Our office was in the El Biar district of Algiers and at lunch time we would invariably go to a little café next door presided over by Abdul, a huge Turkish cook who looked like a menacing extra from Lawrence of Arabia or The 1001 nights. At least he thought he was Turkish, as he explained in his heavily accented French, but he was not entirely sure who his father had been but did not seem embarrassed to talk about that. He produced great fish and meat soups for a fraction of the equivalent cost in Europe, and while the hygiene of the place left a lot to be desired, we liked it for its camaraderie when often other places were not always welcoming to foreigners.

The project also required us planners and demographers to assist our engineering colleagues with their technical work. One night I was needed to assist in measuring the current strength of water supplies and pump pressure throughout the ageing city system. This required hourly measurements of pressure throughout a twenty-four-hour cycle to gauge whether different times of day and consequent patterns of usage had a significant effect on the ability of the water mains to meet demand.

High density neighbourhoods such as Hussein Dey near the airport, or Bab El Oued including the Casbah in the old city, were marked out for measurement and we were required to sit in a car in a darkened street through an eight-hour shift, and every hour on the hour, lift a large hinged manhole cover in the road, descend a metal ladder and read the pressure on a gauge just above the water-line within an inspection chamber. These would have been installed by French engineers anything up to seventy years ago, so were often in a decrepit state with decaying brick work, and broken hinges on the cover. Due to the extent of leakage from the network, the pressure gauges were often under murky stagnant water at the base of the chamber. Difficult enough to do in broad daylight, this became a precarious balancing act at night, with the heavy cover threatening to crash down on your head, descend with a torch not letting go of the rickety iron ladder while squinting into the darkness to read the numbers on the dial. This was the moment for a large spider to drop from its perch under the cover and down the back of your neck. Spider thus installed, the torch was dropped and feet got soaked from having to step down into the murky water to retrieve it. Dedication to the engineers' cause was met the next morning with no sympathy whatsoever, and plenty of ribald comments about how lucky it had not been a rat. Their bite was worse.

In the early 80's, some of these neighbourhoods were becoming very poor, overcrowded and physically decrepit as municipal authorities had little enough money to effect improvements to street infrastructure. This was particularly true of Bab El Oued, the traditional heart of old Algiers near the Casbah and centre of urban resistance to France in the 1950's. The houses are built at very high density and tumble down the steep hillsides linked by a maze of tiny alleyways. This area had been immortalised in the famous Italian anti colonialist film, 'Battle for Algiers'. Resistance fighters would disappear into the maze of streets and by-ways or over the rooftops of houses, pursued by the ferocious French Paras, whose 'ratissage' technique of house-to-house searches - literally 'combing through' the community probably did more for FLN recruitment than any airy rhetoric about freedom and independence. We had to get to know all of these mazes in order to make plausible forecasts of future population, invariably inaccurate for an area traditionally hostile to municipal authority whether French or Algerian. We would explain as best we could the purpose of our mission to curious and often suspicious observers, but I doubt they were really convinced.

I have worked in Morocco, and visited Tunisia and Egypt for business since, and while all of these now have much more orientation towards tourism and the outside world in general, they lack for me, a special authenticity which Algeria's recent forced or chosen separation from western influence has given it. It seems still to be a sad country, alienated from neighbours and among its own people by the horrendous eight-year independence struggle followed by further scarring with still larger casualties during nearly ten years of civil war between left-wing government and fundamentalist forces. Algeria may have got much wrong but it has also been unlucky.

In many ways, it has been rapid development, underwritten by a rich, hydrocarbons based economy, that has brought about these modern post-colonial tensions. Any society undergoing rapid change through industrialisation and urbanisation comes under huge stresses and strains – families uprooted by the search for work and the forces of progress contrasting brutally with those of tradition. We experienced this in Britain albeit over a longer period from the mid-seventeenth century to perhaps the First World War, often with profound but hidden social consequences. So, we should not be surprised if some elements of society in the modern world react to much faster changes experienced in the 20th and 21st centuries, by adopting hostile attitudes to those seen as the agents for change – bankers, financiers, engineers and planners, to name merely those closest to my own profession. But Algeria deserves better, and with peace at last has come the opportunity to open up to the rest of the world and find its place as one of the most beautiful if least known and misunderstood countries in the region.

The Gorge du Roufi, Eastern Algeria where the Independence War against France erupted in 1954

'Alger la Blanche' March '81. Our water supply surveys in the high-density suburbs of El Biar and Hussein Dey were viewed with suspicion by the inhabitants.

Chapter 7 Bolivia and the High Andes

We are stuck behind an overloaded bus descending from the Bolivian altiplano to Chapare in the Amazon in our little Brazilian built VW. Behind us an irate truck driver is all over our back, wanting us to overtake the bus so he too can get on. But the road is too narrow with so many sharp bends and the drop, to the left of the oncoming traffic, so steep we cannot see the bottom of the valley. Suddenly the bus stops with a shudder, dislodging a basket containing a chicken from its roof, to pick up yet another passenger accompanied by her own livestock. The truck driver seizes his chance and roars passed both us and the bus together, his rear wheels spitting stones off the left of the road and into the gaping void. There is an exchange of horn blasts as he weaves his vehicle back to the hillside of the road, as another truck coming around the bend from the other direction emerges out of the rising dust and barrels past and away. Life seems cheap in this wild part of Bolivia; what the heck are we doing risking our necks like this? Not much empathy here and we're too young to die!

I was married in 1977 to Sylvie, my French wife, born and brought up near Barcelona. Armed with new cultural perspectives on life as well as fluency in Castilian Spanish for her, enabling steady improvement in the same for me, we set off on our first long term overseas adventure together in March 1978. The World Bank's affiliate the Inter-American Development Bank, was funding design and construction of a large industrial park and a new town at Santivañez near Cochabamba, Bolivia's second city. Based on an economic agreement with other signatories to the Cartagena Agreement (CA), Peru, Chile, Ecuador and Colombia, Bolivia would have monopoly rights of assembly for all cars and trucks of tightly defined engine capacities to be built in any part of the CA territories. This would transform Bolivia's industrial base. Our consultancy firm from UK in conjunction with CONNAL, our Bolivian partner, would prepare an industrial master plan for the factories, ancillary industries and new residential neighbourhoods.

Getting to Bolivia in World Cup year of 1978 was itself a mission. British Caledonian (now long gone as an airline – more's the pity) to Congonhas, São Paolo in Brazil, then on to Cochabamba via the infamous Lloyd Aereo Boliviano (LAB or 'Yoyd' pronouncing the two L's in Spanish to those accustomed to it), South America's oldest airline, and flying some of its oldest planes. Nearly 20 hours in total. We would become all too familiar with 'Yoyd' over the next year, but the first bumpy trip through the high cordilleras into Bolivia passed off without incident beyond a few white-knuckle moments.

Our first impression of Cochabamba was of a town in the mid '70's but we were not sure exactly from which century. Downtown was Spanish colonial with classic high density but low rise grid patterns, though only a few of the buildings were of modern construction. Out of town, the modernity fell away quite rapidly with progressively poorer habitation and infrastructure to match, mainly evidenced by the bad - often appalling - road conditions. This was four-wheel drive country for most. Cochabamba is at two thousand metres, so middle altitude compared with the capital La Paz at four thousand, and the hot humid tropical oil town of Santa Cruz closer to sea level if not the sea itself, in the Amazon Basin. It was the dry season on the mid altiplano, so there was dust rising everywhere as vehicles negotiated the predominantly dirt roads beyond the city itself including the run in from the regional airport. The recent film Butch Cassidy and the Sundance Kid portrayed Bolivia in the early 20th century and not much seemed to have changed.

During our first few days we were accommodated in the sparsely furnished Capitol Hotel in Cochabamba's city centre, but with the help of the British project manager who had arrived a few weeks previously, we soon found a furnished house with four bedrooms, a small garden and garage – all far too big for the two of us, but useful for all the visitors we confidently expected from Europe. The landlady had fallen on hard times since widowhood a few years previously and was pleased to accept our rent in US dollars. She was a Grande Dame from a bygone age and though living next door in an annexe to the main house, she would drop round with a "Yoo Hoo" and advice and tips for places and people to see - "por ejemplo el Consul del los Estados Unidos" - she breezily recommended. We secretly nicknamed her the Castafiore after the opera diva in the Tintin books whose jewels were stolen at Marlinspike Hall, though sadly, this Grande Dame had probably sold all hers, years back to keep up appearance. A more recent incarnation might have been Hyacinth Bouquet.

Going to a country as a couple to work for a year is a different proposition to quicker in and out visits such as those previously experienced in Algeria and Morocco. Even my three month stays in the US, Australia or South Africa were done constantly on the move, while here we were in Bolivia, setting up house if not home. An 'accompanied long term overseas assignment' was the consulting business jargon, carrying with it a weight of domestic considerations such as accommodation expenses, how to keep the non - working family member(s) occupied and content, and how to integrate project with free time to get to know a new place and maybe meet the locals. This integration was part of our job. After all we were not designing roads or pipelines, we were planning a new town so we needed to understand the people, their anthropology, socio-economy and the way things worked. Ah yes, the way things worked. Or not, as the case may be, because the pace of life was definitely slower here than in Europe and sometimes this being Bolivia, things did not work at all.

For me this was a different assignment overseas to those taken previously. For the first time, I was not alone. I had my life's companion with me and this meant I was seeing things with less Anglo-centric eyes and ears. Nothing wrong in a single national identity as one's frame of reference, but how much better to have two or even three – France and Spain as well as Britain! These three countries have had a huge cultural impact on the rest of the world for both good and bad, but always disproportionate to their size. But the very fact there were three of them as a basis of comparison with new places, lifted me out of my cultural comfort zone about how the world is organised.

Even if there were no new cultural references to assimilate, any new life companion will change your perspective. You think and react often in harmony or counterpoint to your companion. Sylvie's upbringing in conservative Francist Spain of the '50's and '60's was resolutely and understandably liberal, French style. She thanks her father's insistence on the French Lycée in Barcelona for her education, rather than a potentially more oppressive convent-based alternative. Leaving Spain to attend the Sorbonne and the Institute of Interpreters in Paris in 1970, only two years after the student riots and social upheavals of 1968, was mind broadening and probably a source of stress to her caring parents. But as I have observed previously, the right mix of parental control and concern to allow children to find their own way was their family axiom as it had been with my own parents. These are the lasting common elements that bind, transcending narrower national characteristics. They have served us well through forty years together, bringing up a son and daughter of our own, hopefully with the same values.

Everyone sees things a little differently to others – my mind's eye vision of blue or red will be different to Sylvie's or yours, and if that is difficult to imagine, try thinking how you would describe any colour to a person blind from birth! If that is not difficult enough, try imagining an entirely new colour outside the familiar spectrum. Is it dark, or light, and are you bound to reference known colours to get close to describing the new one at all? Different frames of reference also colour our world view, so that perceptions and realities diverge. Those who say to you, "you will love such and such a place, or you will get on so well with so and so," might be right, but they risk stretching your perception to fit their own. Put another way, to be 'depaiser' - as Sylvie taught me to say, literally to be taken out of country or perhaps context – is always going to be a different process for each one of us. But what variety that promises, life is unpredictable. Vive la difference!

Sylvie and I started with a few big advantages over my other working colleagues, all of whom had children – either young enough to accompany them and attend the American (English language) school, or older back in UK, but still needing holiday travel arrangements. A lot of that domestic support has long gone from such overseas assignments nowadays, self-help being the new name of the game, but in the big spending high inflation 1970's, the domestic benefits of the expat existence were a way of life. Meanwhile, just married and without children, we were pretty free to do our own thing. Fluent in Spanish, Sylvie soon found several eager students through the Institut Francais keen to learn French to add to their reasonable proficiency in English. There was a mild local snobbery to follow European rather than 'Yanqui' cultural influences.

Another key difference from most other foreign visitors to Bolivia was our willingness to get a bit absorbed in the local culture. 'Going native', as the Brits used to say in more xenophobic days, was not quite it, but actively seeking out local friends and influences was certainly our priority. We got to know Brazilians, Chileans and Peruvians living in Cochabamba, all of whom were, like us, a little 'depaiser', and therefore more open to other foreigners from further away. One habit of the Brits - and Americans – that we could not get used to was the craving for products from home - Ketchup, Mars Bars, Martini and Gin, even Birds Custard and Salad Cream. Incoming visitors were always being asked by our colleagues to bring such embarrassments on the long-haul flights via São Paolo. It must have puzzled the Customs authorities.

Despite many shortages, fruit and vegetables were plentiful and often exotic. The open-air markets were not for the faint of heart, with unrefrigerated meat and fish for sale in crowded conditions, but once we had identified a few of the more reputable shops with some cold storage facilities, good meat and river fish were easily bought. Seafood in this landlocked country was off our menu for a year. We had to boil water then filter it before washing vegetables and fruit, otherwise some fairly scary bugs and viruses were reckoned to lurk, threatening our delicate European digestions. But we ate well, had great outdoor barbecues and could subsist and better, for a tiny proportion of what it would cost in Europe.

One outdoor restaurant on the main ceremonial avenue through central Cochabamba, was popular on most weekends - the Prado. The tables were laid out on the grass verges of the wide avenue, and just outside of the lamp-light cast by the restaurant's own lighting, a group of beggar children huddled with plastic buckets. As the meals progressed, they would edge closer to the tables and just stand there looking forlorn holding out their buckets and willing you to leave some food for them to scoop from the plates into a mish-mash of leftovers either to be eaten there and then in the semi darkness, or taken home to their families. It was a pitiful display of the contrasts between riches and poverty. Nowadays I suspect, the restaurant owners would shoo away these beggars by hiring security or some such. But in 1978, the world was a little bit kinder and their presence was tolerated. Most diners saw the donation of leftover food as part of what was expected of them in a country where the majority of the population remained desperately poor and undernourishment was common.

The site of our new industrial complex and new town was some 15 km out of Cochabamba in the Santivanez Valley. Difficult to reach if only because of the bad roads, it was difficult to imagine why the government had chosen such a position. The local Santivanistas gazed upon our site visits with initial fascination but declining interest as we came back week after week to measure distances and assess suitable areas for constructing large factories. There was no easy access to satellite imagery in those days. It was as if they knew what we did not, that the chances of a major change to their lives by way of wholesale compulsory purchase of their properties and transformation into a bustling industrial hub were about as likely as Bolivia becoming once again, the prominent economic power in South America. This may have been true in the 17th century, but Bolivia had since become the Poland of South America, picked on during successive wars by its bigger and eventually more powerful neighbours with large chunks of territory ceded by force, first to Peru in the north around the time of independence from Spain in the mid 1850's, then Chile (the Guano wars of 1879) and finally Brazil and Paraguay (the Chaco wars for oil rights in the 1930's). Bolivians were fatalistic about a better future.

This philosophy of 'what will be will be' was partly engendered by the racial and cultural mix – 80% Quechua and Aymara speaking, only 20% Spanish being spoken as a mother tongue. The Spanish speakers ran governments of leftward or rightward persuasion, with power often changing hands abruptly - with over one hundred and eighty coups d'etat in the one hundred and fifty years or so since Independence. Meanwhile the indigenous population mostly watched these comings and goings with resigned detachment, refusing to believe real change would ever happen. Evo Moralles' assumption of power in Bolivia in recent years may not have been the first true native Bolivian in power, but his sustained influence over the politics of the country is a sea change. Such trends were not present in the 1970's.

During the 12 months we were there, there were two forced overthrows of the previous government – 'golpes d'estado' were a way of life in Bolivia. Advised that this was no long term big deal, we closed our project office for a day, staying at home behind half drawn curtains while the army marched importantly up and down the streets. We returned to work the next day to meet the same people from the client authority with the same policies of development using international funding in the name of a slightly different group of people at the top who anyway rarely came to visit the country's second city. "Viva la nueva Revolucion! Viva la Patria!"

Slowly our plans evolved on paper in those pre-Computer Aided Design days, into a fully-fledged development with industrial and residential neighbourhoods covering the whole valley floor of Santivañez. But there seemed to be little urgency from central government to start construction. It was subsequently revealed that this was because the Bolivian Ministry of Industry, whose chief negotiator changed with each change of government, was busy in Argentina hammering out a deal with Mercedes Benz's South American Truck division. Another team were in Brazil with Renault's car division, to agree to ship kits of parts of these companies' vehicles for assembly as if 'built in Bolivia''. This is what we now know as screwdriver manufacturing where vehicles are merely bolted together in country for purposes of employment, tax concession and national pride. Soon after most of us had returned to England in 1979, there was a ceremonial opening of the first factory where two Mercedes trucks transported on low loaders from Argentina were finally assembled and driven over a taped line. This was to celebrate the first vehicle manufactures in Bolivia, to the accompaniment of the massed ranks of the Bolivian army officer corps and repeated renderings of the national anthem. But we saw nothing of this; it was still in the future. Gilbert and Sullivan could have written an opera about it.

The project team was a good mix of different professionals from town planners, through architects and engineers of different specialties. The Planners and

Architects worked in a huddle while the Engineers impatiently waited for our strategic level designs on which they were to lay out their roads, power, water supply and sewerage networks. Then the Quantity Surveyor got to work to price up the whole thing to a level of wholly spurious detail because no-one really believed the Industrial Park would be built quite like that when the eventual industrial operators came along. Joining this team was my close Bolivian friend and sparring partner the magnificently named Antonio Bilbao de la Vieja. 'Tony' as we Brits immediately dubbed him, had accepted a job with CONNAL to tide him over a difficult time in La Paz where he had worked for the former socialist government of Sr. Ernan Siles Zuazo.

But the most recent coup was a right-wing overthrow of the socialists, so he had to keep his head down. This did not stop Tony from expounding his left-wing idealism and we had constant hilarious debates about how much better Bolivia would be under a Cuban style regime. Waiting out the time to the inevitable next coup, he contented himself by trying to convert our sceptical team of semi-capitalistic running dogs, with a good humour that we perhaps did not deserve.

In the course of my work, I was asked to go to La Paz for discussions with the CONNAL company lawyer about extending our contract to include some additional design work. My first trip to the high altitude La Paz was not such a physiological shock as it is for people arriving there from sea level, because living at 2,000 metres in Cochabamba, had helped a lot with altitude acclimatization. I did not get to see much of La Paz on this first visit, but I did get to see the inside of the happiest whorehouse in town.

I met the company lawyer in his office for thirty minutes at the end of the day, before he kindly took me off for dinner, lubricated plentifully with Chilean wine. He then announced his intention to visit a local house of easy virtue. Would I like to join him? He proudly announced he was a part owner of the establishment and well known there. He would be glad to introduce me to the girls. I stammered that I was only recently married and content in my relationship with my wife, but not wishing to upset him and just a little bit intrigued, I agreed to accompany him on the basis of, 'mirar, pero no tocar' – look but don't touch. He thought this was fine.

We arrived in the darkness at a large house in a well-off suburb surrounded by a walled overgrown garden. A gate through the garden wall led downstairs to a well-stocked bar and cellar laid out as a dance floor, empty at the time as we were arriving in the middle of the evening. There were almost no other clients at this early hour, but as many as thirty good-looking girls were sitting around on sofas and bar stools chatting to each other. As I might have expected, they were dressed arrestingly but with style, wearing vibrant colours and leaving little to the imagination concerning shapeliness and what used to be delicately but unambiguously termed 'embonpoint de décolletage'. Truly, some answers to a lonely man's dream.

My lawyer companion was obviously a very regular client as everyone including the Madame of the establishment seemed pleased to welcome him. I was introduced with suitable delicacy as to my motives, and we were soon ensconced in a cosy group with me rapidly absorbing Spanish not normally taught in the grammar books. The lawyer soon retired with a particular favourite lady to an upper room, followed by a heavy silence as the three other girls in our party waited for my next move. I announced with a stammer not fully born from my limited Spanish, that I was recently and happily married and ....

how happy I would be to buy them all another drink! Two of the girls looked distinctly bored by this prospect and wandered off in search of other customers, but one girl Luisa, stayed behind, saying how nice it was to find such loyalty in the face of temptation. At least, that is what I think she was saying.

As I plied her with drinks in compensation for more serious income, I found myself doing a Woody Allen routine from his early movies, asking her why she was ruining her life in this way. Luisa looked surprised and told me her husband earned about a third of what she did, even though she only worked three nights a week and intended to give up when her first baby came along. 'Regardless of its source,' I thought, but I kept that to myself. We got into quite some detail about the ills of Bolivian society and the sad circumstances in which women found themselves. She claimed there were a lot more women 'on the game' than their male partners realised, laughing prettily at how mad they would be if they ever found out. She said it would continue like that until the liberation between the sexes, obviously now occurring in Europe and the US, she was sure. Like so many in Bolivia, it was her dream to migrate to Miami and live in liberated luxury in a mansion on Daytona Beach. I did not seek to disillusion her as to the nuanced interpretation of liberation that operated in countries to the north.

My lawyer colleague came back downstairs soon after, and following another drink and further expressions of mutual esteem, we took our leave of the girls. My Spanish had improved in ways I could not have expected, and I now had insights into aspects of social life in La Paz not appearing in the guidebooks. My lawyer friend lightly suggested that I had missed a lot by not 'going with' Luisa, and since writing this chapter a few of my more ribald friends have said that I would be selling more books if I had stayed behind and enjoyed everything the establishment had to offer, recounting it all here in lurid detail. But, though I had only met Luisa an hour earlier, and we were never to see each other again, the idea of paying for sex with her held no appeal. She was now a friend, as she confirmed in a whisper as she chastely kissed me goodbye. I also confessed this true story with a clear conscience to Sylvie on my return to Cochabamba. To her great credit, she accepted my version of the whole truth of the event.

Our first road trip out of Cochabamba was to Tunari, over the edge of the Altiplano and down into the Amazon Basin. Geography in this part of South America is defined vertically, altitude determining not only the oxygen content in the atmosphere, but also the natural vegetation, climate, scenery, and crop and livestock activity of the mainly farming communities.

The quality of the road surface as we made our hair-raising descents got worse and worse, not helped by the distraction of fine views glimpsed through the thick tree canopies, of steep valleys below and deeply wooded mountain ridges disappearing away into the distance. Occasional traffic coming the other way was the biggest challenge. The few other cars were often of dubious mechanical reliability but passing them was negotiable. The trucks barrelling along in the middle of the narrow road at wholly unfeasible speeds were not. We gave way. Buses were a bigger menace still, hugely overloaded with passengers inside, with every conceivable human artefact stacked outside on the roof. How these loads did not topple over the vertiginous precipices on one, and occasionally both, sides of the road, I cannot imagine.

Despite these hazards and with some suitable European inspired caution, our little air-cooled engine Brazilian built VW managed the whole trip without mishap. A larger four-wheel drive vehicle might not have done so.

Our destination was a small overnight hotel campsite with thatched huts set in a small clearing and an ancient generator for night lighting and little else. As the only guests, we decided the real objective was the trip itself and to say we had spent a night in the jungle. After a night of swatting unwelcome and doubtless blood-sucking insects, we ventured out down one of the many small streams feeding the larger river systems to absorb the atmosphere of deep jungle, expecting at any moment to be savaged by a jaguar or eaten by an anaconda. But the vegetation was so thick and the atmosphere so sticky and hot, we soon called it a day. With all windows open, we retraced our route back up the steep mountain roads and after a further seven hours on the road and our tiny car never missing a beat, we made a welcome return to Cochabamba.

Most travel was more conveniently by air – surrendering to the tender mercies of Lloyd Aereo Boliviano. – 'Yoyd' to the locals. This proud but decrepit airline had been founded in 1924 by ex-German fighter pilots from WW1, flying Fokker tri-planes. By the 1970's the German pilots had been replaced by often-inebriated American aircrew unable to get jobs with more regular airlines nearer home. Things were regularly going wrong with the aircraft – ancient DC4s and the occasional clapped out Boeing 707s – defective ailerons, or burst tyres on landing etc. being quite common. Passengers needed strong nerves but the whole enterprise seemed to function on a high level of good will, trusting to luck and an enormous amount of faith from the passengers that they would survive the experience.

Before 1978 turned into 1979, we took advantage of the extended Christmas holiday to visit a bit of Brazil. We flew down to São Paolo but with sights clearly set on Rio de Janeiro - a seven-hour drive north. Two days before Christmas, the city bus station was a mass of heaving humanity seeking space on Rio bound coaches. Undeterred by the overbooking, we teamed up with other desperate passengers agreeing to share the hire of a VW micro bus. Private enterprise to the rescue! We were finally deposited in Rio at about two am in the morning and here our fortunes improved. A friend from UK, Lawrence Gandar, was on a year-long assignment from Vosper Thorneycroft, ship builders in Southampton, part of a team designing and commissioning six warships for the Brazilian Navy. His bachelor apartment in Ipanema and attendant life-style as an honorary member of the Brazilian navy's yacht club was just the antidote for our more circumscribed mountain environment. He also drove an MG T type lookalike, which VW in Brazil manufactured in those days built on a VW Beetle's chassis. Sounding exactly like a Beetle, it was nonetheless gloriously evocative of the carefree open-topped sports car era of the 1950's. Who cared if it was not the real thing? We scooted round town stopping for Caipirinhas at a beach side bar on Copacabana while ogling the beautiful and scantily clad 'jeunes et jeunesses' parading to and from the beach. How different to Cochabamba!

On return to Bolivia early in the new year, there were only a couple of months left to the end of the project, as we brought our final master plans to fruition. By the end of March, we were planning our route home, making the most of the full month's paid leave, recognizing the 'hardship location'. We did not want to go back the way we had come through Brazil, but rather La Paz, then the train and ferry across Lake Titicaca to Peru, train again to Cuzco, thence by air to Lima, Quito in Ecuador, Mexico City and the Yucatan, and finally a brief stopover in the USA.

Practically the only travel agent in Cochabamba was glad to help us plan this marathon, firing off telexes to train, airline and ferry companies to secure the relevant tickets. Crunching the costs through one of those old fashioned Gestetner calculators, they declared that all this was possible representing a difference to our original ticket prices of US $35 each. Happily reaching for our wallet and purse, the agency lady said, "No, no. We owe you $35 each!" We were returning during low season while the previous year we had been flying on the super high season rates prior to the football World Cup. Happy days; $70 extra went a long way.

In La Paz, we boarded the little train to Copacabana, landlocked Bolivia's only port on Lake Titicaca from where the ferry for Puno in Peru departs. The train was due to leave in the early afternoon, but by four pm we were still stuck on a side platform of La Paz's small central rail station, in the single carriage train, with all its passengers assembled but going nowhere. An Italian priest at the end of the one carriage, pulled out an ocarina – a little clay whistle – from which he extracted exquisite sounds and multiple songs in which the whole carriage joined. It set the tone for almost the whole trip, as all the passengers were travelling the same way across the Lake to Peru and thence to Cuzco following the great Inca trail. A little musical gesture had turned us into a community. It was not to last.

The train eventually wheezed away from the station and climbed out of the great bowl which shelters La Paz from the high winds and cold temperatures of the high

Altiplano, eventually reaching the lake port in the gathering dark and the ferry's due departure time. Copacabana, unlike its Rio de Janeiro namesake, offered little by way of services beyond embarkation for Peru, so the ferry boat was waiting patiently for its sole source of passengers. We eventually set sail three hours late but none the worse for the delay. Bolivian timekeeping is a relative concept.

The ancient steam driven ferryboat boasted a dining/reception room and ten sleeping cabins catering for some twenty passengers at dinner. Built in Hull at the turn of the twentieth century, it had been sailed across the Atlantic and through the Panama Canal, down the west coast of South America to Arequipa in southern Peru where it had been disassembled and carried over a hundred miles and nearly three thousand metres into the Andes by mules, to be re-built on the Lake. It had been doing sterling service to countless ferry passengers for over seventy years since, never exceeding five knots on the invariably calm waters of the deep and hauntingly beautiful Lake. Food on board was simple and we were rocked to sleep to the gentle rhythm of the ancient steam engine and virtually no swell.

But during the night there was some terrible shouting and banging from a neighbouring cabin and in the morning the ship was not allowed to dock as usual in Puno. The Peruvian Police came on board and promptly arrested two of the passengers, a young German couple who had told us they were Lufthansa cabin crew on an early honeymoon. We were then questioned in turn about what might have happened in the middle of the night, as apparently one of the couple, I cannot remember which, had tried to murder the other. Having failed in this attempt, the victim had reported the incident to the captain who was taking no risks with his relations with the Peruvian authorities. Strangely they were both present though kept apart by the police, giving presumably conflicting evidence in each other's presence. All part of the adventure of world travel; you never know what is going on in the minds or lives of your fellow travelers.

The train from Puno climbed steadily to the then highest railway station in the world, Huancayo at over four thousand metres. This engineering feat from the nineteenth century has subsequently been surpassed by a Chinese rail link to Tibet. Huancayo, however, was impressive enough in 1979 with the steep gradients and thin air of the high Andes causing the engine to go so slowly that people could get off and walk beside it, and local kids would hitch a ride and come into the coaches to sell sweets and hot pasties. The comfort level on the train could have been described as 'basic', but a brief visit to 'hard' class a few coaches along, showed us that local people were quite content to travel effectively in cattle trucks with no seating at all. I recall that in our 'soft' carriage, the lavatory was no more than a whole in the floor and an ancient sign, imploring passengers to only use it while the train was on the move.

I recall there was a large group of Argentinians on the train and their conversation was being conducted at that 'listen to me' volume, laced with comments about how primitive everything was – the lack of comfort of the trains, the poverty of the passing villages and so on. The inference we were being invited to draw was that it was not like this in Argentina, but the other foreigners were not impressed by this display of superiority. Argentinians were said to have a reputation for this sort of behaviour, considering themselves more 'European' than their neighbours as if this implied a higher degree of material and intellectual sophistication. It was 1979, and we now know that there were far more sinister things going on in their country, but at the time we kept our counsel. Would we do the same today?

Passing through Huancayo, the train was soon gathering speed again steadily downhill for the long descent to Cuzco, bringing us back into the world of tourism. Nowadays Bolivia seems to be on every student's gap year itinerary, so it is hard to describe how remote we felt there, away from the main tourist trails, back in the late 1970's. When we arrived in Cuzco, we re-joined large scale if not mass tourism and stayed in a wonderful small hotel occupying a Spanish-style courtyard, with an upper floor gallery and rooms lined in dark oak creating a sombre medieval effect, as if back in the sixteenth century. This region was known then as 'The Viceroyalty of Upper Peru' as the previously Inca territory was steadily replaced with a colonial system from Europe from the early sixteenth century onwards.

We visited important Inca sites in the Urubamba Valley - Macchu Picchu of course, Sacsahuayman ("sexy woman") and Pambo, and they were indeed spectacular. Built on vertiginous hillsides for more effective defence, these settlements belied any assumption of the technical superiority of European civilizations. The means to carve large stone pieces so smoothly and create perfect junctions between them without recourse to a wheeled cutting device or mortar was testament to an artisan skill now lost. I also recall the little boy who ran all the way uphill from the rail terminus below Macchu Picchu to greet the bus taking tourists to the ancient site with a wave on every hairpin bend of the ascent. Poverty seemed still to be an abiding contrast between well-healed tourists and local people, but the extraordinary athleticism of someone who could run uphill over four hundred metres of height gain when already at over two thousand metres deserved his few pesos tip each time. Such small gains from extraordinary ability!

The train between Cuzco and Macchu Picchu was a rack and pinion push me pull you affair, climbing the steep mountainsides out of the Cuzco valley via back and forth switchbacks. Like the train from Puno, the speed was sometimes less than walking pace and in the two hours around dawn that it took to arrive at the base of the Macchu Picchu site, we got chatting to our fellow passengers. Everyone had bought their own breakfast and a group of French people had even found croissants at an early morning bakery in Cuzco town centre. We did not see much of them during the day but on the return journey that evening, the train broke down outside Cuzco and we were all forced to walk the last five km along the tracks homeward in the gathering dusk singing French Foreign Legion marching songs. The next day we flew on to Lima c/o Fawcett Airlines with their '60's style pastel shaded aircraft interiors and thus no longer with 'Yoyd' or the other trappings of Bolivian life, led at a seemingly slower pace than the rest of South America.

So, ended our young married idyll in the High Andes, at least until about thirty years later, on a visit to Argentina's northern provinces around Salta. In April 1979, as we headed north from Lima through Ecuador, Mexico and the USA, the world for us pampered Europeans gradually returned to its complacent assumptions of material comfort. Flights left reasonably to time, hotels had running water and electricity most if not all day and night, and the roads became mainly smooth and fast again. But the memories of a simpler way of life, surrounded by poverty and where material comforts of everyday existence could not be taken for granted, stayed with us for years. These combined with a very genuine old world courtesy among the poor people of Bolivia, a tradition of respect, which may by now be diminishing. I recall our gardener in Cochabamba, Luis, who would take all day to cut fifteen sq. metres of lawn with a tiny hand-held sickle and be glad to receive a few pesos for his efforts. Like so many of his race, he was content in his own skin and I occasionally spotted him staring up at the mountains behind Cochabamba as if he yearned to return to his real homeland but for the need to earn some money in the big city. There were no such opportunities in the mountains. His feet were in the city but his heart was in the hills.

We have visited many other parts of Latin and Central America since, from Argentina and Chile in the south to Costa Rica and Mexico in the north. All, have their charms but seem no happier for their obviously superior material wealth to that of the high Andes. There was in Bolivia a special quality of isolation derived from landlocked inaccessibility. It is not just the time it takes to travel over difficult terrain but the dependence on other countries for the means of communication, the quality of road or rail infrastructure, import/export restrictions at seaports or the landing slots at foreign airports which gives Bolivia such disadvantages. Compare Bolivia with Chile for example and the wondrous outward looking but laid back atmosphere of Valparaiso, that stares out from Chile's coast into the uninterrupted Pacific. Previously Chile's capital and still maybe its spiritual home, Valparaiso is its gateway on the world, facing away from the great barrier of the Andes acting like a spinal column to hold the whole continent erect. Since the Guano war of 1879, Bolivia has no equivalent window on the world and they resent Chile deeply, for the theft of their coastal province.

If Bolivia is the Poland of South America, continuously put upon by its neighbours, then Costa Rica is the region's Switzerland – except it is not landlocked. With coasts on both the Caribbean and Pacific, it owns outlets to the world in two directions and a fast-growing tourist industry to boot, based on its magnificent 'Pura Vida' national parks. No such offering in Bolivia, despite many natural wonders. The tourist trail in the high Andes is far too much styled around rucksacks and Jesus sandals to achieve the scale of affluent tourism that sustains Costa Rica's economy.

Then consider a final contrast with Bolivia, the potential and sheer variety of wealth available in Argentina, more than six thousand km from north to south with every geological variant and climatic zone available to farming, minerals and industry alike. Yet there seems to be an abiding sadness underlying so much of Argentine life, as if in mourning for what might have been when in the early 1930's the League of Nations identified it as the next great superpower. This has not happened and the people seem to feel it deeply, expressed poignantly in the songs of the Buenos Aires porteños of which Carminita is the best known. Such aspiration is beyond imagining for Bolivia, yet the Indigenos of the high Altiplano remain mostly content within their own skin.

We can all learn from that. I should like to go back.

Site of our new town at Santivanez near Cochabamba after a rain storm. An unpromising start to our master plan for industrialising the Bolivian economy. July '78

Dinner on the Lake Titicaca ferry, before an attempted murder during the night. Everyone seems very relaxed… or were they?

Quechua children in the Tunari mountains north of Cochabamba with my dad who came to visit us in November 1978

Chapter 8 Four decades of turbulence in the Middle East

The temperature outside the car is fifty degrees Celsius. It is mid-August near - but not near enough - the Al Wufrah oasis on Kuwait's southern border with Saudi Arabia, and we're not moving. Before stopping to take photos, I had warned Hamza the driver as best I could, not to put all four wheels off the tarmac onto the roadside sand, but his English and my Urdu are virtually non-existent, while his Arabic which he should have for a driver's job here in Kuwait, is limited to mosque-based Koranic text learnt in his madrasah in far-away Quetta. Then again mine does not include the need for car tyres to have a solid surface under them to propel us forward. No other vehicle has passed by for ten minutes and it seems down to me to find a way to get us moving. Hamza is the driver only in the sense of guiding the car from place to place. If the car does not now move, that seems momentarily beyond his experience.

I gesture for him to stop revving the engine and spinning the wheels and get out. The heat envelopes me like a blanket, pressing down as if a great weight is discouraging excessive movement and inviting lassitude as an appealing alternative. The heat even suppresses perspiration; perhaps my sweat is evaporating instantly on contact with this stifling air. Stay out in this too long and I will cook.

I go to the door at the back and, risking burnt fingers, open it to reveal two old pieces of carpet on the floor of the boot space. I suspect they are not there by accident and this has happened before, but obviously to a different driver; you would not make the same mistake twice. A shovel would have helped but nothing doing. Luckily the sand is so soft it is easy to shift if I ignore the heat on my hands and arms. I get the carpet pieces wedged in behind the front driving wheels at an angle to allow a turn back towards the road surface. We're going out backwards in the lowest ratio if I can explain that. I learned that trick years ago, in Australia.

But Hamza, observing my efforts from the cool comfort of the air-conditioned car gets it, and with a nod of complicity he starts the engine and gently engages reverse. Slowly the wheels gain a purchase on the matted surface and the car moves backwards a few inches, the off-side front wheel nearest the tarmac now within touching distance to a harder surface. I expect to have to repeat the mat positioning, but the road edge has a hard, rough underlay and the offside front wheel gets just enough traction without the matting to roll us back onto a proper hard surface.

I breathe a sigh of relief and Hamza and I are the best of friends again. But really, am I getting too old for all this pratting about in the desert? After forty years in and out of the Middle East, that may be the case.

In 1977 I had an article published in the respected current and business affairs journal Middle East Economic Digest (MEED). It looked at the capacity for the region to cope with the physical, social and economic changes that were already being experienced and should expect to continue into the foreseeable future. That is to say, massive population growth ahead of the capacity to educate young people and generate employment for them. I argued that there was widespread failure to grasp the essentials of sensitive town planning based on sustainable models of development, and a dangerous overdependence on the income derived from hydrocarbons – the oil and gas being pumped out of the ground at a rate determined by the then all powerful OPEC. I had a cartoon vision of two massive drinking straws stuck into the glass represented by the Gulf and its shorelines, one sucked by the Iranians from the north and the other by the Arabs from the south. Who ran out of the tasty cocktail first would also suffer first, but they were both heading for the same energy drought. I kept this image out of my attempt at a learned article, but it would probably have summed things up faster than all the statistics.

Looking back nearly forty years later, and with the 20/20 vision and wisdom of hindsight, I probably got some of the emphases wrong. The geologists have kept discovering new oil and gas reserves, though Iran's suction power was weakened until recently by decades of sanctions against its nuclear programme, ironically an attempt at energy diversification whatever military objectives it may also have had. I also alluded to the social consequences of un- and under-employment by young people from conservative family traditions in what will have appeared to them to be increasingly dystopian urban environments. Social unrest caused by disillusionment with the benefits of material wealth insufficiently distributed among the burgeoning population was identified as the really sinister threat. But little did I appreciate the depths of violent war and revolution to which so many parts of the region would descend, partly due to the profound rejection of modernist progress as represented by fundamentalist religious movements.

Part of my focus as a planner has always been the physical urbanisation of communities and the importance of planning well laid out and compatible land uses, accessible transport, schools and medical services, adequate water supply and drainage, and landscaped open space. They are the essential ingredients for a civilised life and those of us who have them take this far too much for granted. Those who perceive they are denied these 'rights' simmer with unfocused resentments seeking recompense via migration, and sometimes, if that is impractical, crime, and perhaps the embrace of hollow siren calls from politically inspired ideologies to overthrow those they perceive as keeping power to themselves. Freedom to speak out is the first casualty of such a toxic mix. It does not take long for the superficially mundane principles of good town planning to become the headline issues that underscore the politics of social unrest. Nowhere illustrates this better than the Middle East.

I probably also underestimated the scale of population growth in most countries in the region. Major cities such as Algiers, Cairo, Damascus, Dubai, Kuwait, Riyadh and Teheran, have consistently lacked effective measures to address the overwhelming demand for new housing, physical and social infrastructure and the economic means to provide employment for new urban-bound migrants and burgeoning natural increase patterns. Medical science and life expectancy have outstripped social evolution to cater to ever larger and expectant populations. Add to that the massive movement of refugee groups fleeing decades-long civil strife in Algeria, south Lebanon, and Iraq, Afghanistan, Eritrea, Somalia, Libya, Yemen and most recently, genocidal multi-faceted war in Syria. These do not include the largely failed attempts at 'Arab Springs' in Tunisia, Egypt, Bahrain, Kuwait and even Saudi Arabia, all of which seem to have come to nothing. Then there has been the rise of media-driven terrorism cloaked in the assumed virtue of Islamic purity which has devastated and occupied parts of Syria, Iraq and Kurdistan and lies just beneath the surface in many other countries not just in the Middle East but throughout a Muslim diaspora into western Europe and beyond. I could not imagine in 1977, the massive scale of social upheaval, and the destruction to psychological well-being and physical infrastructure that could be visited upon so many, and then be exported from a single world region and its long-suffering populace to the rest of the world. Truly four decades of turbulence with little prospect of any peaceful endings.

I was probably closer to future truth when examining the roots of social dissonance and cohesion of countries undergoing massive economic and cultural change; reaction to 'modernisation', but not its extraordinary depth. I suggested that the built environment could play a key part in addressing social well-being, by recognising traditional building design and construction methods and well-established Arab urban development principles formed through centuries of experience. The absence of these would have an opposite and adverse effect. In fact, poor design and widespread industrialisation of building systems has condemned too many Middle East towns and cities to some of the most unsustainable development anywhere in the world. Only in very recent years has there been any significant shift back towards more appropriate climate-sensitive built environment, transport and social solutions. But redressing the impacts of many decades of human environment short-termism makes this a huge task.

The MEED article gave me a big early career break via book publishers Croom Helm, whose managing director David Croom offered me a writing and publishing deal. If I would develop the themes in the MEED article into book form, he would publish it, together with an advance to research the subject! It was essential to visit the area, as, until then, I only really knew parts of North Africa at first hand, and my take on the countries of the Arabian Peninsula, was desk-based.

In early 1978, I made my first visits to the Middle East region proper, via a fact-finding trip through the Gulf from Kuwait, via Doha in Qatar, Dubai in the UAE and finally Muscat in Oman. In April I went on a conference and study tour to Teheran and Isfahan in Iran, with the revolution against the Shah imminent and only months away. The end result was, 'An Urban Profile of the Middle East' finally published in 1979, and I have been visiting the region off and on for development projects ever since. 'Urban Profile' was re-published as a Library Edition in 2016.

The projects to which I have contributed vary hugely from city centre redevelopment on Deira Creek in old Dubai, a major industrial master plan in Yanbu Saudi Arabia, and city wide master planning in Abu Dhabi to regional infrastructure studies in Southern Oman throughout the 80's and 90's and, since 2000, industrial strategy in Kuwait and Saudi Arabia, transport infrastructure in Qatar and new town master plans and regional strategy in Saudi Arabia and Oman. Without success but learning a lot from failure, I have chased other projects in Lebanon, Jordan, Bahrain, Tunisia and Iraq, and have pursued - happily with more success - bad debts in Cairo, Riyadh and Kuwait.

Like everywhere else, it has been the people who have made the difference. To those who say Arab culture gets in the way of getting to know people, I say try some different tactics! It is unlikely you will penetrate family lives in most cases, as public and business personas rarely mix with Arabic home life. It is also untrue as wrongly perceived in the west, that women rarely participate in professional work. They are well represented in most countries in planning, project management, architecture and engineering design and represent some of their brightest visionaries for the built environment.

One shining example of a lifelong friendship has been my long-standing colleague and friend 'F al S'. I first met 'F' in Dubai in the early 1980's, when he was Atkins' chief architect there. An Iraqi, he was staying out of his home country while Saddam Hussein was drafting every able-bodied male to fight the vicious border war with Iran. 'F' resembled Demis Roussos, the portly Greek chanteur now deceased, so hardly military in his bearing. He deemed his absence from his country's army as his contribution to the Iraqi war effort and an act of selfless patriotism. How could you not like someone like that?

'F' and I worked on a high-profile project for the Dubai Municipality reviewing plans to upgrade the Deira Creek waterfront opposite old Dubai. This project entailed lots of public consultation - a rare feature in the 1980's – as well as several complex engineering analyses of civil and marine infrastructure. But the most important task came when we presented our recommendations for conserving the Dhow port in the Creek to the whole assembled Council of the Dubai Municipality. Dubai's population is nearly eighty-five per cent expatriate, but the Council is strictly Emiratis only - the guys who really run the place and make the big decisions, then as now. There would be no better chance – or a second one - to get our point across.

Our message was the traditional one; "Don't let the road engineers persuade you to widen the Deira Creek Harbourside and Corniche road! And don't change the mixed small-scale land uses around the gold souk and force the old Dhow port out of the Creek!" This was the beating heart of old Dubai and should be preserved not just for prosperity but also posterity, as it still contributed to the vital if small business commerce of the city. But at our rehearsal the night before the big day, 'F', often given to theatrical gestures, threw the laser pointer we were using for the slide presentation across the room, and exclaimed, "We need to use a camel whip!" He pointed out, in his inimitable style that, "all these buttholes were riding camels when they were six and seven and the one thing they will remember, will be the risk of a thrashing from the camel master and his whip." He had a magnificent example of such an implement, with a shiny little brass ring at the end. "Let's use it for pointing at our slides," he said, so with me wondering how this might be received, that was decided upon.

The next day's presentation was long on detail and complexity. Already by 1984, the Council had sanctioned some bewildering changes to the city in response to major growth. Unimagined at the time, this was going to intensify in subsequent decades down the Sheikh Ziyadh Road South towards Jebel Ali and Abu Dhabi, even though the iconic Burj Al Arab ('our' project in Atkins) and Burj Khalifa were still long in the future. But the Municipality Council had started backing away from some of the worst excesses of modern town planning, and they seemed sympathetic to our message delivered in a mixture of classically educated Iraqi Arabic and my best rehearsed Oxford English. I am convinced that what really got to them was the way we used our camel whip, casually waving it at them and saying menacingly, "don't destroy your city's heritage". You could see their eyes mesmerically following the end of the whip. Whatever, they adopted our conservationist strategy in its entirety and while Dubai is unrecognizable from what it looked like in the 1980's, the city's traditional heart still beats around the Creek. Score one for respect to tradition! Go visit the dhow port in Deira

Creek, still there today with all its cultural charm and human activity, in part because we waved the camel whip.

It is strange how small things stick in the memory while the core of a complicated professional message may be forgotten. Perhaps the complexity behind sound urban planning is the problem. I recall another slide presentation incident in Saudi Arabia a few years later. We were engaged to produce a master plan for the huge new industrial complex of Yanbu on the Red Sea, and, as is customary at the end of these assignments, we were required to present to a gathering of big shots attending specially to hear what their consultants recommended. In the Yanbu case, this included a very senior member of the royal family whose presence was described to us as a great honour and indicative of the importance attached to our recommendations. No pressure then; we rehearsed hard.

The auditorium and the Audio-Visual equipment we were to use were all state of the art. The slide-changing device had to deal with back projection and slides moving in and out of focus. All of this is done via Power Point at the touch of a laptop key these days, but in the '80's the slide changer thingamee used variable voltage like a mini rheostat. You pushed a small lever up the scaled handset for the slides to fade in and out of vision. Simple.

The Royal Dignitary finally appeared after a customary forty-minute delay with his usual entourage of flunkies and bodyguards. After a pregnant silence, we were invited to start. One of my colleagues, Paul Hooper was first on to present the economic case for the industrial growth scenario we believed would be most likely. He took hold of the slide-changing device, but it failed to produce the first slide. Fancying himself as a bit of a techie and as the only one permitted to speak at this frozen moment, His Royal Personage suggested, to embarrassed laughter from his groupies, that Paul press a bit harder to make it work. Paul duly obliged and the wretched device fell apart in his hands with the broken bits scattering all over the floor.

Total silence fell across the room. I imagined the bodyguards stepping forward and hauling Paul off to some dark dungeon to be fed bread and water for a month before a ritual stoning in the market place. The Royal Dignitary broke the tension by saying in a cod James Bond baddy's accent, " I told you to push it, not destroy it!" Cue hilarious laughter from his glee club while a technician took over the slide changing and our presentation carried on, mercifully without further incident. It broke the ice and possibly helped us get the result we sought; another successful application of humour and the human touch, otherwise sometimes known as bullshit baffles brains.

Can you smell revolution in the mood of a people? Journalists in the region have been reflecting on this in recent years as they tracked the pace of social unrest in Tunisia, Libya, Egypt and most tragically Syria. In Teheran and Isfahan in 1978, I was convinced I could also smell social upheaval just under the surface. It is difficult to put a finger on specific symptoms, but I believe that just as you can sense mood from body language, so you can measure morale of a society by the way its citizens behave collectively. Given the fact that crowds also have a different personality to the individuals within them, the process can take on a palpable feeling of menace.

You can gauge the collective morale of people from their public behaviour. I went to Teheran and Isfahan on a British Consultants' Bureau study visit in early 1978 and certainly crossing the road there was a life in your hands experience - respect for life was pretty-well non-existent among car drivers. Taxi drivers appeared more than normally disdainful of their foreign passengers and drove with seeming reckless abandon. Inside Teheran's main souk, the usual range of magnificent herbs and spices, metal and woodwork crafts and carpets were on display. The traders were probably the least likely to foment trouble with the authorities with so much vested business interest to lose, but I felt that the sight of a large group of western foreigners was still unwelcome given the looks on some people's faces. How you are looked at is usually how you are seen, and perhaps we were being perceived as the bearers of unwelcome change in the name of the Shah. Undoubtedly, there was during that visit, a palpable feeling of alienation.

A well-known and respected competitor consultant of ours, Llewellyn Davies International was a star of the study visit, presenting their master plans for a new city outside Teheran called Shahestan Pahlavi (SP) – a shrine in more ways than one, to the almighty Shah as the name suggests. It was designed to be a very high end residential neighbourhood with magnificent boulevards and hanging gardens of Babylon style open spaces and landscape. In fairness to SP, it was also focused on providing much needed housing for middle-class families who were upwardly mobile in their aspirations and some of whom were recent migrants from Iran's country districts. But the style of the architecture and the grandiose geometry of layout suggested to me that the project's consultants had been substantially influenced by a desire or at least an instruction probably emanating from immediately around the Shah, to praise him through great building works.

The result was magnificent, but I could not help thinking, as I looked at their large-scale model, of the Percy Bysshe Shelley poem about 'Ozymandias, king of kings'. I heard myself reciting in my head: -

Look on my works, ye Mighty, and despair!"
Nothing beside remains. Round the decay
Of that colossal wreck, boundless and bare
The lone and level sands stretch faraway

It will be interesting to see if SP lasts the thousands of years envisaged in its initial scope.

At a very posh reception organised by the British Embassy in a down town Teheran hotel, all manner of influential dignitaries and their wives or partners were assembled. There was little doubt from the uniforms, medals and jewellery, sumptuous silks and general swank on display, that they were the sector of the population benefitting most from the Shah's rule. But few people wanted to talk to the assembled foreign visitors at anything other than a superficially polite level. Army, air force and police uniforms were everywhere, but everyone left early in chauffeur driven limos after the speeches and liberal toasts in Persian champagne. An informal curfew was operating throughout the city by nine each night.

The single most unnerving chapter of our visit occurred when a small number of the party flew to Isfahan for a day to see the city known to Persians as 'half the world'. Indeed, if you only visited its huge public spaces such as Nagshe Jahan Square, and its two magnificent mosques, you would have seen in the azure blue of the domes, against a crisp clear sky of early Spring, some of the world's most beautiful buildings and urban planning at its finest – half the world indeed!

But just before the return flight, we encountered trouble at the airport. There had been a mix up over tickets and several of us had flown down in the morning on apparently open tickets, with other names on them than our own. Early in the morning leaving Teheran, this had not been a problem, but late afternoon in Isfahan was a different matter. The Iran Air ground crew spent a lot of time studying our tickets against unmatched passports and held back all ten of us from boarding the aircraft. After much discussion, the Security Police got involved and we were prevented from boarding the plane and instead ushered into a room off the main concourse. Our passports disappeared as we watched the aircraft take off and head north into the night sky.

We were called forward one by one to be interrogated in turn in a separate room. Those questioned were sent through to another holding point so they could not confer with those of us still waiting. When it came to my turn, I was ushered into a semi-dark presence with two policemen in plain clothes seated at a plain table with a single-angle poise lamp, as if from an old war movie. One other plainclothes officer stood behind me and I was not invited to sit. We had heard about Savak, the Shah's feared secret police and the terrible things they were capable of with perceived enemies of the state. But this was surely a case of wrongful identity and among a group of mainly academics - harmless all! Could they not see this?

There was a pervading sense of menace about the whole affair as if we had announced ourselves with this act of identity discrepancy as enemies of the state. When I was called in to answer questions about why I was not Mr Jones, or whoever's was the name on the ticket, most of the others had already been questioned. It seemed to have been such an innocuous error, but the security police were past masters at intimidation. I avoided the temptation to treat the matter lightly and appeal to their better judgment. It seemed better to admit that an offence had occurred of which we were innocent victims, but that we still regarded it as a grave error of judgment and a challenge to the good order and management of security throughout Iran etc. etc. I tend to go reptilian in such situations, that is to say, breathing deeply, slowing the heartbeat and answering questions literally without allowing any inference of dumb insolence.

Perhaps because I was one of the last (thanks be to God that British names predominate within the first half of the alphabet making Roberts one of the last called out even during school days) I could detect signs of boredom among the interrogators. They were serious for about ten minutes, asking every conceivable question about parental origins, whether I had visited Israel, or Iraq - both a no-no for the Iranians – and they wanted details of birthplace and occupation etc. Again, thanks to God for not coming from somewhere anonymous like London rather an obscure place in west Wales; a spy couldn't make it up surely? 007 from Haverfordwest? Get away with you!

I was eventually released into the post-interrogation pen where most of the other ten were anxiously exchanging notes on their own experiences. Every emotion on the spectrum was on display – outrage (getting rarer among the Brits 'wrong century old Boy'!); insouciance (skin deep or a genuine hardened traveller at large?); and one poor bloke who seemed to have wet himself (admission of guilt to the Savak, or lack of mind over bladder?). I did feel sorry for him, but avoided sitting next to him on the flight back to Teheran, which we were graciously allowed to board fully four hours late.

The next day, for the return trip to London, Teheran airport was heaving with families of all kinds – rich, poor, urbanites and country people, and a high proportion of religious types in traditional clothing with their womenfolk fully veiled, all looking to get out. In the endless queues, there was real fear among the travelers that this last check by state security would detain them more permanently. You could smell fear as rank odour in the long lines at passport control. Scattered protests against the Pahlavi dynasty had commenced over 18 months before, and open strikes and street protests erupted soon after. By February 1979, the last royal ruler of Iran had left and an Islamic government had taken over. Sadly, I have not been back since; it was and is a beautiful country and has adopted its own way to development and progress without significant trading influence with the west.

My favourite city in the Middle East is Beirut and favourite country Oman.

Beirut is the Mediterranean gateway to the region and as such a glorious mix of all the cultures of which it is made up. You may have guessed by now I like heterogeneity. Unfortunately, many of the factions there do not despite or perhaps because they all live very close to each other. Many resent their neighbours, or want them expelled or dead. There has been internecine strife for decades and open civil war through much of the 1990's.

Christians, Muslims of every persuasion both political and religious, and those of no strong religion at all, (though they are rarer in the region than in the west) live side by side. The great majority of each persuasion just want peaceful coexistence, but among each group, there are minorities who think otherwise. None of these understand that for every hostile act they perpetrate on their perceived rivals, there will be at least an equal and opposite response. Sadly, and all too often, the net result of hostility and violence is escalation of mistrust and violence reciprocated with fatal results including the seeds of the next retaliatory act. And so it goes on. I sometimes wish there was a country where all those who cannot abide their neighbours could go or be sent, so they could focus only on killing each other rather than the majority of us, seeking a peaceful life. How long would it take them to stop and realise they are made from the same evil ingredients and that their only survival is coexistence? With due deference to the philosophy of Descartes, compromise is the root of, as well as the route to real liberty.

But the appeal of Beirut is precisely its ability to live through these internecine tensions and continue to be the cosmopolitan place it has always been. In the 1950's, such was its appeal in a more stable era, that it developed a reputation as the Paris of the East, with French influence spilling over from the period of French occupation through the '20's and '30's after collapse of the Ottoman Empire, up to Lebanon's independence in 1943. In recent years, after the civil strife and suffering of the 1990's, Beirut has regenerated its city centre with fabulous new shopping streets reclaimed within the previous Corniche area. The result is a bit 'bling' for my taste with little reference to traditional Middle Eastern urban forms, but it is a magnificent statement of confidence in the city's prosperous future. The hills and villages around the city are full during the summer with Arab families escaping the heat in Saudi and the Gulf, as they enjoy the relative cool of Mediterranean breezes. In winter, the high Lebanon mountain peaks of Sannine and Kesrouane provide a snow-clad backdrop to the city and ski stations like Feraya-Wardeh provide the population with the sort of variety which all the world's best warm coastal places should have but too few actually do. Yet still, terrorist acts scar the city with bombings and inter community killings, as if the fanatics cannot bring themselves to permit one of the world's most beautiful places to be enjoyed in peace.

Oman appeals to me because, of all the Middle East, it is the country which has most effectively respected its own traditions and ways of life, while undertaking a judicious level of re-development to bring it into the 21st century. Oman has only moderate oil and gas wealth compared to Saudi, Qatar or Kuwait, and perhaps that is its secret of success. To date, it has not been able to afford the grandiose projects of other countries and is proceeding with its economic and social development at a pace which the population seems to cope with better than elsewhere. It also has two other key ingredients for success; a stable government under a leader, the Sultan who is deeply loved and respected by most of his people, and a rich and varied hinterland of mountains, desert, coastline and in the south even semi-tropical natural vegetation. The Muscat Capital Area is squeezed in between rocky mountainous terrain suggesting it is there only where nature permits. Muscat and Mutrah present a generally low-rise profile of traditional building forms not seeking to emulate the high-rise excesses of Dubai, Abu Dhabi and Qatar. Above all, the people seem far more content with their lot, and usually treat foreigners with respect, provided that it is mutually exchanged. It is no surprise perhaps that the incidence of social unrest and fomented trouble from fundamentalist groups either religious or military seem mercifully to have left Oman largely alone.

I believe this has partly occurred because Oman has deep traditions of trading with other countries across the Indian Ocean to the south into Africa and east towards India and China. That experience gave its people an understanding of other cultures, which much of the relatively inaccessible Arabian Peninsula of former generations never had. If you are outward going towards others, you are better able to cope with inevitable change and social evolution. New ideas do not seem so threatening. It seems to me that Oman is drawing on a deep well of experience to accept change, while protecting what is best of its own to generate a hybrid of traditional and modern in a blend with which we must all learn to live. Tradition is where we gain our culture and change is where we develop stimulus for innovation and social evolution that will eventually make the world a better place. We need them both.

Nowhere represents the contrasts between tradition and modernity more starkly than the Kingdom of Saudi Arabia (KSA or the 'Kingdom' as it is known without irony by many expats). Whether it is physical infrastructure such as roads, airports, industrial estates or new towns, or more subtle but profound factors within the social fabric, the Kingdom sits uneasily between old and new ways. In such a hierarchical society, old and new do not blend easily.

Saudi is by a long margin the wealthiest of the hydrocarbons rich states in the region, and easily the largest. The extent and pace over the last five or six decades with which it has invested in the paraphernalia of modern life has mainly been inspiring. The five big cities of Riyadh, Jeddah, Medina, Mecca and the cluster of towns around Dammam/Al Khobar on the Gulf coast are according to UNHCR, among the fastest growing in the world and are all unrecognisable to me who first visited in the early 1980's. There are some magnificent new buildings and city infrastructure financed by the enormous if fluctuating revenues of the hydrocarbon economy that underwrites everything in Saudi. Each time I return, the extent of change is disorienting. What used to be the way to a particular destination is closed off and another route must be found. It is as well I choose not to drive in Saudi.

A lot of what is being developed in the Kingdom is not so magnificent. The dependence on artificial means of climate control and the huge overdependence on car borne transport are two examples, but it is probably too late to reel back on much of this. Quite simply much of Saudi would be uninhabitable by modern comfort expectations without massive air conditioning.

Good development management in Saudi, by which is meant the consenting of the right projects designed and built in the right way in the right place is not always conducted well. This continues to be a challenge throughout the world, but statutory decision makers in the Kingdom are all too often overawed by private, including inferred royal, patronage to influence the permitting of partial interests to build what and where they like. Too much energy is expended to no purpose about whether such influence amounts to corruption; the point is that the culture allows the inference by decision makers that their best interests are served by allowing the powerful to get their way. The impact on the environment, in particular access to water supplies via the precious deep water table, is profound and unsustainable if permitted to continue indefinitely.

The pace of change is at the root of the huge challenges the country faces, starting with its burgeoning population of young people, far too many of whom are unemployed given the funding for and extent of education available. The fact that there are also so many immigrant workers in the country, at the top and bottom of the labour value scale, is evidence that education and training remains significantly out of touch with employment demand. It also masks the fact that many Saudis are reluctant to accept the most menial or onerous jobs and have insufficient relevant experience for the top ones. At the top end of the labour value scale, I used to observe lots of poor decision-making by young professionals put into very senior positions without adequate experience. With the supply of graduates from usually overseas management schools working up through corporate and government hierarchies, this is steadily improving, but there is still a huge market for consultants. At the bottom of the labour value scale, the mismatch between supply and demand has given rise to armies of guest workers from southern Asia doing menial domestic and often very skilled construction work, sometimes in the most challenging work environments and in the most squalid of domestic accommodation. I have witnessed some of this and would not wish it on anyone.

Measures to 'Saudi-Ize' the workforce across all market sectors are a crude but sometimes effective way to introduce employment opportunities, but too often it leads to tokenism and side-lining of young Saudis nominally on a payroll but all too often permitted or even encouraged to be absent. Accusations of idleness are probably unfair, they are more a reflection of staff resource mismanagement, a further testament to the disconnect between labour need and individual aspiration.

Resistance to change within the most conservative elements of the society including the clerical establishment, coupled with the un- and under- employment of young men is a toxic mix. Modernisation under the guidance and drive since 2015 of the new King Salman, has to be handled delicately at a pace that other societies would regard as glacial, but in Saudi still invites resistance from traditionalists. The government operates one of the tightest security regimes on its citizens as well as guest workers, but that is only because the threat of active resistance fuelled by fundamentalist thinking is very real.

Too much of the blame for this delicate and uneasy situation must be placed at the door of us - not only the 'us' represented by western influence, but the 'us' as planners, architects and engineers. We have assumed that modernity means aping western models of development when a more nuanced Arabist solution would be more appropriate and respectful of local culture. Too much of traditional Arab building design and town planning has been ignored or rejected in favour of solutions that are unsustainable and this will have to change.

Key decision makers in the Kingdom now understand some of these issues better than most outsiders, but their capacity to tackle them is constrained by private patronage, continued traditional thinking at mid management level and the fast pace of change on the ground. Let's hope that Saudis can procure wise council whether from within or without, and ensure that development in the next half century is better managed than the fifty years that have preceded it.

Sometimes the mores and social culture of the Middle East can appear baffling to western sensibilities. I recall once flying from London to meet with the high honchos of Abu Dhabi's National Oil Company (ADNOC), and representatives of the Municipality of that same city. ADNOC were part funding a study to master plan future growth along the main corniche waterfront of Abu Dhabi. They owned a lot of the property there and I formed part of an invited audience to discuss outline terms. As guests who had all flown in from widely differing parts of the world, we were kept waiting for over an hour, not in some ante-room but rather an open majlis or reception salon. The officials who would later be dealing with us, were addressing previous visitors first in open forum. Those waiting ranged from similarly suited westerners and their local business partners, probably like us uncomfortable that their affairs were being conducted in open forum, to people in traditional dress some of whom looked like they had come in from the countryside.

Next up to discuss their grievances were a couple of guys in traditional Arab dress but not the immaculately laundered and pressed variety but clothes they seemed to have slept in. Actually, I knew how they felt, as we had only flown in overnight and come straight to the meeting. They were carrying shepherd's crooks and it turned out they were indeed a couple of shepherds whose grazing rights had been impinged by some recent gas exploration licenses and they were there seeking compensation. I found myself siding with the shepherds who were being outgunned by the ADNOC lawyer's self-assured arguments. I was interpreting most of this through body language as it was conducted in fast-talking colloquial Arabic of which I had little understanding. I have a sneaky hope the shepherds' flocks are still roaming the desert while the drilling machines are prevented from moving onto their grazing land by some ancient bye-law about riparian rights or the like. It is more hope than reality; I expect they are long gone.

The concept of a majlis is actually a wonderful tradition and reminder to the whole community that work in business is just part of the spectrum of community life. It implies that your neighbour's problem is eventually your problem, and we will find a solution together, by the grace of Allah. In recent years, western style preference for confidentiality in business seems to have taken over traditional ways of doing business, and the majlis is becoming a corporate rarity, though it remains a thriving custom for family matters. You need patience to follow and accept the natural rhythm of the exchanges and plenty of extension time on your flight schedule. But respect is garnered to those who offer it in return by observing traditional custom and taking time.

The concept of 'face' is different in Arabic societies than in the west, but we should not, as some believe, peddle an idea that we westerners are innocent of the vanity which loss of face implies. We just do it differently. It is often said that in Arabic society, it is an offense to directly contradict someone. Rather, a response may be nuanced to give you an answer you may want, though too often that may not fit with the answer you actually need. Do not be fooled however, because westerners do the same, or rather with breath-taking hypocrisy avoid the issue altogether by answering a straight question with a tangential answer. How many times have you encountered a dissembling reply to a straight question? It is as common in Europe or the US as it is in the Middle East.

On the positive side, Arab society is very welcoming and overwhelmingly hospitable, especially if you can get to know people beyond the confines of the office. This comes straight from ancient traveller tradition, that you are welcome as an honoured guest while passing through, though some have told me that by becoming resident, the rhythm of friendship changes from passing acquaintance to a more permanent one and may not survive the ultimate test of, "Do I like you? Do I want to spend my precious free time with you?" Not much difference then with western tradition, at least as regards longer term relations. I have had many effusive early encounters with people in business only to have this drift into indifference as the possibility of longer term friendship presents itself.

I referred previously to what was, a few years ago, optimistically called an 'Arab Spring' or social revolution – glasnost Arab style. Sadly, most of the countries where this was starting to happen have moved on to a disappointing summer and in some cases a winter of civil war and continued social strife which shows no sign of going away. Tunisia, then Egypt, Bahrain, Libya and most tragically Syria showed such promise to become societies opened-up to more freedom of expression and accountability of governments. However, despite the will and the evident literacy and education of the people, the habit of open and universally accepted democracy seems not to be robust enough to encourage those who cannot trust their people with the freedom to think for themselves and act upon it. Instead they continue making every effort to maintain tight social and judicial controls over everything from social and printed media to democratic systems. The control seekers who run so many Middle Eastern governments can come equally from the religiously conservative or the militarily dictatorial – two extremes which, despite their often-visceral differences, are cut from the same cloth of mistrust for the people at large or 'Umma' as they are known to the Koran. The people sit uneasily between the two extremes, not knowing which will dominate next while the vast majority only wants peace and tranquillity to raise their families in the knowledge that they are safe and secure. Both the religious fundamentalists and the military dictators claim to espouse safety and security while doling out precisely the opposite. We take open democracy, peaceful changes of power and the right to speak out against authority too much for granted in the west, but they remain an illusion for much of the Arab world.

When I look back to my first real experience of Arab culture in the built environment – the traditional M'zab architecture across the southern rim of the Atlas Mountains of Algeria (far more an Arab tradition than its more metropolitan and Mediterranean influences to the north - see Chapter 6), I realise how far the region has moved away from the environment in which so many who now control national destinies, themselves grew up. Admittedly the M'zab was, and hopefully still is, one extreme of traditional desert fringe urbanism. This is now practically extinct in Egypt or the UAE, and only rarely to be found in Saudi Arabia, Jordan or Oman. But the disappearance of traditional respect and courtesies by which such small communities were also characterised, is also as true as perhaps the diminution of their equivalents in the west in previous decades or centuries. For both societies – western and Arab, the internet and instant access to social interaction and retailing on line has made us all both globally connected but individually self-absorbed and thus removed from an older more proximal sense of community. Let us hope that one other impact of the internet age is the inability for repressive governments to continue denying their citizens from gaining access to news media beyond government control. Access to the world beyond that immediately around you is a catalyst to think for yourself.

That last wish is my most important for this troubled region that has afforded me so much pleasure as well as a good proportion of my livelihood. I hope that people will not mindlessly slip into a consumerist led world of instant online marketplace access, to guard and nurture their communities while protecting the precious asset of thinking and judging for themselves. That too will safeguard against the continued march of extremism that so blights the Middle East. There is no substitute for the

right and means to think and judge the world for yourself;
the ultimate lifetime journey which never stops!

Beirut regenerating after years of civil strife,

Falaj and Qanat irrigation in mountainous Oman are a wonder of ancient technology as effective today as hundreds of years ago. They render agriculture and human settlement viable in arid environments.

Shanty towns are the only accommodation for too many new urban dwellers in many Middle Eastern countries. But despite the squalor and 'living on the edge' these are among the most vibrant communities to be found anywhere.

Chapter 9 Eastern Europe before and after Communism

"From Stettin in the Baltic, to Trieste in the Adriatic, an Iron Curtain has descended across the continent."

From the 1950's to the late 1980's, we grew up and grew accustomed to the consequences of Churchill's ringing words from his 1946 speech to Americans in Fulton Missouri. Looking back, the apparent threat of nuclear annihilation was borne first with incredulity and later with the equanimity of over familiarity. This seems odd now in our multi-polar world. In 1970, my first attempt to visit a Communist country was singularly unsuccessful. I was thrown out.

Three of my mates from Oxford, David and brothers Mike and Anthony and I, had decided that summer to do a grand tour of Europe, borrowing Mike and Anthony's mother's ancient Sunbeam Rapier. This trip was not well planned. With a large boy scout tent held up with 1940's style wooden tent pegs and an ancient primus stove etc., we decided to go where the roads would take us. We crossed southern Germany stopping briefly in Cologne, Ulm (with the tallest spire in Europe) and Nuremberg before deciding it would be nice to visit Czechoslovakia to see the beer town of Pilsen and thence to Prague. We would then swan off to the fleshpots of the Mediterranean. Nice! Only two years before, the Prague Spring had broken out in the then Czechoslovakia under the leadership of Alexander Dubcek, and we had heard vaguely that it was now easy to get an entry visa at the border for a country breaking its former ties with the Warsaw Pact, Russia's answer to NATO in the west. What could go wrong?

Our information was of course based on the most cursory research as only students would be so lax as to try; we would have done well to verify facts before leaving.

Suspecting it might not be quite so easy, we chose a relatively remote crossing point between Nuremberg and Pilsen, specifically on the forested road between Furth-im-Wald in eastern Bavaria and Ceska Kubice and Domazlice in Czechoslovakia. If you look at these places on GoogleEarth now, you will see peaceful rural scenes with a crossing point virtually fallen into disuse since the Iron Curtain was raised and the Czech Republic assumed full membership of the EU in 1998. Not so in 1970, as we were about to find out.

The last few kilometres up to the frontier passed through dense forest and increasingly de-populated farmland. Here towards the end of WWII, advancing Russian and American troops had met on uneasy terms belying their allied status. The formal physical division between east and west came later in the early 1960's, but crossing the frontier had been hazardous since Czechoslovakia fell under a communist government from the late 1940's onwards.

Arriving at the frontier, the West German border guards looked at us a bit quizzically, searching through our heavy blue British passports of the period for signs of visas to enter Czechoslovakia - finding nothing. They asked us politely how we intended to enter the neighbouring country, to which we blithely replied in halting German that we could apply for visas at the border. There were few enough Germans crossing and no cars from other countries, so perhaps the border guards did not know what entry requirements applied to the Brits in those pre-EU days. They did not argue, though their sceptical gaze should have been a clue as they released us to drive the half kilometre of fenced off road through No Man's Land to the Czech barrier.

Except they were not Czech border guards – they were "Rujjians", as I heard my Dad saying to me in my head, recalling as he would have done, his own last tumultuous days of WWII in the four power-occupied Vienna of 1945. These Russians had obviously taken over border duties from their Czech 'allies' as the Prague Spring was definitely over, Dubcek and his party arrested and exiled, to be replaced by the deep winter of a cold war freeze again. They were not amused by our halting explanations that we wished to enter Czechoslovakia for tourism and cultural exchange in the beer-kellers of Pilsen and Prague, and told us to go back to Germany and apply for visas in Bonn. Apart from the disruption to our suddenly urgent schedule, this was not going to be an easy manoeuvre. The road had been deliberately narrowed, with a single strand wire fence at low level on either side, beyond which was a well signposted minefield. The Iron Curtain was still emphatically in place over this remote part of Mittel-Europa and the 'Rujjians' wanted to keep undesirable elements such as British students well and truly on the German side of the border.

By now there were local cars, Wartburgs, Trabants and the occasional ancient Mercedes taxi, stacking up behind us. Their drivers were showing signs of irritation at our evident stupidity not to know the procedure. We made a sixteen-point turn to get the heavy old Sunbeam facing west again into Germany without straying into the minefield. The German border guards had been watching with semi-detached interest from half a kilometre away, and as we approached them again there was great amusement in which we reluctantly joined.

"You are lucky, ve let you back into Germany," they said, suddenly finding some English with side-splitting merriment, "ozzervise you drive up and down the frontier for the rest of your lives like Wagner's Fliegende Hollander!" Ho, German humour at its best, quite good really, though at the time, we struggled to see the funny side. No Czech beer for us on that holiday.

My second experience of a Communist regime was four years later during a student study visit to Poland during my Town Planning Masters course in Cardiff. A group of fifteen of us were to visit the magnificently rebuilt centre of Warsaw, then take the train south to Krakow, Zakopane and Katowice in the Silesian coalfield district. This was just before the rise of Solidarnoscz in the Gdansk shipyards on the Baltic in the mid 1970's, which did so much to eventually break the previously impregnable power of Soviet regimes over eastern Europe. Not yet in 1974, though there were already discernible rents in the curtain through which some sort of light was shining.

On our first night in Warsaw, we went to the Krokodil bar in Rynek Starego Miasta Square, almost entirely destroyed in 1943 and 1944, but now magnificently rebuilt in traditional Polish style. It is a perfect recreation of the old medieval square of which communist town planning can be justly proud. The pub was obviously a meeting place for students of every nationality who by the mid '70's, were coming to Poland in increasing numbers. A group of very attractive girls seemed keen to talk to us in halting English standing nervously nearby. This was very encouraging, until we realised they were Russians and frankly scared of talking to local people whose distaste for their big neighbour to the east too often bordered on hatred. We expressed fraternal goodwill as only students know how, exchanging addresses yet knowing full well we would be most unlikely to see them again. I recall they were from Volgograd – previously known as Stalingrad before its name change after the death of their iron leader Stalin in 1953.

Next day, we travelled south in a steam train, through flowering cherry and plum orchards arriving in the mediaeval city of Krakow in the early evening. Amazingly, the war had not damaged Krakow's city centre, a pact being somehow agreed between the Russians and Germans in late 1944, to leave the magnificent centre alone – similar to Paris around the same time. Our guide in Krakow and throughout the south of Poland was an Economist major from Katowice University, Helena Tendera. Like many in Poland, Helena did not conform to the western stereotype of the ironclad propagandist official tourist guide. She was no heroine of communist rectitude, but rather a subtle brand of deep national pride and social dissent bordering on outright insubordination to the Communist cause. The rents in the curtain were beginning to show at a personal level.

We did not stop long in Krakow despite its evident tourist appeal. We were bound for the much grittier western coalfield district around Katowice in Polish Silesia, with its worthy attempts at social and industrial reconstruction through the '50's and 60's. This was a planning study tour after all. We attended worthy lectures from Katowice's city planners about population statistics and economic forecasts, together with production data on coal and steel production – all good Communist Five-Year Plan stuff. Yet all the while we could see through the windows the leaden grey skies and pollution that were the legacy of this concentration of unrestricted manufacturing activity. Though now much cleaned-up, in the mid 1970's this area of Poland was a by-word for Soviet era industrial production – at the cost of seriously depleted environmental conditions and doubtless the lung functions of the local populace, if they were not already coping with a forty cigarette a day habit to relieve the stress.

This was still not enough to prepare us for a stop on the journey back to Krakow to visit the mildly named town of Oswiecim – better known in the west as Auschwitz. So much has been written about this hellish place that I cannot contribute further without being accused of superficiality or triteness. Should a museum be maintained in such places? Undoubtedly yes, for we should never forget the capacity for Man to be genocidal about his fellow Man, regardless of nationality. Given the same complex circumstances, I believe this could have happened anywhere. The impact of such places is for me in the little things; for example, the room with a huge glass screen down its middle, the other side of which were piles of spectacles frames stacked high to the ceiling, the sole remaining artefacts of those slaughtered on an industrial scale in the gas chambers. Arguably worse, because it spoke of current reactions to past events, there was an offer of a restaurant meal in the well-appointed museum restaurant at the end of the visit. I was astonished that anyone could eat so soon after what we had seen, but I was in a minority. Where does people's empathy reside after such an experience? Does it even exist?

I left Poland with a profound sense that things were about to change, but not quite knowing what shape it might take. We had been brought up in Britain after nearly thirty years of cold war, to believe the Iron Curtain was impregnable. After brutal repression of democrats in Poland and elsewhere in the late 1940's, then the Hungarian uprising of 1956 and the failed Prague Spring of 1968, the Soviet Union would surely never allow things to change among its satellite countries to the west. Yet amazingly within a few years, the very working class whom the communist revolution of 1917 sought to liberate, rose up in Poland and threw out its puppet government under Soviet rule. I would have loved to hear Karl Marx or V. I. Lenin's theoretical explanations of what was happening here. Any political system or ideology which espouses the principle that the ends justify the means to the extent that Soviet Socialism eventually did, could not, like its bastard sibling National Socialism, expect to survive for ever. You cannot theorise about social control without arriving at uncomfortable truths and the day to day reality about the need to be ruthless, corrupt, exploitative and eventually genocidal in pursuit and the protection of power. The unavoidable adjunct of violence eventually consumes itself. Social change can only ever succeed when dealt with more slowly and organically from the grass roots upwards. It can never be imposed top down.

I remember through those early '80's days, watching Solidarnoscz at work in Poland as we waited with dread for the expected overwhelming reaction of force from the Russians. But it never came. The Soviets too, were undergoing profound upheaval and a bending of their will to resist not only external opposition but that of their own people, fed up with the blind authority of a broken social and economic system. Glasnost or 'opening up' and Perestroika roughly 'reconstruction', were two terms carefully explained in our own media as emerging all over the communist world aided at last by an enlightened Soviet leader Mikhail Gorbachev. The long night of cold war to follow the hot variety which had so dominated the young lives of our parents a generation before, was finally coming to an end. It was hard to believe.

But just before the cracks became fully visible, in November 1977, we were invited to visit Moscow for a long weekend, by friends John and Penny, working at the British Embassy. John was in one of his first overseas postings as a lowly Third Secretary, but went on later to a stellar career through the Foreign Office and the UN. His wife Penny had been my neighbour in far off Haverfordwest, ten years previously. Their own apartment accommodation was so small that we had to stay in the Intourist Hotel, two blocks from the Kremlin and Red Square, but that made our various visits to city centre sights very easy.

The tone for this visit was set by our official 'guide' Ludmilla, who met us off our flight at Sheremtyevo Airport, outside Moscow. Perhaps 'minder' would have been a better description. She was not like our friendly Polish guide of three years previously – more the ironclad battleship type. Immediately outside the airport, there was a destroyed German tank monumentalised as the furthest point of advance of the Nazis during the war thirty-four years previously. No carefree trip this one, more like ploughing through recent historical archaeology. The Russians were not going to let us forget it.

The Intourist hotel was right out of spy movie fantasy. The décor was circa 1955 with little sign of refurbishment since. The lobby could not be crossed without close scrutiny from Reception and Concierge desks. Guest registration procedures included very close inspection of our passports – who was this British man married to a French woman – a cunning NATO inspired plot to subvert or confuse the proletariat revolution? The lifts were staffed by muscular attendants in field grey suits, probably moonlighting for the KGB. On each floor as we emerged from the lift, we were confronted by a large table behind which sat a matronly guardian of public morals, as wide as she was tall, with absence of humour to match. She spoke only Russian, so how she would have advised foreign men not to bring Russian women back to their rooms, I could not imagine – unless, as now seems likely, she included martial arts in her range of skills. Her body language made it clear she was not there for the benefit of guests, rather to keep us strictly in line. Such was the concept of service Soviet style in the 1970's. Our passports, one blue the other red, were inspected again, giving rise to deep suspicion that this was another clever trick to subvert morals if not the security of Matushka Rossia.

With these forbidding first impressions, we finally got to our room, and started to look behind the black and white photos that were the sole decoration in the bedroom, searching for microphones - James Bond style. We found nothing; perhaps they had been built into the heavy mattresses or under the industrial grade carpet bolted to the floor.

But outside, the first snows of winter were blanketing these sinister impressions. We walked through a fairyland atmosphere as the city's traffic noise was deadened by snow, across Red Square to view the impossible fantasy of St Basil's Cathedral and its confectionary of coloured domes, lit up in the gathering gloom of late afternoon. Then to the GUM stores facing the impenetrable façade of the Kremlin on the other side of the square. Inside, it was revealed as a magnificent late 19th century edifice with a central atrium constructed of filigreed ironwork. We visited the food hall where the pro-employment policies of the Soviet Union were on full display – one person to serve the somewhat limited food fare, another to issue a price ticket for you to pay at a third attendant's ancient cash machine, while yet a fourth wrapped the goods to be taken away, strictly on production of your receipt paid. Clearly there was no messing with this lot, whose perception of shopping service seemed to exclude anything so frivolous as a smile of welcome or thank you for your custom or a friendly, "come again!"

That first night, we attended the Bolshoi ballet theatre alongside the Kremlin, and though the Bolshoi company were presenting abroad, we saw an amazing mixed show of Cossack dancing and classical ballet in the cavernous and highly decorated auditorium. On other occasions, this venue had doubled as the location for each annual Communist Party Praesidium. Some of these I had watched, previously televised to the west in grainy black and white together with all its mind-numbing predictability of subjects debated with their block-voting inevitable outcomes.

The next day we queued to enter the Kremlin museum where there was still an amazing display of Fabergé eggs and other decadent Czarist jewellery, the better to remind visitors of the sheer wasteful luxury in which the previous regime had immersed itself. As we waited outside in the snow to gain entry, I stepped briefly out of line to take a photo of the queue of people against the high snow-curtained russet brown walls of the Kremlin and the partly iced up Moscow River. A guard immediately blew a whistle and marched up to me shouting in my face in colloquial Russian, leaving no room for doubt that stepping out of line was not permitted. Amazingly he did not confiscate my camera, but I did not argue further. Many of those in the queue sniggered at my humbling (presumably others from the west), while the locals among us stared dumbly at this extraordinary behaviour of someone so stupid as to indulge in blatant displays of civil disobedience. The latter were clearly used to such abuse; we were not. It was a metaphor for our differences; individualism vs. collective rectitude.

If this begins to sound like a rant against Communism, it is more aimed at autocracy in general. I had studied some Russian history since the revolution as a minor specialty at Oxford, and Russia was historically a ruthless maintainer of law and order whether in Czarist or post-revolutionary times. It maintains that reputation to this day. Most revolutions seemed to me to take very little time before starting to consume themselves through ruthless power politics and personal vendetta. When in 1921, the sailors of the Baltic Fleet, some of whom had been in the vanguard of the revolution leading the attack on the St Petersburg Winter Palace four years previously, rose up against their political commissars demanding greater democratic rights, they were ruthlessly gunned down for counter-revolutionary behaviour. The Kronstadt 'Incident' as it came to be known, set the tone for a gradual descent into the dark autocracy of the post-Lenin era under Stalin and his successors. No dispensation for fellow revolutionaries; maintaining control was paramount. The Jacobins in early 1790's France who doubted the loyalty of fellow revolutionaries through little more than an innate human capacity for distrust, behaved in the same way, effectively replacing the previous despotic aristocracy with something worse. All violent revolutions ultimately consume themselves.

For a change of scene, we had a wonderful visit out of Moscow to Peredelkino and another fairyland castle within a snowy setting, to see Boris Pasternak's grave, deep in the woods. This was a rare glimpse of the great Russian landscape beyond the city, just enough to remind us what a deep tradition of literature lies within the Russian soul, set within the vast and endless country which is one of its sources of inspiration.

Our friends in the British Embassy lived an interesting double life, steeped in high diplomacy one minute (Test Ban treaties were on the agenda between East and West) and rushing to the international shop on the other, to stock up with salads and fresh tomatoes, paid for with foreign currency when a new consignment was shipped in from Finland. They taught us to refer to the KGB as the 'Kiev Gas Board' as the initials spell out the same meaning in Russian and it did not do to be mentioning their name in public. The all-powerful secret police had watchers everywhere, eager to report counter-revolutionary behaviour. The collective rectitude had perhaps become as tight as in Czarist days.

I recall on our last day in Moscow going to a restaurant behind the Lubyanka and well known to the locals for occasional seafood and river fish – ironically called the Berlin. But, on the day we ate there, the interior fish pool, which was a notable feature of the restaurant, only had dead specimens floating on the surface. No one saw fit to scoop them out. Fish only on the menu of course, and it did taste like last week's catch - another monument to the indifference to good service in the late Communist era. As we left the restaurant, we stared at the sightless windows of the neighbouring Lubyanka, headquarters of the KGB.

I spent the next twenty-five years with little difficulty avoiding further contact with the 'eastern bloc' as we were neutrally taught to call it by non-aligned academics. Some of these had been fellow travelers with Communism, but most had long since abandoned hope that the version being applied in the Soviet Union would lead to the hoped-for liberation of proletarian spirit and creativity. 'To each according to need; from each according to ability' was part of the original promise of the revolutionaries when overthrowing the outdated and tyrannical Czarist regime.

How far they had departed from this worthy cause! It seemed more like 'To each according to influence and power; from each according to infinite capacity and patience of the downtrodden proletariat'. Shame on them, for calling themselves champions of the world's downtrodden and lumpen masses – they were anything but, once the lust for power and its retention took hold.

However, in 1999 Sylvie and I ventured back into the country, which had so summarily rejected me in far off 1970 – the Czech Republic. Gone were almost all the trappings of the former regime, with Prague decked out in early summer flowers and a welcome to match for the tourist hordes. There remained a degree of Bohemian melancholy if you scratched beneath the surface, as perfectly encapsulated by the national music of Smetana and his tone poem to the River Moldau. But the spirit of self-expression and free enterprise was also burning brighter than before, giving an eventual happy outcome to its early flowering under Alexander Dubcek in 1968. Such a pity he did not live to fully appreciate his country's emergence form the long dark night of ideological and sometime military occupation.

A couple of years later we went for a long weekend to Budapest, capital of Hungary, arguably the first of the previously eastern bloc countries to fully embrace a capitalistic economic model, after the fall of its previous regime in the early 1990's. Hungary seems to sit apart from its neighbours both culturally and linguistically, its language being usually impenetrable to others outside the Finno-Ugric group. But Hungary is also famous for its mathematicians, composers and such left-field inventions as the Rubik cube and the ballpoint pen – the Biro - named after its 1930's inventor.

The setting of Budapest on the Danube is magnificent, with the royal palace in Buda on high ground above its west bank commanding a magnificent view beyond the city, eastwards into the vast Hortobagy Plain making up much of rural Hungary. We stayed in a hotel called the Gelert, which had been completed during the city's carefree affluent days just before the First World War. It incorporates plumbing from some of the finest warm water natural springs, converted in 1911, into Roman style baths to which both locals and hotel guests flock to spend happy hours in the steamy balm of warm sulphur-odour waters. Nakedness is acceptable in the steam baths but it was so foggy that there was a lottery of emotions from repulsion to vicarious pleasure as contrasting body shapes revealed themselves through the mist.

We journeyed out of Budapest by train to the town of Szentendre to see something of rural life. But by the early 2000's the tourist dollar had already taken over and local crafts were priced squarely with foreign visitors in mind. There was little sign of rural tranquillity among the avaricious stall holders. A saintly sounding Norwegian choir could be heard, gathered in the village square entertaining the crowds to Nordic national songs and a few international favourites. People gathered around from all sorts of racial and cultural origins with smiles on their faces as they took the simplest enjoyment from four-part unaccompanied singing – a universal form of common pleasure to any culture.

That night, in stark contrast to the middle European setting, the Rugby World Cup semi-final was due to be played between England and South Africa, so we got back to Budapest early to secure two precious places at the only pub in town we could find intending to televise it. Because of some peculiarity of upper atmosphere physics, they had tuned the TV to S4C, the Welsh language programme little known outside my native Wales, but broadcasting from the game with pre-match deep analysis - all in Welsh. The South Africans (and the English for that matter) did not understand a word, assuming it was Hungarian. I heard one puzzled South African turn to his mate and remark "Jeez, these Hungarians reeelly know their rugbee!" I love this mix up of cultures to the point where no one really knows what they are looking at or how to understand it properly. It just does not matter that we are all different!

But Budapest and the typical mood and pre-disposition of Hungarians seemed to me to be melancholy bordering on moroseness. While Poland even during the heavy burden of the late Communist era and the Czech Republic alongside it, seemed to retain an uplifting spirit of irrepressibility, this was not so evident among Hungarians. I expect I can be proved wrong, but it seemed to me that the intellectual effort to grapple with a Rubik cube probably exhausted any propensity to joy at the mere prospect of being alive. I like their wine though.

The pulling back of the Iron Curtain marked the end of an era of either open or clandestine warfare which had endured with few interruptions since 1914 – nearly eighty years impacting at least three generations across all of Europe and beyond. I lived through the end years of this period, mercifully missing the hot war stages of it which so marked both my father's and mother's early adulthood. The Hungarian Uprising of 1956, the equivalent in Czechoslovakia in 1968 and the rise of home grown revolt against autocratic rule in Poland in the mid 1970's, then Russia in the late 1980's, all came close to spiralling into far worse international conflagrations from which we have been mercifully spared. Without doubt, communism initially liberated millions from the serfdom of despotic feudal regimes, but replaced them gradually with similar chains of conformity to a cause serving only those at its apex. All the worse for the hypocrisy with which Marx, then later Lenin, Trotsky and Engels claimed to be liberating the masses. They ended up not even liberating themselves, but living in a world of perpetual menace where lack of trust and non-accountability were the cancer to destroy their originally worthy cause.

I will return to this theme of social and cultural control in my final chapter. However, I feel privileged, educationally at any rate, to have experienced something of such societies during their enslavement to a corrupted cause, and then to see them liberated. Now they are societies with faults like ours in the west but including at least the freedom to admit this and think for themselves. As my generation grows older, the privilege of experiencing this contrast first hand will get rarer, only afforded to a few who lived at the right time on either side of a huge social divide with some opportunity to experience at least a morsel of both. I know which I prefer, but the ability to contrast and compare was hugely significant.

Katowice, Poland, April '74. Brutalist architecture accompanied by an iron-bosomed, battle-ready heroine. Not much empathy here!

Waiting to visit Lenin's Tomb, Moscow, November '77. No stepping out of line!

The Berlin Wall in 2016. Now just a tourist trap.

Chapter 10 South Asian Mosaic

Thailand

There is a pulse to life in south Asia, specifically, in my experience, Thailand, Sarawak in east Malaysia and most extensively India, which seems to beat stronger than elsewhere. The people in these countries contain an unstoppable belief in progress, and while the original tiger economies referred to four other countries, the term could equally apply to these three. How else to explain the following: whole city block scale retail re-development in Bangkok in the 1990's; taking more than an hour to overfly new industrial development along Sarawak's north coast. In 2012, we must also contemplate the wholesale loss of development land to river flooding in southern India a few years earlier, because of intense development upstream. In this latest case, the massively increased run off downstream with consequent loss of development land where our new town was due to be built? So, 'there's a river running through it' is not just a film title and the basis of river hydrology. It is a metaphor for the hyperactive circulation through the blood stream of these supercharged economies.

In Bangkok in 1996, I was asked to broker a project, to manage refurbishment of a large scale multi-tenanted retail mall in one of the city's many commercial centres, on behalf of a major Chinese/Thai property investor. I had to find someone within our UK businesses willing to manage the city block wide re-development works via a three-year commitment to live and work in Bangkok. From my innocent perspective, I thought this would be difficult, but I had bargained without a wide range of Brits of a certain age apparently fleeing from 'domestic strife' at home, and eager to seek oriental 'R & R' in their down time. Having weeded out from the shortlist a few obvious lotharios, I set off armed with some suitable CVs to meet and be briefed by the Thai investor in his palatial offices in Bangkok as to what they wanted done.

One of his bright star underlings was deputed to escort me around the city and visit the site. Huge city block sized buildings are a feature of many south east Asian cities designed and built in the tradition of the Chinese 'Go-Down', a shop house on several floors selling a wide range of goods. The modern interpretation is typically a massive concrete structure over one hundred and fifty metres long and typically built over five floors, at least one of which is dedicated to parking. There is usually an 'anchor tenant' such as a big department store occupying one or more floors and the rest of the building is configured to accommodate a large food market and smaller retail outlets, together with some residential space for those who wanted, as in the oriental tradition, to live 'over the shop'.

The key strategic decision was whether to undertake a progressive refurbishment or knock it all down and start again. Like property companies the world over, my client was interested in the best return in the medium term: receiving regular income and managing tenancies by providing the maintenance, or building new developments and filling them with fresh tenants either as residents, retailers or office clients. One looks like steady income for mature companies, the other works wonders for a growing balance sheet. The fundamental for both business models is a strong and growing revenue, keeping the property company solvent and its big bosses and shareholders in the manner in which they like to become accustomed. Capitalism property style.

We soon agreed a refurbishment brief and after the usual contract wrangles, our project manager was installed in a company flat on site, starting work about a month later. They like to work fast in Thailand. I went back a few months later to see how things were getting on, and he was happily co-habiting with a new live-in partner – a nubile young lady more than half his age amidst the noise and dust of the demolition of most of the building's interior. He was also enjoying the delights of Pat Pong, Bangkok's down-at-heel but very vibrant 'entertainment' district. 'Louche' describes it perfectly; English seems too puritan to have an equivalent word.

Much changed now, Pat Pong consisted in the mid 1990's of a multitude of bars and restaurants, most offering food and drink, but also the company of disconcertingly pretty girls, whose company was purchased for a few Baht more than the cost of the drinks and food. Depending on the quality of the establishment, their conversation ranged from stilted to sparkling, but most offered back massages (in public with your clothes on) and doubtless other services progressively more private elsewhere in the establishment. Remembering my chaste days in La Paz retold in chapter 7, I applied the old principle of 'Mirar, pero no tocar' - look but don't touch. Some of the girls, who must have been Filipinas, immediately recognised this from the Spanish mixed up in their Tagalog native tongue. With glee and laughter, they named me "Milarpelo!" Any attempt at empathy through humour being fair game for either party in the faux-intimate environment of the girlie bars. Fundamentally they seemed melancholy places.

Pat Pong's other feature was the Thai boxing rings where inebriated foreigners were persuaded, against better judgment, to take on local kick-boxers. Some of them were falsely encouraged by the discrepancy in size and appearance between themselves (big and pink) and their professional opponents (small, brown, lean and super fit). There was hardly ever a real contest, the foreigners invariably coming off worse with kicks all around the body and (leather helmeted) head. It usually took less than 3 painful rounds for it to be all over, but I did see one Australian go twelve rounds with a local and push him all the way with money changing hands frantically round the ring as it got harder and harder to see who would win. He did not, but he got a standing ovation from the baying crowd at the end.

Bangkok life was lived very much in the raw; dog eat dog, whether doing business, cruising the bars or sizing up the boxing ring competition. A few years later, I travelled with Sylvie to Chiang Mai in the north of the country, where we found a gentler existence infused with Buddhist like tranquillity. But Chiang Mai is rapidly losing its tranquil reputation as it gets overrun with mainly low cost but very high end Chinese tourism. But as I relate in the next chapter, Thailand's tough almost survivalist hard work ethic made people more than able to respond to the Tsunami disaster of 2003. My empathy with Thais starts and ends with a deep respect for their ability to live with adversity on many levels and to triumph over it.

Malaysia

Malaysia is superficially at least, much more staid and traditional to its various cultures than Thailand, probably because of the Muslim majority, though China Town in Kuala Lumpur makes a serious effort to match the vibrancy if not opportunities for sin of anything in Bangkok. I recall a weekend in KL with our local office director once in the mid 1990's, who invited me after finishing work one Saturday morning, to join a cross-country run with the renowned Hash House Harriers. This international and slightly eccentric club of long distance runners was founded in KL in the early fifties spreading its unique amateur pastime across the world ever since. There are now Hashers everywhere. Everyone pitches up to an agreed start in suitable running gear, to be sent off around town or in our case through thick jungle, following a course with just enough markers en route to avoid becoming completely lost. In places, our course was up or down vertiginously steep hillsides with the aid of lianas growing out of the jungle, or across brown and turgid streams, in which, I imagined, there lurked unspeakable blood-sucking insects and probably larger creatures who would fancy an opportunity to revert to man eating.

The other hashers consisted by the late nineties of a multi-racial mix of runners of both sexes. I soon detected that the KL founding HHH had become something of an informal marriage bureau. Several Chinese and Indian girls turned up in the very latest figure-hugging lycra and displayed disheartening fitness. There were also lots of Brits in standard Saturday afternoon running gear – worn out trainers, socks round the ankles, knee length shorts probably previously owned by their Dads during national service, and a sweaty T shirt that had not been washed for months. I doubt they won fair maidens' hearts given the self-assurance of the fair maidens who were looking for much fitter and focused individuals.

We all finished the 'race' without being poisoned or eaten on the way and everyone repaired to the upper room of a Chinese restaurant in town where a gargantuan meal with copious volumes of beer and wine was on offer. That much seemed still to be frightfully British in style – lose all your inhibitions getting filthy and lost, but laugh about it over a copious drinking session afterwards. Many Brits seem to use playing the fool and alcohol in equal measures to overcome their pre-disposition of shyness with strangers. The formula was working for a range of cultures present as demonstrated at the ribald prize-giving ceremony to end the evening.

Sarawak is as different to West Malaysia as northern Thailand is to Bangkok; the contrast of old country versus metropolitan values re-appearing again. In 2012, I went to Kuching, capital of Sarawak to review plans for a new city with the unprepossessing name of Mukah. It is situated half way up the eight-hundred km long coastline of the island of Borneo of which Sarawak forms most of the northern third, facing the South China Sea, stretching west and east from Kuching, to the border with Brunei. During British colonial times Sarawak was almost the personal fiefdom of the Brooke family, who 'owned' vast areas of jungle via obscure concessions dating from the 18th and 19th century East India Company. They progressively granted part of the land to subsistence farmers and more recently palm oil plantations. The Brooke family ruled as Rajahs from 1841 to as recently as 1946 when the British government, unpopularly for many, converted it to a more conventional colonial status until it became part of federated Malaysia in 1963.

My local hosts were fellow planners, architects and engineers, a mix of both Malays and Hong Chinese, most of whom were themselves immigrants to this east Malaysian state. I delicately probed the apparently benign landlord/tenant relationship based on the Brookes as Rajah/landowner and local people as their tenants and rent payers. To what extent had they become subjects of the landowner and did this stand up to post-colonial scrutiny? To my surprise, the reputation of the Brooke family and the last Rajah - Charles Vyner deWindt Brooke -

was stoutly defended by my hosts. The Brooke reputation also baffles western Malays who experienced a different colonial experience at the hands of less altruistic rubber planters on the peninsula. Claims to property ownership were invariably contested more strongly after a short run and unsuccessful communist insurgency, as the country moved towards independence.

The Brookes were canny rulers, banning Christian missionaries while outlawing native head-hunters with punitive expeditions into the jungle interior to stop this practice. They managed the influx of immigrant entrepreneurial Chinese with the more traditional native population of Dayaks with a skill many would envy today. They seem to have been a throw-back to a period pre-dating the mass colonial age, when genuine respect of local people including a deep cultural knowledge and awareness of their language and customs was expected of titular rulers, compensating for their own racial and religious differences. Something similar existed in parts of India before the onset of large scale European immigration after the Napoleonic Wars. The first one hundred and fifty years of British influence in India saw much more social interaction between the races when intermarriage, between Indians and Europeans, became common. This diminished from the mid nineteenth century onwards, evolving into near apartheid between the races after the Indian Army Mutiny of 1857.

With only one day available for my site visit, a proper impression of the development prospects of the large and remote region around Mukah would have been a logistical impossibility without helicopter transport. So, my Malay Chinese hosts who had invited me to join their bid for the future master planning work, arranged for my fifteen hour flights from London to Kuching and back, and a suitable charter flight on arrival over the development region. Jet lag was not on the agenda.

Our two hundred employee consulting firm had recently completed its sale to a larger Australian organization, for whom staff safety was deemed paramount. At least the bureaucracy of safety was paramount – the completion of all necessary documentation in minute detail about travel plans, including verification of the proper maintenance procedures for all means of conveyance, all completed and signed off in advance of departure; no forms – no travel. The prospect of a helicopter flight over unknown jungle territory with a previously untried charter company ticked all the high hazard boxes. I had previously been responsible for all my own business travel, but our new owners had appointed a new head of business who turned out to have significantly less experience than me of the hazards of travel in remote places. Selling your business comes at a price, so biting my tongue, I submitted to his interrogation around the safety procedures. The trip failed every test imaginable, despite my having obtained from eight thousand miles away an airworthiness certificate for the helicopter. I was inordinately proud of that. So, a wondrous fudge was concocted. I would make the visit 'in my own time', thereby exonerating the new owners of blame for any accident liability. When an employer states that staff safety is paramount, consider in whose interests such worthy statements are made!

By 2012, the scale and pace of new industrialization and urban development around Mukah was awe-inspiring, despite the fact that the Sarawak state government had not yet confirmed Development Corporation status on the new town. While the pace of change typified an Asian tiger economy, rather than the staid pace of development to which we are accustomed in Europe, I found myself relating to very British concepts of development management.

Many of the senior professionals in Sarawak from both public and private sectors, had been trained at British universities. In fact, several of my colleagues on my Masters Town Planning course at the University of Wales in the early 1970's had been Malays or Chinese from Sarawak. Sadly, I did not meet any of them during this visit nearly forty years later, but our local consultant colleagues had also trained in Cardiff, while others remembered Glasgow and Nottingham with equal affection. I listened while Chai Long Sen, my architect bidding partner for the project got quite emotional over his memories of Sauchiehall Street in Glasgow on a Saturday night while he was a student there thirty years previously. His own son was now a post-grad dental student completing his clinical experience in the cranio-facial unit at University College Hospital Cardiff, where Chai had bought him a house. Common academic experience, despite living and working half a world away, runs deep through relations between Britain and Malaysia, as for many other parts of the Commonwealth. We will reduce our intake of foreign students to vocational degree courses at the peril of losing this deep loyalty and affection for student days spent in the UK. It is very good for business, in case the cultural arguments are not enough for our British Treasury.

Up and down the coast either side of Mukah, the Sarawak state authorities had consented the construction of aluminium smelters, manganese plants, power stations and associated port facilities, deploying a mix of Malay, Chinese and Japanese capital. It took us well over an hour to overfly the region from south to north. Layouts of new residential neighbourhoods already resembled suburban USA or Europe and the construction of wide haul roads for heavy industrial equipment and pipelines into formerly remote coastal jungle was visible across a wide area. The energy, pace and thrust of new development was immediately apparent and I concluded that if it carried on like this for a few more years, Malaysia would be a net exporter of processed mineral products and manufactured goods to the traditional industrial heartlands of Europe and North America or even Japan. Times are changing.

The viability of such investment is underwritten by lower costs of labour in south east Asia than the west or Japan, but the extent and speed of change also signified a worrying pre-disposition to assume development will always be prioritised over environmental interests. As far as the eye could see at two thousand feet above the landscape, there were palm oil plantations where only a few years before, native jungle of hardwood species would have prevailed. Palm oil is a highly lucrative crop representing one of Malaysia's most valuable exports for detergent and foodstuff processing worldwide, but at what cost to indigenous vegetation, and loss of tropical hardwoods?

On the way back to Kuching, we had to cross a range of hills about eight hundred metres high. But afternoon storm clouds had gathered and the top of the ridge running unbroken across our route was partially hidden in curtains of rain. During a brief landing to refuel, the pilot contemplated this problem, together with his contract commitment to deliver us back on time for the next stage of our pressing schedule. I wondered idly whether time-keeping or safety would win, thinking of the distant safety procedures I had signed up to. As far as the company was concerned, I was on leave so 'on my own'. Time keeping won and we took off into the mounting gloom, which pretty soon converted itself into a raging storm with thunder rumbling all around while lightning flickered through the blackness. Unlike my little Chipmunk in north Oxfordshire long ago, helicopters deflect a lot of rain with their main rotor blade, but the bucking and banging was even more alarming because of the inherent instability of a rotary winged aircraft. There were fifteen minutes of sheer strap-hanging fear for me, while affecting the insouciant demeanour of a well-travelled 'helicopteristo'. My fellow passengers were doing the same thing, but when we finally landed thirty minutes later, safely back at base, Chinese emotions erupted and the pilot was hugged for preserving our lives. Like all pilots everywhere, he just shrugged modestly. All in a day's work.

In the end, our proposed consortium of Malay, Chinese and Australian/British consultancy failed to win any master planning commission to plan the future new town. I believe that (at last after much development abuse over recent years) the Sarawak government has been reviewing the extent of loss of native species resulting from the ever expanding intended development. Policies for protecting virgin jungle for ecological interests would have appeared as a given within our scheme, but I suspect that the government has been re-thinking the whole concept of extensive development. For the local environment, this will not have come a moment too soon.

India

I have visited India three times, twice on project assignments and once on vacation. Lucky as I am to have chosen a career I love that is also related to the life of the people, there is no huge difference. It remains one of the most challenging countries to visit and understand, thickly layered with deep traditions, multiple cultures, castes and religious sects.

My first visit took me to the southern state of Kerala in order to master plan a new media city to be built by Dubai developers immediately inland of the coastal city of Kochi. My team and I had been hired by Arab investors I had known from Dubai after a successful similar project planned for them in Malta, briefly described in chapter 11 to follow. This occurred during the years immediately before the 2008/9 world banking crisis and resultant recession, so we little guessed what commercial loss of confidence was looming over the predictive horizon. Our Emirati clients wanted to replicate the Maltese model of a business park for IT and media industries, with residential and high end retail facilities in many more of the world's time zones and major growth markets. Kerala was just the latest in their planned series.

Their idea was soundly based to the extent that Kerala currently supplies some of the most literate and IT numerate employees speaking good English throughout the Gulf. Why not offer a homecoming for such skilled people to establish an IT and media industry in their own home state? A joint venture between the Kerala state authorities and our UAE investors was the obvious route forward. It takes two to make an agreement, but either one of them can break it. Kerala state and their Arab investors inhabited very different worlds commercially and contractually, as regards expectations of the outcome of such a collaborative endeavour. Neither party did their homework properly concerning the other.

Kerala state has exhibited an independent streak from mainstream India politics for decades and the state did not even join the new union of India for several years after the British left in 1947. The Congress Party and BJP who dominate states further north, get regular trouncings in elections and though the state government was desperate to attract foreign investment, with this project, Kerala sometimes had odd ways of showing it. The Arab investors meanwhile were unfamiliar with the expectations of a state that has many communists in its governing class, who blithely assumed that such investors had bottomless pockets.

The Arabs made little attempt to warn the Keralans that reciprocal investment would be expected, such as roads, and good communications facilities off site enabling fast access from Kochi and its international airport. Their franchise agreement was silent about such matters. They also used outdated rainfall data and one-hundred-year flood incident mapping, drawn up by British hydrologists in the immediate post-independence early 1950's, thus allowing both parties to assume the extent of available flood-free land was far greater than was actually the case. Climate change and a huge increase in impervious surfacing from building development upstream in the river basins had caused a significant reduction of buildable land near the river courses over more than fifty years, since the flood maps were drawn. Was there a river running through it? And some!

Most damaging of all, to be placed at the door of both parties, the state government offered, and the Arab investors accepted, to take on, long-term leases rather than freeholds for the land subject to development. Individual Indian house buyers are rarely able to borrow money to buy residential property on lease rather than freehold terms. We pointed out that this could have been overcome if freehold transferred to individual owners on purchase of single properties, but neither the developers nor the state were interested but the facts were telling. But the facts were telling. Very few final property buyers were coming forward.

After our preliminary site visits to southern India, a good deal of our early master planning time was spent in Dubai rather than Kochi, spelling out the significant commercial and cultural differences of perception as to how a development model might evolve. Meanwhile back in Kochi, the state authorities had agreed to share the decision-making structure via a Special Commissioner appointed by the federal government in Delhi, a further unexpected event, and this time with significant tax implications. Though the Special Economic Zone status would be free of state tax liability, Federal India still intended to tax the project. Again, the Arabs had not expected that.

Perhaps in a more buoyant economic climate, there may have been time to overcome these difficulties, but this was early 2009, and financial circumstances for attracting partner investors in the UAE were growing tougher by the day for its proud but steadily over-reaching property companies. Foreign ventures were especially vulnerable. Early in April that year, I was summoned to Dubai with my chief urban designer Peter Dijkhuis, expecting a mild telling-off for being a few weeks behind schedule with design development, only to be confronted by the client's whole project management and legal team lined up on the opposite side of a huge board room table. "We have called you here to terminate this contract,", they announced in sepulchral tones. Taking a deep breath, I asked if this was due to any perceived failure on our part. Poker player eyes across the table elicited the response "That depends on the outcome of the terms for closing the contract". In other words, play ball with us over your severance costs to close down your team's work prematurely, and we will not argue over 'lateness' or 'insufficient quality'. Put more realistically from our viewpoint, it was a case of seek too much compensation and we will exaggerate our critical interpretation of your work to date!

Charming. We had warned them that their business model was flawed but had been straining every sinew to deliver designs to demanding deadlines. But it would not now be enough. I did not know it at the time though I had a good guess, that our client's company capitalisation was in dire trouble with projects all over Dubai and elsewhere being terminated prematurely. They were not alone, this was a widespread phenomenon at the time, and with no employment protection and bank overdrafts deemed illegal in the UAE, a lot of expatriates were exiting the country fast. The atmosphere in Dubai was febrile. Expatriates who had been buying their cars on fast track money hire-purchase terms with only 10% deposits down, but who had now lost their jobs with no means to continue payments, were driving to the airport and abandoning their vehicles leaving the keys on the seat for the hire purchase companies to retrieve after they had fled overseas. Better than ending up in debtors' prison! Bankruptcy is a criminal offence in Dubai.

The next two days with our soon-to-be ex client were a negotiating challenge while I sought to recoup fees for work completed by our small company but not yet at a contract milestone for invoicing purposes. Set against the darkening sky of the local economy close to free fall, I realised that if we hung on for all we were owed, I would get nothing, as our client could be declared insolvent at any time. I began to wonder if we would get out of the country safely as each evening, the bars in the free drinking hotels were host to excesses of behaviour brought on by expatriate despair that the good times were over. It was 1929, Dubai style.

I eventually got out of Dubai with about 70% of what we could have expected in more stable times. We parted on reasonably good terms, and the money agreed to be owing was settled within thirty days. Just as well because less than two months later, the client went into liquidation. Face is everything to Arab business practice, so complete collapse will have been devastating psychologically. I was not too happy either, but after more than thirty years in business by then, earlier financial vaccinations kept me upright.

I should have seen the signs earlier perhaps. So much of the hopes of the state of Kerala were based on the dubious promise of vast investment. In turn this hung on the premise that local people would flock to their new town and borrow money to buy leasehold property. All around Kochi, there had been ten-metre high advertising hoardings selling the dream of the new town good life soon to be had living in 'Dubai Heights', or 'Emirates Village'. These were portrayed as havens of the future rich if you were lucky enough to be employed by the IT and media companies confidently expected to arrive soon in Kerala. But like so much forming the boom and bust mentality worldwide, this was a dream built on sand, perfectly portrayed by one of the hoarding images of a Dubai Heights, high-rise block with an Arab dude in turban and full white dishdash, sporting his Armani sun shades with his foot casually resting on the front fender of his recently acquired Mercedes sports coupe. The Bollywood cool did not cut much ice with local people.

My third visit to India was a holiday with Sylvie, through Delhi, Amritsar, the Punjab, Shimla in the

Himalayan foothills and finally through the ancient fort cities of Rajasthan. We arrived in Delhi in miserable early February wet weather and headed north to Amritsar, with its Golden Temple, the holy shrine of Sikhdom. Magnificent even in the cold driving rain, the thousands of Temple visitors are invited to a free meal of dahl and rice and I was welcomed to join the team of cooks stirring the huge vats of gently steaming lentils. It was simple fare but a great way to start a journey to a part of India steeped in history and religious tradition, not all of it with a happy outcome. The British Army massacre in the Jallianwala Bagh in 1919, and the sacking of the Golden Temple by the Indian Army in 1984, illustrate the extent of racial and religious intolerance with violent results, of which all humanity can be both perpetrator and victim.

There is a great spectacle to be watched at the India-Pakistan frontier as they close the gates between the two at dusk each day. On the way there, I passed thousands of lorries parked up in interminable lines kilometres long, their drivers patiently waiting for Customs clearance and right of entry to Pakistani Lahore and beyond. There must have been identical queues on the Pakistani side. The magnificent vehicles, known in the past as 'jingly' trucks because of their multi-coloured decorations often with little tinkling bells, remain to this day the life force of commerce in India, Pakistan and so much else of southern Asia. They ply their trade across the sub-continent carrying every conceivable legal and illegal item, between the cities, towns and small villages wherever there is a demand to be supplied - small vehicles, white goods, clothing, fresh vegetables and fruit, tobacco, whisky, hashish and more. Decoration of these ships of the road cover every flat surface of cab and sides, invoking blessings and safe passage from Hindu gods, Buddhism, Islam, Sikhism and

Christianity. Often all religions are represented on a single truck as the drivers are nothing if not pragmatic preferring to hedge their bets. Barcelona, Bayern Munich and Manchester United also feature, depending on driver preferences, symbolizing a common popular alternative religion with which we all live. The drivers and lorry traders are India's most effective missionaries of modern culture.

The patience of such truck drivers is legendary as they wait in endless long lines for clearance to pass a border or pay a motorway toll. Faced with yet another bureaucratic barrier to progress, they stop, brew their tea in a chai khana and swap tales with fellow truckers of where they have been and where headed. They work ridiculously long hours, often driving wholly under-serviced vehicles giving India a bad name for major traffic accidents. Few westerners except those on the leanest budgets, have the bravery or patience to seek lifts with them. But as an occupational way of life and if you have the temperament with a substantial dose of local karma, it must be preferable to working in a sweat shop factory or as a three-wheel 'tuc-tuc' taxi driver, taking life in your hands around the crowded centres of cities.

At the India Pakistan frontier gates, after the last buses of the day had passed through, crowds of onlookers on either side of the arbitrary line separating the two countries assemble to watch the nightly border closing ceremony. Each set of magnificently uniformed border guards from India and Pakistan seek to outdo each other with exaggerated drill gestures, play acting aggression and defiance. The potential for a real incident – diplomatic or worse - seems high until you realise the whole thing is carefully choreographed as a piece of theatre. In fact, they must rehearse together, strictly in private, to avoid things going wrong. "Pakistan!"/"Hindustan!" the crowds either side of the gates chant good-humouredly in turn, outdoing each other for volume and fervour.

The Indian army seemed to have recently got one over the Pakistanis by introducing female guards with film-star good looks and full make up, to add to the normal complement of tall Olympian males. They must have calculated that the deployment of border guards of both genders was not something Muslim culture would be inclined to copy. The Indian girls seemed to revel in the perceived discomfort of their Pakistani opposite numbers as they glared at each other crashing to attention only inches apart, immobile while the last post sounded on the military trumpets. May all their international tensions be reduced to this style of good-natured theatre! A good principle for the rest of the world as well, perhaps?

From Amritsar, we took a train to Chandigarh and thence by road and light rail through the Himalayan foothills to Shimla, once the summer capital of the British Raj. The railway to Shimla does not start until Kalka but the hundred-year old train was very slow, so we opted to take only part of the journey by train from Barog Tunnel to Khandaghat. There, we jumped back in our following taxi. Barog station is located at the end of a kilometre-long tunnel designed and built by a Scottish engineer of the same name, in 1903. Starting his excavations from both ends, his calculations were slightly out at the meeting point in the middle – no more than a couple of imperial inches. The Government fined him a nominal one-Rupee probably as a joke, but he failed to see the funny side and was so ashamed of this slight to his engineering precision that he later committed suicide. Such was the stiff upper lip of the Raj.

Shimla is much larger than it was in colonial days, now approaching two hundred thousand souls. Their houses cling to the steep hillsides relying on vertical integration in perilous structures accommodating extended families. But many of the old features of the town remain, particularly in the centre, where the shops with their mock Tudor timber framed facades and the Anglican church appear for all the world as if they were Godalming or Leamington Spa. In the church, there are brass plaques to the Glorious Dead not only of two world wars but to many previous imperial adventures such as the Crimea and South Africa. Casualties of the Mutiny of 1857 seemed no longer to be on display.

Leaving the Punjab, we passed through Delhi again en route to Agra and the Rajasthan forts, arriving in Delhi's Main Station by train in the early evening. I was there the victim of what must have been a well-rehearsed robbery routine. So-called porters jumped on the train as it slowed on arrival in Delhi, only to have our bags eagerly carried away for us to the platform without our express consent. While focusing on chasing the eager carrier, keeping track of where he was in the crowd, my passport and I-Phone were quietly lifted from my tightly zipped shoulder rucksack, the loss only to be discovered later, on arrival at our hotel.

I immediately returned to the station, but earnest enquiries of the nearly supine Indian Railways Police when their office was eventually located close to midnight, yielded nothing. Early the next morning, I was ringing the bell at the British High Commission office seeking a temporary passport with only the rest of the day available on our tight schedule, to obtain a new entry visa, without which it would not have been possible to leave India ten days later. Armed with my new cream cardboard five-page temporary passport, I set off to report the theft again and seek a post-dated entry visa from the Indian Internal Immigration Department. IIID sounds like a nasty illness and that is how it seemed.

If ever there was a descent into bureaucratic hell on earth, the visit to the inland office of the Indian Immigration Service was it. It is worth recounting what happened as a study in the effectiveness of applying - or failing to apply - empathy to a stressful situation. The interminable waiting which comprises the bulk of the process offers little other diversion. Hundreds of people were queuing for emergency visas of one sort or another in an aircraft-hangar sized hall. There was ample time to speak to fellow sufferers in the queues, many of whom had been victims of robberies far worse than my own, including violent muggings. Some had been forced to beg lifts over long distances to Delhi, penniless and devoid of ID. There was a prevailing ambience of tense expectancy.

With the exception of Afghans, presumably deemed to be an additional security risk, some three hundred people were corralled into a large seating area in the centre of the huge assembly hall. Any Indian guides accompanying the better off tourists were banished in case they started influencing the Immigration officers. There were a series of numbered desks – 1 to 20 – located around the vast hall's perimeter. Each desk represented a separate stage in the bureaucratic progress from initial application to the eventual nirvana of a stamped entry visa with which the passport holder could leave, safe in the knowledge they could later exit the country. This final accolade to the interminable hours of waiting, was ultimately bestowed by the magnificently named 'InCharge' (all one word), a gentleman whose sole right it was to declare each victim's halting progress, through the bureaucratic labyrinth, to be finally complete.

The supplicants for each progressive stage were ordered to sit in the middle of the room from where they would be called forward to answer minor queries on their forms. Control was maintained by strict positioning of applicants and processors. Applicants would only be dealt with when called forward, you had to sit down first. Only rarely were people listened to if they initiated their own enquiries – a subtle and fiendish form of crowd control that kept the officials 'in charge', the abiding principle by which the whole place operated. There were many who were sent back for adjustments of fine detail to one or more of the previous stages, almost in tears about the certainty with which this was adding hours to their wait. There was no scope for a free-for-all as a group of Nigerians unused to the concept of queuing learned to their cost, being sent back to the beginning when they finally lost patience half way through and demanded priority attention. That much at least was satisfying.

I did not start well, having completed my initial application form by hand only to have this politely rejected at the first desk as it was not completed 'online'. "How was I supposed to do this?" I asked. 'Online/Outside!' came the peremptory reply. Suppressing my own tears of frustration, but with growing despair, I left the building and quickly found the perfect metaphor for the Indian condition – crippling bureaucracy but a lively adjacent private enterprise sector ready to respond. For the price of a soda, a samosa and a ten-rupee fee, the soft drinks vendor was running a form-filling service. Flipping open his laptop, my stall holder, come bureaucratic guardian angel, typed out my application, applied one of my photos (always take spares with you when travelling abroad) and printed it off within the space of three minutes flat. He and his kind should have been running the Immigration service in the first place.

Despite the delay, I was back queuing at the first desk again within ten minutes, now applying the sharp elbow techniques needed to repel more boisterous West Africans for whom standing in line was outside their experience. Learning fast how to behave, I graduated from Desk 1 and settled down to watching the passage of my forms from 'out' tray on each desk to 'in' tray on the next, with the gimlet-eyed concentration of a starving bird of prey. If my forms got lost in the pile and did not move for twenty minutes or so, I would approach the desk from the central seating area oozing humility from every pore, to ask politely if the clerk could be so good as to apply the appropriate stamp and move the documents on. Through frequent displays of unctuous handwringing, I maintained the all-important demeanour of humour with goodwill, essential for cooperation with any bureaucracy worldwide. Progress seemed geological in time scale.

We had delayed our departure from Delhi to the evening, but were dependent on catching a last train that night to Agra to regain our schedule. I deployed several conversational devices to keep my forms moving along, such as my obligation to attend a British/Indian wedding in Agra the next day, after which I modestly declared myself due to play in an England vs. India veterans cricket match. These blandishments were met with smiling goodwill by the officials. They had probably heard them all before, so may have appreciated the originality of my excuses or not. The whole atmosphere was affable provided you stuck to the rules, but it mattered little to the officials how long it would all take. A TV mounted in one corner of the hall was broadcasting a cricket match, giving the officials ample excuse to pause and admire the ground strokes or the spin bowling from their favourite players. Steam rose quietly from the long-suffering applicants, especially those for whom cricket was a mystery.

There was a personal crisis at about Desk 12. I was called forward, to be told they had no separate record of my having entered India. I insisted on the date, approximate time and airport of entry, but of course I had no documentary proof without the stolen passport. I faced a Kafka-esque situation that if the only record of my having entered India was in my stolen passport, there would be no means of getting out. I was a non-person! By good fortune, the absence of the necessary separate documentation on the issuing of Entry visas was not uncommon, so grumbling about the whole situation clearly being my fault, the official reluctantly stamped my papers and they were moved glacially onwards. After seven hours, and with merely ten minutes to spare before they closed for the day when they would be asking everyone to come back in the morning to start again, I was called forward to the final desk, the penultimate clerk signing my papers with a flourish and a humorous shake of the head.

"Oh yes, the cricket player!" he stated with mock sincerity, as he placed my forms in the last in tray for His Majesty 'InCharge' to approve.

'InCharge' displaying his authority over everyone in slightly egg-stained jacket and club tie, despite the failed air conditioning, sat on a slightly raised pedestal above all us lesser mortals as undisputed arbiter of final exit visa issue. Two of us were summoned before him simultaneously, a four-ring Taiwanese airline pilot in full company uniform unusually allowed an interpreter because he spoke no English, and me. 'InCharge' flicked through the pilot's bright blue Taiwanese passport and glaring at me, exclaimed, "This isn't you!"

Up until this point, I had maintained an icy almost reptilian calm, with monosyllabic responses so as to avoid offence or ambiguity. But at this very last of seven hours of procedural fences, I nearly lost it. "No!" I cried, "That's him, he's the airline pilot!" Luckily, 'InCharge' saw the funny side rather than sending me back to the beginning. The China Airlines pilot and I got our passports stamped together and we were out of there with blessed relief and a quick farewell to each other, before parting company for ever.

An experience never to be forgotten and if I never see the inside of an Indian civil service office again, it will still be too soon. The sense of overwhelming helplessness in the face of mindless process and paperwork stays with me even years later, but it was and remains, a nice metaphor for modern India – almost religious adherence to procedure regardless of the time it may take, but all done with goodwill and charm – provided you obey the rules.

Thankfully the rest of our visit to India unfolded broadly to plan, through Agra and Rajasthan with all its attendant magic of fabulous sights seen, invoking wonderment at the inventiveness and creativity of those who had built the Mogul empire. The Taj Mahal is a shrine to love expressed as a monument to craftsmanship of the known world in the fifteenth century. Stonemasons, sculptors, painters and others came from India of course, but also China, the Middle East and Europe to design and build an edifice that stands among the finest structures in the world.

Rajasthan is a favourite among foreign tourists to India probably because of its strong sense of history of the Moghul emperors, manifested in well preserved fortified cities such as Jaipur, Jodhpur, Udaipur and Jaisalmeer. Here the latent class consciousness of Europeans - the British more than most, perhaps - can be reassured of the innate familiarity of Maharajahs who, like Lords of the Manor in rural England, ruled their people with, more or less, benevolence and foresight. They did this with such a high degree of social control that most were permitted to maintain nominal independence from the British Raj. After all, they had almost identical social objectives to the British, stability, modest technical evolution provided no boats were rocked, but principally 'noblesse oblige'.

The Maharajahs have perhaps also been the Indians whom the British admired most, their fabulous wealth being wondered at while emphasizing their dependence on an external military power and conservative stability that by the nineteenth century, the Rajahs could not have hoped to maintain alone. This faded opulence shines forth in a large number of glorious palaces, built with intricate sophistication at the height of Moghul power during the fifteenth and sixteenth centuries, putting to shame the more basic architecture and construction of the militarily superior but utilitarian British, even two hundred years later. Only railway architecture and the bungalow seem to have survived as ubiquitous, meritorious and thus enduring examples of British Indian architecture. Lutyen's New Delhi is a notable exception for municipally magisterial town planning.

Slightly off the well-worn tourist track, we visited Deoghar, home to one of the smallest Raj palaces. This is now a 'haveli' (hotel) preserved and refurbished in traditional but slightly down-at-heel 'distressed' style, to a lived-in perfection of multi-coloured glass, ornate and decrepit antique furniture, mirrors, fabrics and wall decoration – 'shabby chic' Indian style.

Perhaps the most charming aspect of the Deoghar haveli is its urban setting. Tourists walking through any typical Indian shopping street must run the gauntlet of every trader enticing them into their shops, sometimes to the point of outright harassment, to admire and buy fabric, clothing, 'genuine' antiques, jewellery and carpets - whatever - at 'never to be repeated' prices. Resisting politely is hard work. But Deoghar is different, because the current Maharajah, and having met his wife, the Maharani briefly one evening in the hotel dining room, hold sway amongst the town's traders. They own most of the commercial property in the tiny town where the guests at the haveli are almost the only source of external earnings. Noblesse oblige again.

The unwritten message through the few narrow shopping streets of the town is, 'don't harass the tourists - well not too much - for they are our sole source of incoming revenue and we want it to continue that way'. Shops only line about three main thoroughfares and are therefore identifiable even to the most inexperienced visitor, otherwise likely to get lost. So, over-exuberant salesmanship gets reported back quickly to the town's only foreign tourist hotel. The reporting is actively encouraged of guests when they arrive, and makes the experience of wandering through the bazaars, the pleasure it once may have been anywhere - unlike larger towns where it is only for the strong-willed, determined and tight of pocket.

Some of the more domestic imagery of real urban India was therefore available to us for discreet observation and photography; women without running water at home, washing their laundry and themselves in the town's 'tank' or artificially retained water source; goats happily grazing on festering rubbish heaps; school children in their recognizably European style uniforms hanging out together - equally European style - on their way to or from school; and the un-intentioned comedy of the magnificently uniformed traffic policeman trying to keep order and free flow among the crossroads chaos of local urban transport. This was 'Indiaah profonde'!

We took a morning ride on a regular passenger train from the nearby Khambli Ghat Station to Marwar Junction through the nearby the Arawalli Hills. Marwar is famous as the starting off point for 'The Man who would be King' by Rudyard Kipling, later a film with Sean Connery and Michael Caine. Our journey passed through some of the driest and most inhospitable country over which engineers had to build the line in the early twentieth century. It reminded me of the 1950's film North West Frontier - an evocative if shameless propaganda piece to the selfless devotion of Kenneth Moore as the best of the British Army in India. He was serving the long-term interests of peace and stability, while all around him was division and national break up in post-independence partition between India and Pakistan, in the late 1940's. The drive back from Marwar in an open-topped jeep was a return to reality with a bump - in more ways than one.

Two issues are regularly cited as those holding India back from being the fast growth economy that its human potential offers. First is corruption and the second is the caste system holding millions in poverty without the means to achieve their real potential.

During my work in India, I luckily had no personal experience of corruption so cannot speak of it first-hand. However, what I have observed within the property development sector, tells me that the bureaucracy of decision-making is so loaded against new development that it can only ever progress when the wheels of consent are oiled with cash or favours. Putting aside the moral issue, you could argue that additional payments to decision makers is a means to fast track development, because it gets things done faster than a more equitable but endemically bureaucratic alternative. It also filters the wealth of investment down through progressively lower layers of officialdom who are otherwise lowly paid. But that ignores the deleterious effect on project viability imposed by necessary payments, as corruption has its own way of calculating market value like any other service. What is market value in such circumstances? Why, whatever the beneficiary can get away with of course!

Corruption also attracts crime of a worse sort including large scale embezzlement, intimidation, violence and murder. But the lower grade stuff is much more common because it is less likely to attract media attention. However, the delays attendant on so-called 'clean' transactions (if indeed they ever exist) is enough to blunt the will and motivation of many honest people, seeking to conduct themselves without recourse to bribes. Once again it is perception not reality that rules people's lives, and while there is little faith in processes devoid of corruption, bribe free business remains difficult to establish.

The second prevailing constraint on India's unfettered development is the caste system. How long it might take to supplant caste prejudice with a more egalitarian system, is more the concern of the social anthropologist than me as an urban planner. Even then, given the infinite variables in human behaviour, ambition and social attitudes, the onset of greater equality would be hard to predict. British influence during the Raj probably gave caste divisions a boost, as the British, when they first arrived in the seventeenth century, were nearly as hidebound about class as India remained about caste. But I conclude that we British learn about class-consciousness via our social education, while in India caste remains embedded in people's DNA.

India is the most exciting of countries with huge potential to succeed and become one of the world's dominant economies. Freeing up all its people to contribute to this growth and evolution, unfettered by ineffective bureaucracy, remains the country's greatest challenge. It deserves to succeed.

The future of India part 1. Curious schoolboys in Deoghar Rajasthan, February 2013

The future of India part 2. These Udaipur schoolgirls are unlikely to accept the subservient position of their mothers and grandmothers.

Chapter 11 Island Postcards

This royal throne of kings, this sceptered isle,
This earth of majesty, this seat of Mars,
This other Eden, demi-paradise,
This fortress built by Nature for her self
Against infection and the hand of war,
This happy breed of men, this little world,
This precious stone set in a silver sea,
Which serves it in the office of a wall
Or as a moat defensive to a house,
Against the envy of less happier lands,
This blessed plot, this earth, this realm, this...... Island!
Shakespeare Richard 11.

I am fascinated by islands. Not just their physical separation from 'mainlands' (a relative term) by various distances of sea, but the isolation in various forms that they manifest in their flora, fauna and most subtle of all, human inhabitants. My travels about the world have included a variety of islands in different settings, and I do not forget that in relation to the world's largest contiguous landmass, as a citizen of Great Britain, I am an islander myself. Apologies for mangling the last line of Shakespeare's marvellous death bed speech for John of Gaunt above, but this is not an essay on national exceptionalism, rather a celebration of islands as a geographical entity.

The first one fulfilled occasional boyhood daydreams of isolation and remoteness.

Stack Rock, Pembrokeshire
My birthplace county is surrounded on three sides by sea with an indented coastline and the most diverse

physical and historical structures found in any single county of Britain. The whole geological table from Pre-Cambrian to the Paleontological Age is represented here, and the place names reference Welsh, Norse, Flemish, French and most recently English as the languages of choice.

Surprisingly, given nearly 150 miles of indented coastline Pembrokeshire has only a handful of islands, some inhabited such as Caldey off the little Regency town of Tenby, where Cistercian monks and a few farmers still live off the balmy southern climate growing flowers to make perfumes, Skomer with its bird sanctuary including the county's National Park symbol, the humorous Puffin, and Ramsey with one farm accessed by a wild crossing from the St Justinian's lifeboat station near St David's. But the uninhabited ones - Skokholm, Grassholm and the Smalls with their lonely automatic light, twenty miles out into the Atlantic, are more fascinating - the remoter the better.

For a fourteen-year old with occasional pubescent dreams of inhabiting his own private space, there was one smaller one within reach, and one warm summer day in 1965, I persuaded my elder cousin Doug, with his small boat Lucy with her three hp outboard two-stroke engine, to mount an exhibition to Stack Rock. Situated about a mile off the coast and two miles from our favourite seaside village of Little Haven, this was an hour's sailing time at Lucy's maximum speed. The sun was high, there was hardly a cloud in the sky and the sea was unusually millpond calm. Time to go!

I had prepared a flag declaring UDI (Unilateral Declarations of Independence were 'in fashion' that year, after the style of Rhodesia) for 'my' Republic of Stack. Human Population: occasional; Seabird Population: too numerous to count (and v aggressive); source of Gross National Product: guano. Stack is two blocks of rock about forty metres high, connected by a lower causeway, all of it about one hundred metres long and fifty metres at its widest, so, not really big enough to sustain independence, but big enough for dreams!

We landed on the modest high tide swell in the one small sea inlet and tying Lucy fore and aft we climbed up through thick plantains to the island's summit. We planted my flag with due ceremony, watched by some puzzled seals in the sea below and the island's entire colony of disturbed seagulls, cormorants and gannets. Gannets were so common off the Welsh coasts at that time, that the 'Min of Ag and Fish' as they were known, would pay you a shilling for each one you killed, as they ate their own weight in fish every day. Doubtless gannets are now protected, but mackerel have no voice in Parliament.

Views were long and clear in all directions; to the north across St Brides Bay to the St David's peninsula, south to the nearby St Brides village with its then derelict Kensington isolation hospital (now a high-end spa resort), and eastwards back to Little Haven where we would soon be regaling the locals with tales of derring-do. But out to the west there was almost nothing except the seaward horizon, the western Atlantic in its most benign state, with Grassholm far to the west and the remotest of all Trinity House lighthouses on the Smalls (still manned in the 1960's) even further west again and just visible on this clearest of days.

At times like this, I tended to daydream of what was to come; storms lashing the coast, the wind so strong as to carry foam off the top of each wave and the seagulls driven before it like so much flying flotsam; no weather for venturing out in small boats such as ours. But this was high summer and warm weather, so why could I not continue being a will o' the wisp dreamer, listening to the waves lapping the rocks, the seagulls' call with the soft warm wind ruffling the thin grass on the summit? My own special island.

We waited half an hour for the Air Sea rescue helicopter from RNAS Brawdy to come and check us out, perhaps accompanied by Interpol to arrest us for the treasonous act of independence. But eventually growing bored at the world's indifference, we made our way home to Little Haven, trailing a mackerel line unrequited by an evening catch. The next year 1966, I went back and there was of course no sign of my flag, blown away landward on the first winter gales to where someone would wonder at its strange incomprehensible message But, amazingly my bamboo flag pole was still there, slightly chewed by a curious bird but just about upright offering little resistance to the wind. I was proud of that.

Thus, ended my first island love affair, leaving me with fascination for remote places, most of which have offered slightly more human stimulus than Stack. Motivated by pure nostalgia and boyhood memories, I have been back there in recent years. Not much has changed; thicker vegetation, smellier guano, fewer cormorants (the fish must be pleased) and no seals to be seen, but no flag pole either after nearly forty years. My Republic rests merely in memory and imagination.

Goultrop off Little Haven Pembrokeshire and Stack Rock in the distance, my first Island of Dreams in 1965.

Malta

At the other end of the lonely island spectrum lies Malta, a highly-urbanised community of over half a million inhabitants and, being Mediterranean, with opinions at least double that number. I was asked in 2006 to form a team to plan a new town - a 'Smart City' no less – to integrate into Malta's crowded settlement pattern. This was required to comprise specialist business space for the media and IT sectors and associated high end residential and retail facilities all surrounding an up-market waterfront with berthing for million-dollar maritime gin palaces. No pressure then, a bit different to Stack, but hey, another day, another dollar!

Our clients were Arab property developers I had met in Dubai for whom a subsequent project in India was described in the previous chapter. They had hit on the idea of providing this specialist business space throughout every time-zone in the world, starting with Malta. Supposing Malta to be the soft underbelly of the EU, where planning consent would be a pushover and tax-free incentives would be plentiful, the objective was to attract back, young educated Maltese IT and media professionals who had migrated to new opportunities in Italy, Britain or the U.S. Create some high-end business units cheaper than in Rome, London or Silicone Valley and the Microsofts and Siemens of the world would flock to the project. What could be simpler?

They had reckoned without the individuality of island people and the Maltese in particular. The government might be the willing partner of one of its biggest foreign investments for years, but that was not going to make their own Environmental and Planning Authority (MEPA) roll over and have its tummy tickled. The chosen location for Smart City was near Kalkara and adjacent to one of the island's prized historic forts, which had defended the island against all comers through the centuries, from Arab invaders in the 14th, Napoleonic navies at the end of the 18th, and the Italian and German air forces throughout WW2. Military archaeology is now one of Malta's fastest growing tourist attractions and the island was not about to give up one of its major un-refurbished forts without suitable compensation.

Because of previous disdain for examples of ex-British colonial influence, the old wartime anti-aircraft batteries and massive bombproof shelters had fallen into disrepair, to be slowly taken over as shelters for cattle and sheep. The smell from animal faeces from recently departed livestock was a powerful deterrent to site visits.

But slowly public opinion was evolving to a realization that most of those killed and injured in these wartime structures were indeed Maltese, and they have become shrines to the war dead. There was also now a potential source for reviving these features as shrines to the war dead, so half way through the project, we made major alterations to our scheme to plan a sensitive lower density housing development in a quiet parkland setting with excellent views out to sea. Conservation is not a low-cost town planning solution, and it does not always mix with providing housing at accessible prices.

So, Malta were no pushover for their new Arab invaders. Elsewhere across the site, we discreetly pointed out to the men from Dubai, that a mosque on every street corner was not what the deeply traditional Catholic population had in mind. Malta had survived the Mufti of Jerusalem's three-year siege in the 1400's, and successive waves of would-be Arab migrants escaping the turmoil of nearby Libya in more recent years, so the Maltese welcomed investment but not an associated threat of cultural change. Islanders may spend a lot of time compensating for their detachment from the mainstream, but ask them to join that mainstream via someone else's definition of what it might be, and lines are drawn in sand.

Crete

My only visit to Crete was shamefully short; in and out on the same day. The Minotaur would have been disappointed but I hope Hercules was impressed.

Working out of our Athens office for the Greek Cadaster (a.k.a. the Greek Ordnance Survey) we had been commissioned through a European Union grant, to map property plot boundaries and ownerships so the authorities would know for certain which occupants wholly owned their land, or who else might be a landlord or other claimant to development rights. Of course, the Greek tax authorities would also quite like to know who in far flung Melbourne, Malmo, Manchester or Milwaukee might be good for some absentee property owner taxes. Only that in Greece, inheritance is, by default, split evenly between all sons and daughters of a deceased owner. With multiple previous diasporas world-wide, to the U.S., Australia, Latin America and so on, claimants were hard to find and in some cases deceased.

First off, map the assumed titles. The town we were surveying that day was Episkopi to the west of Crete's capital Heraklion, requiring an onward flight to Chania and a drive up into the hills over-looking the Mediterranean. Our surveyors were locally contracted students from Heraklion University supervised by a young British GIS surveyor harassed by the complexity of his task and very little Greek.

A recipe for extensive confusion then. The students were loving it - bright, talkative and fully understanding the problems - while every property occupier also had a lot to say, either claiming sole ownership and thus unfettered rights over the property, or where they feared extra taxes, their tribulations with absentee part owners, comprising their distant relatives living in Sydney, New York or Buenos Aires. Mapping this was becoming a nightmare and a six-month exercise to record ownerships throughout the whole town of Episkopi was falling way behind schedule.

I flew in to review the situation on the morning flight from Athens, but the supervision budget restricted me to one day only, returning to the mainland on the last flight. After a frustrating morning, we retired to a local Taverna, as is the Greek custom, to discuss the problem with the student surveyors, trailing some of the more aggrieved occupiers in our wake. The problem was quite obviously intractable. Even when we had mapped and registered ownerships, the appeals process would take months especially as the Cadaster insisted on appeals in person; a bit difficult if you were a subsequent generation living on another continent with no deeds of part ownership and your Greek might now be rusty.

Sadly, I forget the year - maybe mid 1990's - but time seems infinite in parts of Greece, and Crete in early April was beautiful, with wild flowers everywhere and that pale blue sky which reflects a landscape whose luminosity seems to strike you physically coming from Northern Europe and the recent darkness of winter months. On returning to Athens, I wrote my report on project 'progress', declaring that there was very little of it. Not for the first or last time, the EU's money was not being well spent, and I forget what the outcome of this optimistic attempt at order out of chaos was. We had started a similar survey process in the north, near Alexandropli close to the Turkish border, but I had no need to visit; I could probably have written my 'progress' report location unseen.

So, I can claim no real knowledge of the physical attributes of the beautiful island of Crete, but I was instead able to glimpse the labyrinth that is Greek property ownership - especially that which applied to this independently minded island community. It will take an 8th Labour of Hercules to sort it all out.

Gomera, Canary Islands and Boa Vista Cape Verde Islands

Sometimes it is good to look at two islands in parallel to reveal their differences not only with mainlands but with each other. Why so?

Two islands in the eastern Atlantic off Africa's coast struck me as having the right ingredients for comparison. They are broadly the same shape and size, emerging from the sea through volcanic activity millions of years ago, with human settlements by the fifteenth century recorded by two separate Iberian empires, removed from their nearby continental neighbours but with markedly different cultural references. Boa Vista (BV) in Cape Verde and Gomera in the Canaries fit my definitions of separateness nicely, but how similar are they to one another?

The answer is hardly similar at all. Boa Vista in the Cape Verde Islands, now independent from Portugal, comprises predominantly dry rocky desert, vegetation only breaking out around rare surface watercourses or, on the coast where plants are salt tolerant. By contrast, La Gomera in the Spanish Canaries is more mountainous with vertical climate separations and a remote interior frequently covered in cloud and mist, supporting a dense vegetation, while the lower slopes and coastal edge are often in bright sunshine whipped by lively Atlantic gales.

La Gomera had an indigenous population known as Guanches since at least Roman times, though these people were either absorbed or wiped out by the colonising Spanish from 1489. Boa Vista was apparently uninhabited until 'discovered' in the 1460's by British sailors and only colonised later by Portugal. The British left them alone as they were allied with Portugal for over five hundred years since, one of the longest alliances in European history. That did not prevent a few sea battles around the islands particularly (as so often) between the British and French, particularly during the Napoleonic Wars, and Cape Verde has long been a haunt for pirates, smuggling to and from the African mainland. Forlornly deserted shipwrecks going back centuries lie scattered on remote beaches, their remoteness rendering salvage unviable, their stark and rusting hulks exposed at low tide in Sal Rei harbour or on more exposed stretches of empty coastline.

BV is now growing faster than Gomera, having gained funds from the EU and tour companies to build a new airport allowing direct flights from Europe with their influxes of large tourist numbers, intent on winter sun. Gomera also boasts an airport but it is one of the scariest approaches and take-offs, for small aircraft only, being so mountainous as to have no suitable space for a longer runway. Most visitors arrive by the Olsen Lines fast ferries from Tenerife and if lucky, they leave by the same means, but not if there is heavy weather when the island can be isolated for days. That is when island life really kicks in, with outside influences cut off and island communities becoming reliant on their own resources. It does not last in our hyper-connected world, but that is when I am most interested in island life!

Gomera has another charming and unusual feature testifying to its inaccessibility - its Silbo Gomero, or whistling language. Some of the mountain pastures for sheep and goats were so remote and difficult to reach that the local shepherds would communicate with each other often unseen across the valleys with a whistling language. For outsiders, it has to be heard to be believed, let alone understood. It became a means of bad weather warning or danger from predators, as well as a clever early indication that the legal authorities were on the trail of some local miscreant. After all it was only whistling! While the Spanish authorities were able to police the coastal communities, the Silbo ensured they could never really control the interior.

The main indigenous life of BV is to be found in the small town and capital of Sal Rei, though its modest mix of Portuguese and African style architecture also now hosts an interesting range of hustlers from the African mainland. On my walk through the streets of Sal Rei, I was harassed by several such ambassadors of the world's second most common form of capitalism, and I made the mistake of pretending not to understand them in Portuguese or the universal English, by replying in French. This only induced a renewed assault on my attention as one seller of cheap tourist trinkets claimed to come from nearby Dakar in Senegal while his fellow tormentor with yet more overpriced tourist tat hailed from Nouakchott in even closer Mauretania. Both claimed French as their mother tongue though I doubted that. Local Boa Vistans were either too shy or polite to hustle tourists.

Both islands now boast big tourist trades in relation to their other economies. If tourist development did not exist, these islands would remain as they were for centuries, isolated from the world with the ambitious and enterprising among the population migrating to where their aspirations could be realised. The choice is stark; stagnation as a remote backwater of the world economy or leave and join the globally connected rat race. Depopulation is the inevitable outcome. As an urban planner, I have frequently faced the dilemma of master planning for new industries bringing economic progress, while threatening the natural ecology and manmade environments. Where appropriate, we always propose 'offsets' to the negative impacts such as improving natural drainage systems and subsidised improvements to power and water supplies, but sometimes the developers resist and the indigenous population are suspicious of newcomers bearing gifts.

Gomera and BV suffer and benefit equally from their island remoteness, enjoying much of the magic in the world attendant on remote and wild places while suffering the loss of their dynamic and ambitious young people. Little changes in the never-ending contrast between progress and stagnation.

Phi Phi Island off Ao Nang, Thailand

Phi Phi is immortalised in one of Leonardo di Caprio's first films - The Beach. It is a paradise island by any visual standards bathed in the tropical warmth of the East Indian Ocean and detached from its more prosaic populated neighbouring settlements on the Thai mainland of Phuket and Ao Nang.

Just as in the film however, where di Caprio's character has an unlikely escape from a shark attack, every paradise has a reverse side. I was lucky enough merely to hear second hand about Phi Phi's dark side, rather than experience it myself. We visited in early 2005, merely three weeks after the infamous Tsunami on 26 December 2004. In fact, Chatri, our ferry captain out from Ao Nang only some four weeks later was making his first visit back to Phi Phi having been shipwrecked there when the tidal wave struck.

Chatri described in vivid detail how he had carried about thirty sightseers and snorkel divers out to the islands on 26 December, and that the sea seemed unnaturally calm and the sky a peculiar purple blue. His boat was in one of the sheltered bays when the massive wave washed without warning out of nowhere across the island. He had landed some tourists to collect things from their hotel while others were sunning themselves or swimming in the quiet waters of the lagoon. The boat was lifted with the wave and driven several hundred meters into the dense tree foliage rising steeply up from the beaches. He remembers nothing except regaining consciousness maybe several hours or perhaps days later, stuck in the branch of a tree but feeling no pain. For a time in the silence, he wondered whether he was actually dead or still alive. His boat had disappeared and nothing was moving, until he heard helicopters approaching from the mainland to start the search for survivors. He was still not sure only four weeks later how long he had lain unconscious. Maybe it was days, because the destruction and toll on human life was so enormous that rescue resources had taken a long time to arrive.

Chatri was lifted back to the mainland where he later learned that none of his passengers who had returned to their two-storey hotel had survived, trapped by rising waters, while those on board his boat or on the beach had miraculously survived. They had been thrown into the sea and like himself after a doubtlessly terrifying washing machine tumble, they were caught up in trees as the tidal water receded. He did what most would do after such an out of body experience in a devastated country; he went home to his family, hitching a lift northwards to Chiang Mai in the country's far north, through the national emergency impacting all of Thailand. He then just stayed there for several weeks until he felt it time to return. In typical resilient Thai fashion, he had, only three weeks later, been allocated captaincy of a new boat and was making his first trip out to the islands again. Little had we suspected what dark and recent memories hid behind his confident air of competence displayed towards his passengers that first day back.

Amazingly, the islands seemed almost unaffected by the damage, trees were mostly still standing and the underwater marine flora, so spectacular at the best of times had also survived the worst of times. Perhaps the famous lagoon that features so prominently in The Beach, had reduced the physical impact of the huge wave. We swam and snorkelled in clear blue water as if there were no cares in the world or tragedies in very recent memory. Phi Phi Island remained a most magical place even only a few weeks after one of the biggest natural disasters to have befallen it since its peculiar karst landscape was formed from the surrounding limestone. Perhaps that was the best epitaph - affirmation that life goes on even in the most remote and vulnerable places.

L'Ile des Pins New Caledonia, Central South Pacific Ocean

So, to the remotest of islands visited, deep in the South Pacific Ocean and even then, set apart from its mother island of New Caledonia (NC) to the north. The Ile des

Pins, reached by a rickety half hour plane ride, from Noumea capital of NC, the Island of Pines is a recent tourist resort if the single modern hotel qualifies it as such. Previous visitors had experienced a very different provenance, as the Isle of Pines was a former penal colony a hundred years ago, to the unyielding justice system of the faraway French Republic. There are various ways of encouraging immigration to one's overseas possessions, but this would have been among the most brutal. As the sad war memorial in the single urban settlement on the island testified, there was one way back to the French homeland in 1914, to join the army, and probably die in a trench at Verdun probably as part of a punishment battalion. Were any of those who volunteered or later drafted, survivors of the war? If so, were they then either granted their freedom or sent back to the penal colony? Those were much harsher unforgiving days, but penal servitude ceased there soon after in the 1920's.

The island is almost circular and about twenty km in diameter, so big enough to support cultivation and its own subsistence farming. The native population are Melanesian Kanak people with a separate language to those in Vanuatu or the Solomon Islands to the north, and Samoa and Tonga far away to the east, their nearest island neighbours hundreds of miles away across the trackless Pacific. Some within the local Kanak independence movement protested violently against their perception of French suppression as recently as 1988, but while a major hostage incident at the Ouvea Caves was eventually settled, the great majority of the population now seek an amicable relationship with France, especially while the Gallic Metropole continues paying substantial grants to maintain the local economy in return for minimal increases in local productivity. Independence movements come at a price.

Sylvie and I took several trips round the island by ancient taxi, then on our last day, out to desert islands and tidal sand cays way to the south. Exotic sea birds including sea eagles nested on rocky promontories and huge skuas which glide for hundreds of miles across the ocean vastness, were especially invocative of the remoteness. So too were the sea turtles, tame enough to swim up close to our boat, going nose to nose with those who dived to swim with them.

The boat's captain and his crew comprising his wife and lively six-year old daughter, decided without consulting us, to drop us on a tidal sand cay about half a mile long and a few yards wide to go to another island and prepare a barbecue. We were out of sight of other land and the width of the sand cay seemed to be getting narrower still as the tide encroached. As their boat disappeared over the horizon, I wondered idly whether we would see them again, but we had not paid them anything yet and had our money and cameras with us, so we assumed all would be well. There were a few dried out and long dead trees clinging to the higher parts of the cay, but not even enough to afford a sun-shade canopy - just the sound of the small wavelets edging the brilliant turquoise sea and the brightest of white sand in the clearest air imaginable so far from man-made pollutants. It is strange what warm sun and lapping seawater can do to your general sense of wellbeing.

The boat duly returned after half an hour and the smiling boatman and his small crew sensing our relief, took us on to a larger island about two km long and a hundred metres wide with dense vegetation and convenient shade across its middle. They had prepared the promised barbecue of delicious fish with rice and salad, shared with a small group of Japanese honeymooners who had arrived on another boat - as you do these tourist-driven days - in the middle of the Pacific. Sylvie was presented with the largest lobster we had ever seen, over a metre long and over ten kilos in weight – known locally as a porcelaine because of its brilliant bone china colouring. It was apparently dead and pronounced too old and tough to eat, so likely to become a trophy on the boatman's wall at home. We were horrified when it went back into a very large bucket and started moving around lightly flipping its enormous tail.

The boatman's little girl scampered off into the undergrowth and came back holding by the tail a small black and white striped snake called a Tricot Rayé or 'Striped Pullover' in English because of its resemblance to one of those quintessentially French garments from the far away métropole. She seemed completely fearless as she swung it round. They have poison in their bite, but have such small teeth and jaws they can only do you damage if they bite you in the soft webbing between the fingers. So, that was all right then. Luckily the little girl's mother also thought her behaviour with the snake was at least disrespectful, and persuaded her to let it go. It slithered off into the low vegetation, on which we kept a close eye for the rest of the meal.

Returning from that boat trip seemed like returning from the very ends of the earth with the sea breeze and bright sunlight sustaining a warm sense of wellbeing. However, remoteness has a peculiar quality of melancholy because of the sense that you will never go back. Parting even from places as well as people is a sweet sorrow.

En route the Isle of Pines, New Caledonia across the trackless Pacific. The white bits are the only land above the water, the light blue is coral

Cuba

Nowhere in Latin America has quite the romantic appeal of the in-your-face joie de vivre and revolutionary fervour of Cuba! Sitting near the linguistic fault line between the Anglophonic North and Hispanic Latin America, differences of culture would have thrown up misunderstandings and tensions of whatever scale, regardless of the ideological extremes between its northern neighbour and this most Latino of countries.

Havana was the jewel in the crown of Spain's American empire through the seventeenth and eighteenth centuries as the magnificent buildings of Havana Vieja illustrate, now confirmed by its World Heritage status. There were successive attacks through these centuries by British, Dutch and French fleets jealous of the riches residing there, but real distinction between the wealth and poverty of Cuba became most marked from the end of the nineteenth century when the local grandees expelled the Spanish. They were supported, when it suited them, by the opportunistic Rough Riders, 'gringo' adventurers from the USA under Teddy Roosevelt, before he became President in 1901. Despite subsequent claims, they seemed intent no more on liberation from imperialism than to replace it with a more modern form of exploitation of the rich over the poor.

From the start of the twentieth century, Cuba became a playground for all the activities frowned upon in the more puritanical US. Gambling, liquor consumption, smuggling during the prohibition years and prostitution grew to such proportions by 1959 that they were a key motivation behind the revolution and overthrow of the Batista government led by Fidel Castro in that year. This was not evolutionary Marxism as neatly defined in Das Kapital, but rather, the end result of a visceral vomiting up of all that was corrupt and venal in the previous regime. You would have had to be heartless or seriously on the make yourself in pre-revolutionary Cuba, not to cheer as Castro's forces entered Havana. Placing their muddy boots on the coffee tables at the Hotel Nacional they rejected the mob's offer of a share of their gambling and prostitution proceeds, inviting them to depart or get shot. Most departed; a few got shot.

The next few years represented a folly of the human condition which nearly brought us all to the point of self-annihilation, as the two vastly unequal protagonists, the USA and Cuba, the latter aided and abetted by the Soviet Union, faced off against each other. Even in faraway

England we expected nuclear war to break out any day of the month of October 1962. I cannot tell who played their cards less well than the other; sufficient that we should wonder at, and be grateful, that we somehow survived the real risks of mutually assured destruction.

Leadership succession politics after a revolutionary beginning are often a Latin American weak link and Cuba has been no exception. A benign explanation would claim that such fervour of continuous revolution could only be entrusted to those nearest the great leader; a more prosaic explanation is that revolutionary leaders are no better at yielding power than any other. Power corrupts. The Castro brothers Fidel and Raul have clung to power long after modernisation has become acutely necessary and long since the support of the Soviet Union melted away with the USSR itself in the mid 1990's. Cuba is now emerging slowly from great poverty, a testament to the failure of communism here as elsewhere, to make room for the spirit in all humanity to strive and do well for oneself and family and retain some of the material rewards.

To its credit as an independently minded society, it has survived the almost paranoid embargoes and cultural isolation imposed by its giant neighbour to the north, egged on by those of its own sons and daughters who escaped to the US and represent the most zealous of those opposed to the regime. But Cuba now desperately needs to return to the mainstream of international relations and commerce. Slowly this is happening and we should hope that the spirit and individuality of the place is not homogenised into some ghastly repeat parody of the pre-1959 regime, as America's playground of sin. Future reality is likely to be, like the Curate's Egg, good in parts, not in others.

Local answer to Havana's Buena Vista Social Club: Street Band in Trinidad, Cuba 2015

Iona, off Mull, Scottish western Isles

One island I have visited for work in recent years is in fact an island off an island off another one. Getting there is a mission in itself, and part of the experience. Most visitors start at Glasgow and travel via one of Scotland's finest scenic rail journeys up along Loch Lomond and over the mountains before the long gentle descent to Oban. From here you catch a ferry to Craignure on Mull passing some of the best mountain scenery and ruined castles in the west of Scotland. At Craignure you board a coach for forty km across the base of Mull, via a single-track road with passing places, through tiny hamlets such as Pennyghael and Bunessan. Almost there, you reach Fionnphort on Iona

Sound with the island finally visible five hundred metres away across the water; a twenty-minute ferry crossing to your destination at last. Some mission, for some a pilgrimage!

Missions were what going to Iona has been all about for many religious people through the centuries visiting the birthplace and nursery of British and Irish Christianity in 6th century. Remote islands had real advantages in those days as their settlements were more trouble to attack and destroy if your raiding parties had to expend so much time getting there. That did not stop the Vikings and others doing just that in 806 and probably other years during what we inaccurately term the Dark Ages. In fact, they were a period of disparate Celtic and Nordic influences inadequately documented across northern and western Britain between the Roman occupation over most of England and parts of southern Scotland, and the onset of a more unified Scottish clan system north of the border and gradual unification of Norman influence post 1066 throughout England and Wales. In fact, by 1100, Norway was also Christian and the first Benedictine monastery and nunnery foundations were established under the protection of the King of Norway from 1203. So, the Vikings were not all mad, bad and dangerous to know.

The current Abbey dates from the end of the nineteenth century so it is now difficult to imagine what things were truly like there before that time. The Victorians were very good at building things to extinguish previous expressions of culture or faith through architecture. Not the best conservationists, they thought they knew better. The Iona Christian community was formally established in 1938 and has flourished there ever since.

My visit to Iona was motivated by far more prosaic purposes. The Sound of Iona Harbours Committee had become concerned that the sheer numbers of visitors, especially through summer months, were causing traffic congestion and slowing movement on the ferry slipways to an unacceptable degree. The ferry passengers were also not the sole source of the problem. More and more shellfish are being landed at Fionnphort for export to Spain or China and each year, there are more daily boat excursions to the outer islands of Staffa and Treshnish. The mix of freight and passengers was ever more likely to cause accidents which would slow traffic still further.

To complicate things further, the Caledonian MacBraine ferry boat could not berth overnight on the jetty at Fionnphort having to anchor in a more sheltered sound a half hour away. This required the crew to attend to boat drills for at least an hour a day before and after passenger and car traffic revenues could be earned. Of such small margins was the ferry company feared to be susceptible, to reducing the frequency of crossings or even stopping the service altogether.

Our brief as master planning consultants was to assess these issues, together with the sad fact that very little money was being spent by visitors in the embarkation village of Fionnphort. Hardly surprising perhaps, because the single shop and pub were a walk uphill from the main coach drop off near the slipway. The main car park was also a good distance away. Pockmarked with potholes, it encouraged motorists to risk a ticket parking down near the ferry embarkation point – a common case of no footfall no expenditure.

Another master plan was called for and this came together slowly, aided by stakeholder evidence and measures to support improved signage and street furniture to enhance the 'visitor experience'. But the main task, as always, was not a nice design on paper, but rather a process of communicating possible solutions to the two communities around Fionnphort and the harbour on Iona itself. Here is where a big contrast arose with a non-island culture. Normally such public meetings held to discuss development matters would expect to attract an audience of between five and ten percent of the people likely to be impacted. Around the Sound of Iona, interest in our proposals was sky high and the two meetings, one on Iona in the morning and an evening equivalent in Fionphoort Village Hall that night with autumn rain lashing down to discourage a big turnout, still attracted virtually the whole community.

The meetings were lively affairs. I found myself emphasizing my Welsh origins, thus deflecting any tendency for the locals to perceive that here was a consultant 'up from London' claiming to have all the answers. This seemed to chime with my Scottish colleagues on our small team, and gave me a bye into the trust of an otherwise sceptical audience. Our recommendations for improved slipways, a large breakwater to provide pleasure-craft shelter at Fionphoort and a change to the land use policies to encourage more commerce near the ferry's embarkation point met with broad approval. Consultants bearing gifts, but who would pay?

Highlands and Islands Enterprise are the public-sector body set up to channel funds to worthy infrastructure projects from the Scottish government. In the summer of 2013, they were keen to emphasise their preparedness to fund the right scheme, which probably had a lot to do with the looming referendum on Independence for Scotland scheduled for the Spring of 2014. No political party wanted to be seen as opposed to funding access improvements to one of Scotland's iconic tourist hotspots. Sadly, but perhaps not surprisingly, this visible support for Iona melted away after the referendum and, to date, I am not sure that the island community has had much new infrastructure installed. At least this sustains the underlying perceptions of remote and island communities, that they are largely on their own when it comes to making do and fending for themselves as regards better public facilities with which to make everyday life easier. 'It's all the fault of those on the mainland!'

Great Britain

I never forget that GB is an island. Growing up in the 1950's, we were educated to the virtues of island status, our parents and other grown-ups having only a decade before, survived the worst onslaught on our freedom and way of life in living or written history. As youngsters, we were taught how important it was to be separate both militarily and - applying a substantial leap of logic – culturally. There was, through those post-war years, a deal of reluctance to embrace our near neighbours in Europe, largely seen inaccurately but collectively, as responsible for bringing us so close to disaster only a few years previously. This prejudice lives on among some.

However, I still needed some of the benefits of this island status spelling out for me. Neil G, a Jewish friend at Oxford in 1969, whose father had escaped Nazi Germany in 1936, was the first to point out to me, that most countries of Europe would have given anything to have Britain's island status. Taking Shakespeare as his inspiration, he pointed to our island status as the reason for absence of effective invasion and occupation for exactly nine hundred and three years since the Norman Conquest. This provided the welcome quarantining against political and social extremes. No fascists (except a few ridiculous ones thanks to our innate capacity to laugh at demagogues), no real diehard communists, (at any rate the sort who had any real influence), and a ('Glorious') revolution in the seventeenth century, to curb monarchic influence one hundred years before that of France. But this shift of power to Parliament retained the king as head of state with significant limits on his previous divine right to rule, the better to safeguard national loyalties above and beyond the temporary approval or otherwise of our current set of chosen politicians. How civilised!

This posits a very benign picture of our history over the last three hundred and fifty years, but if you count up how few are the countries in the world to have avoided the major social upheavals of civil war or unrest, together with the absence of militarised foreign occupation, you come to realise that Britain's homeland has had a pretty easy ride through recent history. Substantial responsibility for some terrible episodes in our imperial history and huge contributions to foreign wars are all thoroughly documented nowadays, but with the fighting mainly on foreign soil. One downside of all this is that we tend to take our history for granted and assume that it owes more to good judgment than good fortune; complacency by any other name.

Some now mourn the parting of a more tranquil and respectful way of life where everything seemed ... well, so British, naturally assumed in the 1950's to also mean 'best'. But by the 1970's our island – not to say siege – mentality had reached such a state of complacency and loss of confidence as to render us incapable of keeping the lights on during yet more industrial (in) action and strikes. Quite apart from the details of each dispute - job demarcation, workers' rights, wage rates, terms and conditions etc. etc., - there was an underlying class tension, a febrile 'us' against 'them' atmosphere, felt as deeply by either side whether you considered yourself 'one of the workers' or 'part of the management'. As I was preparing to leave University, in the early 1970's, our island race seemed ready to tear itself apart socially.

Since Britain has become tangibly and mentally more cosmopolitan, things have evolved from a former assumption that 'British is best'. Depending on the newspaper you read, this entry of people, material goods and more important values from foreign parts has either been a disaster for our way of life, or generally beneficial as different ways of doing things have been good for our more diverse society, economy and future prospects. There are, as always, a certain proportion of society cut off through poverty from the generally greater prosperity enjoyed by the majority. But we are broadly speaking immeasurably better off than we were in the mid 1970's. Of course, news media of all persuasions rarely espouse optimistic views, as this tends not to sell copy as well as doom and gloom.

After the 1970's, the British seemed to pull themselves together and wake up to the fact that the world does not owe us a living. While we are, like so many others a less caring society, the deep-seated mistrust of each other which I recall from the early 1970's has melted a bit. Despite the referendum result of mid-2016, to choose by a narrow margin to leave the European Union, and the underlying motives behind it, we seem to be more tolerant and probably more welcoming of recent newcomers than was the case four decades back, a little less inclined to racist or other unfounded branding of the bad habits of others. More of this to follow, because of course, it is not universally true.

Unexpectedly I became an agent for reducing Britain's island status in 1986, when I joined the growing team planning for, designing and building the Channel Tunnel. My employer, the large development consultancy WS Atkins were an integral part of the winning technical bidder submission from Eurotunnel to the French and British governments, to construct two rail tunnels and associated service tunnel and cross passages, connecting Britain to mainland Europe for the first time since the last Ice Age. This became known at the time as 'le Grand Twin Bore', in a famous poster depicting PM Margaret Thatcher and President François Mitterand.

I initially joined the project for six months but stayed six years, all through the statutory procedures of the Hybrid Bill in the UK Parliament and the equivalent D.U.P. legislation in France and early delivery of many of their statutory commitments. I finally left after the tunnels met up in mid Channel in 1992, but went back for the grand opening ceremony in Folkestone in 1994. I was lucky enough all through that period to observe the changing attitudes among my fellow islanders because, with Peter Middleton, my boss in the Maitre d'Oeuvre (technical audit) team and best leader I ever worked under, I ranged around Britain and parts of mainland Europe presenting about the project to a huge range of audiences as part of a concerted hearts and minds campaign to promote the project.

Our presentations were necessarily pretty technical, describing tunnelling methods, signal-controlled 'train paths', and methods of evacuation and escape in the event of train breakdown or fire, but audiences seemed to like that. My own interest as a planner was the economic benefits of regional connectivity between Kent and the Pas de Calais, but these impacts were longer in gestation so less noticeable. The human side of things – how did the French and British workers get on across the project, and how would it all work operationally - were the repeated questions with which we were faced. Younger people, particularly school children were our most incisive interrogators. They also demonstrated the greatest enthusiasm for the project's potential, though the well-off children of one school in Perthshire, Scotland, seemed not to care less for the possibilities. Understandable perhaps, given the call of the grouse moors nearer home.

Looking back, it now seems unimaginable that we would not have a terrestrial connection with our near mainland, as most of over twenty million passengers a year now carried by the Eurostar trains and Eurotunnel shuttles would agree. Less than three hours between London and Paris or Brussels has contributed hugely to why we have become so much more cosmopolitan in outlook. After all you can buy olive oil in the supermarket now, rather than, as in 1970, at the chemists… progress!

But in 2016, we have once again been beset with a renewed strain of Little Englander mentality, understandably, if sometimes unpalatably, presented under an anti-immigration banner. In mid-year, it created the first of several shocks to a worldwide connectedness agenda with the referendum decision to leave the European Union – 'Brexit' now being a part of everyday vocabulary, though no better understood as to its implications, than before the term was first minted.

Later in the year Donald Trump was elected against pollsters' predictions as the USA's next President, on a self-styled 'Brexit ++' ticket without any previous experience of government, and precisely for that reason. This rise in populist politics will not stop there, and the threat that other EU members might be similarly sceptical about our economic and political unions – almost anti-politics given their rejection of the preceding liberal political elites – is said to be as momentous as any industrialization or revolutionary upheaval. The rise of extreme parties of 'right' or 'left' (sometimes both together, as they care little for old ideologies) now espouse protectionist policies and a style of communication with voters capturing the need for instant even simplistic problem solving. ("Too many immigrants? We'll build a wall"!)

I agree with neither these simplistic solutions, nor on the other hand, the direst predictions of the dumbing-down of how we will be governed. The so-called thinking media of written and broadcast journalism, (I do not count the Twitter sphere as 'thinking media') have now gone too far in their recent desire to correct previous myopia about what the man in the street thinks. Now every news item about changing political directions seeks the common man view preferably from middle-England, middle-America or wherever, to reflect new media sensitivity to views that even the pollsters had misjudged or ignored previously as of no consequence. It is as if the avowedly metropolitan scribblers and talkers had lost sight of the plight of the common man or woman, (views which might have reflected their own non-metropolitan roots in some cases) and were now atoning for their sins of elitist thinking.

Starting during University days and countless times since, I have listened to some of my more academic colleagues declaiming on anything other than their own specialism, quietly thinking to myself, you are the most intelligent idiot I have ever met – since the last one! There seems to be a common if not universal principle that the more you know, the less you retain the ability to make sound judgments and take appropriate action. That is the root of the new populism: stop worrying over the information overload and get something done!

The loss of faith in a government class and the people who had come to inhabit it is guttural. It is the reaction of people too often bathed in the soft soap of undeliverable promises and the sophistry surrounding excuses later as to why promises remained undelivered. What does worry me is that the plain speakers who espouse the new populist cult have no more ability to deliver than those they are rapidly replacing. I fear for their supporters' reactions when they find that out. Governing is predominantly coping with events rather than maintaining a tight course towards a pre-defined long-term strategy. As a planner, this might sound like indictment of my craft, but I hold the view that we tinker at the edges of change, rarely influencing social or economic trends that are bigger than any one country's means of governance. We will see!

What has all this commentary on recent political events got to do with Islands and Empathy, you may ask. Well, to my mind quite a lot. It tells me that Channel Tunnel or no, the days of our island status are long past. In the last years of my career, I spent as much time dealing with people elsewhere in the world than in the same office or meeting room with me, not only by phone, but by Email, Text, WhatsApp, Conference Call, Skype, Webinar and other systems. This was regular fare, communicating across the globe and thus in differing time zones. We now talk but do not perhaps connect, with people worldwide and are expected to build empathy and understanding – trust would be a better word in business terms - on the basis of blurry images on screen and a half hour of chat on a Monday morning.... sorry Monday night in Australia, and still Sunday night on the US west coast. Technology delivers us a tough call compared with business only forty years ago!

Much of this ignores human nature. It takes time to relate to other people – whether as business colleagues or neighbours down the street – but the vast majority of us still seek ways to get along, build positive relations with each other and eventually find time to understand a different and sometimes conflicting point of view. People remain essentially decent citizens and know that they have to get along, but they struggle to do so, using electronic communications rather than the face to face real thing.

Despite recent and probably temporary evidence to the contrary, it is good to remind ourselves that Britain has a history of embracing foreign influences. A bit different to welcoming it with open arms perhaps, more a begrudging acceptance that foreigners can sometimes do things better and teach us a thing or two. Whether it was the sixteenth century Italian influence on our architecture, the seventeenth century Dutch impact on marine and flood control systems, the eighteenth-century French Huguenot skills with silver and gold or the nineteenth century Jewish expertise in the London clothing industry, Britain has always eventually made the best of its foreign influences. Immigrants are usually by definition enterprising and filled with energy to justify their presence in a foreign land. Mercifully for our future welfare, such people of enterprise continue to want to come here and long may it be encouraged!

I am an optimist and expect that we will slowly come to accept the twentieth century cultures to have joined our society from the West Indies and Africa, India and Pakistan and from the current and twenty-first century, Russia, China and the Middle East. Of course, this is putting pressure on our towns and cities while our housing shortage seems rarely to get better. But if you doubt me as regards assimilation, compare the way West Indians were originally received in the late 1950's in west London or Birmingham and consider how they are now accepted by the great majority of the 'indigenous' population, if such a category still exists. Not perfect by any stretch, there is still ugly racism under many surfaces, but accepted as near neighbours by the vast majority of a white population who trace their 'British' ancestry through centuries rather than decades.

After all, as I sometimes point out to my English friends, we Welsh have just about come to accept them, now they have clocked up some fifteen hundred years on 'our' island! Tolerance and empathy but above all humour will always remain the vital ingredients of getting along with the neighbours. Lest we forget, almost everyone in the world moved from where they were born to somewhere else, so really, we are all migrants. No man is an island.

Chapter 12 France and Spain. My alter ego.

It is all well to journey about the world ready to absorb as much as possible of other cultures and ways of life, but without day to day domestic involvement, can you really see over the garden wall and understand how and why things are done differently on the other side? Probably not, because you are normally looking through the gate, fully open perhaps with everything on view, but not fully part of what is going on.

Through marriage for nearly forty years, I am lucky to be able to see two non-British cultures at very close quarters and thus more hands-on engagement than merely wide open eyes. Married to Sylvie with Catalan and French parents, previously brought up in Barcelona with French nationality, I have spent over half my life exposed to subtly different ways of doing things to us Brits. As an insular race, it is far too easy for us to assume that when we do something in a particular way, it really is the only way to do it. It is probably worse to accept that there are other ways, but that they don't stand comparison with our own. This 'Little Englander' mentality has diminished in recent years but was very strong in my growing up years. There was an underlying mistrust of all things ' foreign', as if we could cope with our own bad habits but rejected those of others. Understandably perhaps given recent history, but inexcusably, too many of us took comfort in the fastness of our own little sea-girt island, quietly satisfied that 'British was best'.

We were certainly not so insular in previous centuries. We frequently looked to 'the continent' for fresh ideas about everything from political philosophy, art, food and fashion. We also roamed further afield for exploration and imperial exploitation, away from Europe as much as possible, but our preference for a world view still led to constant changes in our outlook. The third quarter of the twentieth century when I grew up may just have been a very insular but brief episode.

At the personal level, proper exposure to other cultures has meant new languages, and accepting different ways of looking at the world, all within the family. This has led me to question many of my own values - not to reject them, but examine them from a new perspective. I hope I remain open to new ways of doing things throughout my old age. This would provide at least a mental elixir of youth, a means to realise that the world still has lots to teach with surprises around every corner, mostly pleasant ones not the opposite - glass half full rather than half empty.

Through marriage, I was gradually weaned off certain national stereotypes. As a teenager, I had dreamed of an entirely different exposure to France. By the age of seventeen I had sampled the Art House films of Jean-Paul Belmondo, lusted after the ice-cool Cathérine Deneuve, and wished to sample the life style immortalised by Peter Sarsted, counting the Boulevard St Michel, St Moritz and Juan les Pins on my regular itinerary, the better to meet Sarsted's Marie-Claire and 'the rest of the jet set' in the words of his evocative song – "Where do you go to my lovely?"

My stereotypes of Spain having not even visited there until aged twenty-six, were even more far-fetched and tenuous. I imagined leading a Laurie Lee type itinerant life as in his book, 'As I walked out one midsummer morning', busking through hot sunlit villages in Andalusia, for the price of a meal, or fighting heroically with the International Brigade alongside similarly doomed idealists in a remake of the '36 to '39 Civil War before drinking the bodega dry with Hemingway, Martha Gellhorn and pals. Completely irrelevant to today's world of course, but this was easy to imagine if inclined to romantic dreams born of Anglophone literature of a certain vintage.

Married to someone with origins in two other countries and thus less attached to either than me to mine, gives a very different perspective on what constitutes a motherland. First off, what is it that is so important about national identity anyway? Many mainland Europeans understand this better than Brits, with our more easily defined sea borders, though the movement of people in a mobile world now renders us as permeable as every other European nation. If only the little Englanders among us would appreciate that fact.

There is also the language issue. If, like Sylvie, I had learned one language (in her case Catalan) at my mother's knee, another (French) at the international Lycée, and a third (Castilian Spanish) to speak in the street (the Franco regime being distrustful of foreigners and minority Iberian languages), I would naturally have grown up with a different outlook on world affairs. Then for good measure, to come and live in England and learn a fourth language would have left little choice but to adopt an international perspective. Some Brits are uncomfortable with all this, because we do love to classify people by single nationality, the better to pigeon hole them on our mental world map.

Unlike many Brits I am not scared to make mistakes in other languages, especially those false friend varieties, where you assume something in one language will translate directly when it does not. This level of ability gives adequate means to communicate day to day matters, but leaves you short of the ability to understand idioms or slang, regional accents and lots of humour and witty repartee, unique to each language. This is a pity, for these are the areas where so much of the real colour resides in any cultural dialogue.

I get all this language stuff out of the way early because I am convinced it is a more dominant factor in culture than other perceptions of nationality. Nationality counts for less and less now that we are all bombarded with the same stuff on the Internet, bonding us together as consumers more effectively than as reflections of our national stereotypes. People of similar age and background progressively wear the same clothes, eat more of the same food, watch the same films, read the same books (if they read at all), play with the same IT hardware and drive the same cars made across any number of countries such that their original source nationality is impossible to define. How different to 1960!

Time for a breath-taking generalization. British people have had an innate lesser ability to see the world multi-culturally than our continental neighbours. Being an island has not helped here, but the main issue seems to have been language and on that issue alone, things are only getting worse. As English dominates international discourse more and more, motives for learning any other language have diminished. It is too easy for Anglophones to remain overly self-absorbed.

There are so many happy experiences of France and Spain, which I could relate, and most of them would serve to explode durable British myths about the unfriendliness of French people or the haughty pride of the true Spaniard. These myths survive because too few Brits take the trouble with local discourse, and assume a lack of empathy or humour when the locals cannot or will not speak English and they don't get the joke. Luckily for us, a great many more 'locals' do now speak English than half a century ago, even in France, the pre-war holder of a status of the oddly name 'Lingua Franca' of international diplomacy.

Many happy memories of family holidays in France and Spain, provided deep immersion into Provencal or Catalan culture and hospitality and have been the route to a fresh perspective on these different cultures. Most years, while our kids were little, we would drive south and stop at Sylvie's aunt and uncle's place near Salon. We could tell we were in the south by the flat hard light of the Provençal summer accompanied by the incessant rattle of the cicadas in trees and undergrowth. We knew we were close when passing the car graveyard on the edge of Pelissanne village, the central feature being a red double-decker London bus - vintage early 60's. Left by Cliff Richard and Una Stubbs no doubt, after that Summer Holiday, the corniest musical of 1961 but a memory of happy innocence to most of our generation, Europe wide.

There was a different atmosphere in the south, released by summer heat and torpor; one of letting go of conventions of offices and timekeeping that went with the warmer clothing of the north. Mornings spent shopping in the village market for Cavaillon melons, salads and cheese ahead of the midday heat, followed by gathering Oncle Meline's awesomely large tomates de Pelissanne from his plentiful irrigated vegetable beds, to be served with a few black olives and goat's cheese as a simple lunch time hors d'oeuvre. With a barbecue fire made from arch dry twigs and logs well lit, it was time for a swim and a pre-lunch Pastis, before sitting down to the simple but two-hour long meal in the shade of the old oak tree, outside the kitchen.

Relations and neighbours, Italian, Spanish and French in origin, would be invited over, some from Marseille, regaling us with lurid horror stories of the city's growing racial tensions between Corsican criminal gangs and the expanding population of immigrant Algerians. There was little sympathy for either faction and this being the 1980's, it was coupled with substantial contempt for the Mitterand government in Paris, regarded as running France into the ground with too much socialism. Being Provence, not much good was said to come out of Paris, and slightly surprising to me, there seemed to be broad admiration for Margaret Thatcher, 'La Dame de Fer' - as the type of leader needed in France. After the Falklands/Malouines war of 1982, this became more pronounced, as she was widely regarded as having put those uppity Argentines in their place. This sort of stuff seemed more insular than we Brits!

Counter arguments - just for the sake of a debate you understand, but probably interpreted as representing irredeemable left-wing tendencies - provided some after lunch sugar and spice - with the coffee. But it was too hot to get over-exercised about and meals would drift through the drowsy afternoon, lubricated by rich dark Cotes du Rhone, sold in litres from the nearby co-operative in Lambesc, before settling into a siesta with everyone finding their favourite shade under the trees. Not much more to wish for from this quintessential French atmosphere of sun, red wine and moaning about the government up north; a better setting for improving my French than schoolrooms in England of distant memory.

Many and varied have been subsequent visits to France, for work and pleasure. Everywhere the welcome has been the same and curiosity about our way of life as heart-warming as its reciprocal about those of our hosts. This was never the stereotype of France with which I grew up.

Exposure to Spanish ways were originally confined to the Barcelona area, but in 1990, still the early days after that country's accession to the European Union, I set up a planning and engineering consulting business in Madrid. I would spend one week in every four in the capital networking obsessively to gain client and partner contacts for our firm, aided and abetted by a recent engineering graduate. Despite his impeccable English name, Paul Hamilton-Smith had been brought up in Colombia with Spanish as his mother tongue. He taught me more slang and business idioms than I could have read in a textbook and we chased consulting work from Bilbao in the north to Seville in Andalucia, including attendance at that city's Expo in spring 1992 to present about the Channel Tunnel.

There were many non-starters among our project pursuits including one madcap scheme for a master plan for a provincial Comunidad near Burgos north of Madrid. They claimed delegated discretion to design and construct an industrial estate and freeport with EU regional aid money, being attracted into the country at that time from Brussels. Site visits ahead of preparing the master plan were two-day affairs up from Madrid by car through the cold winter of 1991, but always ending with splendid early afternoon meals in local tavernas with officials from the local Council. These lasted through to early evening such that very little work was done each day.

The local government officers took comfort in having engaged a British firm to do their planning, the better to convince Brussels bureaucrats that this was a multi-national concept, not some elaborate local scam. But it turned out to be both; the project never got beyond the feasibility report stage. The government in Madrid finally intervened applying a merciful coup de grace to this flight of fancy, confirming the need for central sanction - and that they would not grant! It was all fun while it lasted and I smile when I see similar examples of empty regional airports in remote Spanish towns, which did better than ours by getting past the bureaucrats in Madrid in time to get built, but still hardly ever used –infrastructural white elephants.

My role as visiting director was self-evidently a stopgap and we needed to appoint a local boss for our putative Spanish business. We scoured the employment market for the right engineering trained candidate but one with a commercial mindset, not always an easy combination to find. There was a wide choice from people seeking escape from firms such as Arthur Andersen. Andersen had recently been hiring young engineers in large numbers from the best Universities across Spain, only to be losing them when they realised they were in the wrong business. I instinctively avoided these candidates seemingly intent on big managerial salaries with as little technical project exposure as possible.

We eventually chose our candidate - I will call him Guillermo - whom we thought would fit the bill. He proved demanding in his expectations of financial reward - about fifty per cent higher salary than we expected, together with a seriously expensive company car - but with the economy booming, we ratcheted up our expectations of what new business he must win via his splendidly portrayed network of contacts - and hoped for the best. As the visiting director, I was expected to keep an eye on progress and support G when the British end of our service offer needed deployment in front of clients. We also recruited a PA for the new office, a young lady whose good looks and arresting figure cheered every red-blooded male who came to visit us. Apart from having the figure to cause a Jesuit priest to question his calling, she happened also to be the best candidate for the job and ran our office and its accounts like a tight ship.

Our highest profile piece of work audited the construction of Spain's first fast train link from Madrid to Seville, the AVE. Covering a distance of little more than four hundred kilometres, RENFE, the Spanish national rail operator had nonetheless seen fit to award the construction to no less than twelve companies. With scarcely more than thirty-five kilometres of track each, the task of connecting up an integrated system to one set of operational and safety standards proved beyond the best project management skills available at the time. It took several years for construction quality to be improved, and the AVE only started travelling at its two hundred and fifty kph design speed over seven years after the line was opened in the mid 1990's. Despite enormous physical constraints of mountainous terrain, Spain remains well ahead of Britain in the extent of its fast rail network.

Guillermo also proved a big challenge in terms of generating new business. He simply could not convert prospects into projects, while claiming that the fault lay with the British end of things as we seemed ill-prepared to commit to necessary upfront work for free. Each prospect we encountered needed work at risk to a point where client funding might prove possible. Then one day, I arrived in the office unexpectedly early, to find him in what might be called a warm embrace with our PA. Nothing wrong with that I suppose, though he was married, and it was probably inappropriate behaviour in the office. I thought about his preparedness to cheat on his wife so why not our business too? Then I reflected on the last few months of his finding too little new work, and reluctantly reported back to head office that I could not work further with him.

I moved to another part of the business, but head office eventually lost patience with him and passed the whole enterprise on to another subsidiary offering Quantity Surveying skills instead which turned out to be much more saleable. Something of a closed shop for planning and engineering skills from outside Spain continued for several years, and only now more than two decades later, can a freer market in professional services be said to exist across the different Spanish regions. I climbed that learning curve at great expense, but I learned a great deal about business success and failure along the way – mainly to choose your staff with great care.

I have learned by witness to first-hand experience that the dark chapter of the Civil War still marks the memories of old people in Spain. Its memory is slowly emerging again in the form of the first few chapters of my father-in-law Henri's book of life memoirs. He has been several years writing it, starting with his vivid memories of teenage years as tensions between the Republic and traditionalist sentiment grew steadily through the mid 1930's. As French nationals, his family were to some extent insulated from taking sides in the ideological struggle, but Spanish families were not so lucky.

My parents-in-law confirmed that both sides in the civil war were as bad as each other in terms of atrocities committed and ruthless attempts to root out their opponents within each community. Claims that one side was worse than the other have usually originated from their opponents, as history is usually written by the victors or at least those who survived. Often it was what you were perceived to be that mattered. If you were better off or a devout Catholic you were assumed to be an enemy of the Republic; if you were working class or inclined to social modernism in whatever form, you were assumed to be a Republican. Perhaps the real tragedy lay in that there was no room to avoid classification. There was simply no room to be somewhere in the middle and it tore families apart.

Henri was only fourteen when the civil war started, as the oldest of three brothers. His father decided it would be safer to get out of Spain and go back to France for the duration of troubles. Henri finished schooling in Marseille and in 1940 went on to read chemistry at Toulouse University by then in the Vichy controlled south west of the country. With Spain at last at peace again after 1939, his family returned to Vinaroz, though like the rest of the country it was much impoverished after the war. But after only eighteen months in University in 1942, the Germans occupied the south west of France, so with a Jewish friend, Ben Bassat, Henri caught a train to the Spanish border in the Pyrenees, and they both got out of France only hours before the border was closed for the next three years.

The Spanish economy was on its knees and while Franco kept the country nominally neutral, there was little hope of building a decent living with which to support a family. So, in 1946, Henri returned to Toulouse to finish his degree. By 1949 he had returned to Catalunya and married his new bride Pilar, but in 1951, he went back to Marseille again with wife and baby daughter and my future wife Sylvie until 1953. Then, Barcelona's economy, if not the rest of Spain, had recovered enough to offer a return to good employment. They have been there ever since.

I write this now, not only because it is a good and true story that bears personal witness to the agonies that France and Spain underwent over seven decades ago, but to reflect a wider truth. After as long a period of relative peace and growing prosperity that Europe can recall, we are once again exposed to threats of social unrest of the sort that disrupted the lives of previous generations and tore some of those lives apart. The issues may have subtle differences; uncontrolled immigration from Africa and the Middle East may have replaced the upheavals of competing political extremism of right and left, but these latter were only the effects not the cause of previous threats to ways of life resulting from the folly of war and its aftermath. Nor should we British consider ourselves safely quarantined from such effects now. As we have seen in recent years, sea borders are no more effective than the relatively meaningless lines on maps denoting land borders, when the pressures of human movement become too great.

As I write, my father-in-law is a living testament to previous social upheavals attendant on man's inability to settle aspirational differences peaceably. We will do well to heed this experience before it loses its living impact, and use it to find ways of resolving our troubles avoiding the tragedies of the past.

The capacity to flit from Spain to France and back again to avoid the worst extremes of nationalist and ideological sentiment characterised Sylvie's family and outlook on life from the 1930's onwards. Who knows if, in our more febrile world with its recent adoption of populist politics, it may be needed again? Will a similar principle of keeping a foot in more than one country come to apply to us here in UK? To retain a pre-disposition to see oneself as a citizen of the world, rather than of just one national culture, may yet become again an essential talent for survival. I would once have found non-partisanship unsettling, but given my own capacity for travel, this world-view has grown on me.

France and Spain my alter ego? More like everyone else's too in our world without boundaries; all our yesterdays; all our tomorrows.

Long lazy lunches shaded from midday sun. Pelissane Provence France 1980s

Chapter 13 Back where I started? Empathy found?

Does travel and ranging about the world merely broaden the mind, or does it change the traveller for ever, by developing empathy for those whom you meet, where you are and what you see? Broadening the mind could be defined as understanding why people behave in a particular way, hold certain opinions or react to given situations as they do. Empathy goes further – it helps predict how strangers might behave, what opinions you might encounter, and how people might react before a given situation develops. In short empathy is all about anticipation with which to nuance your own behaviour, to not seem so strange to strangers.

Exposing yourself to other cultures is one of the best ways to develop empathy – not just by getting to know people, but living among and working with them. For real insight, raising families together or living as neighbours, might attain the necessary familiarity through every day language and study of behaviour. This all takes time and is likely impossible with more than one culture at a time.

Why would you want to achieve empathy rather than mere understanding? Quite apart from the satisfaction of human relationships taken to a higher level, there are incalculable material benefits in finding empathy. It is the single most valuable device in the briefcase of any diplomat or businessman. Dealing with other countries or enterprises offers great benefits, but only lastingly so if there is mutual benefit. And knowing what is mutually beneficial calls for understanding of the other person's agenda and thus knowing when to stand fast when negotiating and when to yield. You will need to do both and anticipating a protagonist's response to a set of moveable positions, might even generate peace and harmony between nations, or at least avoid war. There is not much more important in the affairs of men than that.

Do I now view my values differently from travelling the world? Have I found greater empathy working and living among people of other cultures, languages and points of views? Let's examine what has changed and what has stayed the same.

I cannot see much change in my values over time, by which I mean, what I like and respect in most people and what makes me inherently mistrustful of a small minority. I don't recall this respect being instilled by parents, but they probably had a discreet hand in it all as values grew on me like the extra inches of height, absorbed unconsciously but through life experience. Parental influence was effective but invisible – the best kind, as we have learned as parents ourselves.

However, my prejudices have probably changed from those with which I grew up. Making judgments in ignorance of the facts needs a pre-disposition to think you know better without evidence. While that is stupid, it is very common and probably emanates from not wanting to be bothered to find out, or sheer rejection of the unknown that is an alternative to fear, contempt and eventually loathing for strangers of a particular kind. So, that has been a change; I would once have merely accepted, or even wallowed in the preconceived - usually negative - perceptions of other cultures – German authoritarianism, French vanity, American brashness etc., Sadly, country areas like the one where I grew up may be more prone to prejudice than urban ones, because there is less variety around – all outsiders are strange. But in the best countrymen and women, this is quietly compensated for by more time and perhaps interest taken to understand outsiders and their circumstances more profoundly –

empathy pursued through having and taking the time to listen.

In the quiet times of very early morning while still only half awake, I reflect drowsily on such matters. Despite being half asleep, ideas can often seem very clear. Is this the origin of Australian Aboriginal dreamtime, deemed to be of equal status as time awake in their culture? Some of my half-awake reflections revolve around what it would have been like to have lived a very different life back in the place of my birth – one perhaps where contentment was gained from much simpler life values than rushing about the world as I have been, always hungry for the next impressionistic experience. What use all this empathy without the time to savour it?

In my Pembrokeshire birthplace, self-deprecatory soft humour is very common and, with a nod to another language and culture, 'mañana' is laughingly regarded as an invocation to urgency ("you mean you want it mañana – as soon as that?"). If I had never gone away from there, I might have found myself living next door to people content in their own skin by just knowing how their own corner of the world is toddling along; the pub and the post office on the corner, what Rhys or Myfanwy were doing with the house down the road and whether the weather is set fair or coming on to rain. I can hear them now … "How you been keeping? Why aye boy, mustn't grumble, fair to middlin'!" spoken in that wonderful west Wales lilt, a hybrid between Welsh and west country, perhaps containing more wisdom about time passing and things all being the same tomorrow, than any fevered quest for deeper insight.

Do such people have a wiser take on life? Will they meet their end in a more serene state than those of us who cannot keep still? I cannot say, but sometimes when recounting tales of adventure or strange experience in a far-off place (i.e. anywhere east of Carmarthen) there is a look in the eye of such tranquil souls, as if to say, "do you really find your God through such thrashing about the world?" I cannot answer this convincingly, but for me, choosing to leave such a contented place, was an act of commitment to a different way of being. However, much as I love to go back, it would have driven me nuts to have stayed.

The benefits of learning other languages are self-evident as the most basic building blocks towards understanding. But limited language ability can also be an advantage. Deaf and blind people develop acute faculties to compensate for their loss of hearing or sight; deaf people often being among the most observant, while blind people frequently have the most acute hearing. Applying a similar principle, inability to understand a conversation can sometimes be replaced by acute observation of body language. It is astonishing how much you can learn without understanding a word, but from tone of voice, posture, juxtaposition of movement, chosen seating patterns at a meeting, but more than anything else facial expression.

Surprisingly, of the seven hundred muscles in the human body, there are only forty-two in the face, but these combine to provide an almost infinite range of expressions that only the most skilled (non) communicator can hide. Stranger still is the fact that only six muscles control eye movement while as many as seventeen control the lips. Learning a bit about what facial expressions are engendered by critical sentiments such as scepticism or doubt, irritation, rising anger, wry amusement or acquiescence and approval, often reveals as much about what is going on as merely hearing what people are saying. Words can often send the wrong signals and given that what people do is always more important than what they say, body language observance will always be critical to empathy.

One such occasion comes vividly to memory from Algeria nearly forty years ago, while my French was still little better than schoolboy level. The occasion was a high-level business meeting between directors of the Algerian national steel company SNS, and the suppliers of some the necessary industrial plant, from Mitsubishi, communicating in French through an interpreter. They were discussing terms whereby Mitsubishi Steel would install the new steel mill at Djijel, between Algiers and Annaba. I was invited to attend to estimate the need for new residential infrastructure for the steel workers, ancillary trades and their dependents in this comparatively remote area.

Despite considerable difficulties with the heavily accented interpreter's French, and no Japanese at all, I was able to see where things were heading through the wide range of body language and particularly facial expressions on offer. Mitsubishi had been granted preferred bidder status, but the Algerians were still anxious to convince their chosen contractor of the value of a steel plant in the area. Having obtained a modest advantage of preferred bidder status, the Japanese were evolving from supplicant to supplier. The commercial advantage was shifting in their favour. All this was on display despite the hatchet-faced SNS directors to whom I had grown accustomed, and the apparent inscrutability of which Japanese businessmen are said to be famous. Once understanding of language intervenes, comprehension of what is being communicated intentionally or otherwise via body language, diminishes, but there was already a lot on offer while understanding hardly anything of what was said.

As a geographer and town planner, I probably view the world slightly differently to most people. I am always looking at why a place works or does not, measured against various prosaic factors such as transport, environmental management, population growth or decline etc. When working on a client's project, this becomes a bit formulaic, because a master plan for a new community, industrial complex or future land use policy, must be generated as an end-result. But even when I am visiting as a tourist, I often apply these faculties subconsciously and as often as not I get my analysis wrong. It does not stop me trying.

This 'professional place review' is usually restricted to physical evidence; I consider the social and community issues to be too complex to call without a lot more evidence not readily available at first pass. However, this is not always true, growing communities are by and large healthy ones, as people flock to where there is work, and where things function effectively if not always fairly. The shanty towns and informal housing areas which accommodate a growing proportion of the world's urban poor, particularly in countries with limited planning restrictions, are among the most fascinating communities and physical layouts to study. Left to themselves without interference of municipal planners, architects and engineers, the physical infrastructure of such communities would evolve pretty successfully on its own. That might be true until the inhabitants seek formalised electric power, water and sewage treatment systems, against which city authorities might trade long term occupational rights reciprocated by the right to charge municipal taxes.

A lot of town planners working in the developing world espouse a socialistic model in response to informal edge of city building – "let the people develop in their own way," being their mantra, "they are solving their own housing crisis!". However, they are actually dealing with informal communities operating a fairly capitalist system of day-to-day welfare and control with services traded between people on a barter or formal money basis. Shanty-town dwellers are usually there because there is work and they are earning money from it to support themselves but also their relations elsewhere, until the time the two can be reunited. They understand the ways of the market better than most. Allocation of living space and building materials may seem unorganised, but usually works on a free market basis, sometimes in the hands of groups who operate at the edge of the law.

City authorities have to work much more closely than hitherto, with leaders of shanty-town communities, to enable the self-help principle to facilitate access to building materials, before setting up the means to provide physical (e.g. water supplies) and social (e.g. schools) services against the payment of taxes. This is no more than working with the grain of how things operate anyway; authoritarianism of either leftward or rightward inclination never works within informal but very vibrant communities.

Such pragmatism influences my politics in the developed world as well. If it works, let it continue and place the ideology second. I have voted at one time or another for all three mainstream British political parties Conservative, Labour and Liberal and their various offshoots. But I have never had any time for any of the extremes to right, left, so called nationalist or anarchist. That probably owes something to empathy which has taught me that for every action there will be a reaction, and the more extreme the former the greater the latter. One pace forward and two paces back, accepting the principle that less happens in politics from action than from reaction. There is no point in espousing extreme solutions to governance, because someone will always push back with interest. That much is evident from even the most rudimentary study of history.

With the final collapse in the last decade of the twentieth century of an avowedly communist system in almost all societies, ideology has become far less important to good government than enlightened leadership. People and individuals at the top of a political party are what matter more than their espoused ideology or cause. Sadly perhaps, it has proved true that most ideology will get more or less corrupted in the end. Events are what dominate the governing agenda rather than high ideals and dealing with events is hard enough.

While this may seem cynical, it is still a value system judged on fair play. I think most people regardless of culture, historical context and experience inherently understand what this means, though there is a fond nostalgia in Britain for our having invented fair play through sport. I also believe that prescriptive political ideologies may have been suited to a simpler time of relations between rulers and the governed, but are ineffective in a heterogeneous era of multiple communication media. Who for example one hundred years ago, would have imagined that the greatest threat to personal freedom would now be cyber controlled data, but that the greatest opportunity for democratic accountability would also be electronic media? How can you wholly embrace any ideology in such a fast-changing technical world? Better to adopt pragmatic principles of doing the best for the largest possible number of people, and keeping a wary eye on those who seek to lead including those in the communications industry. Those who influence opinion are as pivotal to good government as those who make the decisions.

At their extremes, of course, autocratic governments claiming either left or right leanings become one and the same thing, namely the pursuit of personal aggrandisement by those holding power via suppression of those who do not. Fascists, communists and demagogues of no particular ideology except egotism deploy the same tactics of suppression of the individual; their ideologies always default to the single pursuit of social control. If I espouse any ideology, it is a bit libertarian - to promote individual freedom of expression and resist autocratic behaviour of any stripe. I hope that is not the purest form of anarchy, but if I am intolerant of any one thing, it is intolerance.

So, 'not much change over four or five decades,' might summarise my broad values and politics both home and abroad, but what of cultural values, prejudices, preferences and eternal verities transferred with mother's milk (nature) or just 'the way we do things around here' (nurture)? These ingredients of greater or lesser empathy for different ways of life are tougher questions. Here I think my lifetime of journeys has affected me profoundly.

Wide experience of other geographies, cultures, people and both odd and everyday events happening along the way, poses questions such as why we travel, what we seek on the way and whether the elusive empathy gift can be found at the end of the rainbow. Maybe what I mean is, have I now changed my perspective on life with which to gain new impressions of what I see and find, based on the experiences of the past?

Wait a minute. Is that not simply what age offers you? The exuberance of youth replaced by sage reflection, filtered through the wise contemplation of hard won experience. But why this reverence for age? Mentally speaking, I don't feel any age at all! I can be more frivolous now than fifty years ago. Back then, creating an impression of sober maturity was necessary to seem credible, while now I want anything but! Remember that great 1955 photograph of Albert Einstein sticking his tongue out for the camera? Forget the genius bit. I could not aspire to that, but Einstein's sense of mischief is exactly what I want for my ageing years - to shake if not shock comfortable assumptions about what and how I think and behave – the better to make people I meet look afresh at their own world and themselves.

Gaining empathy through travel often requires journeying alone, leaving oneself open to fresh human company and physical impressions, not so easily gained while travelling within the comfort zone of friends or family. I have always been a bit reluctant to travel in groups. You carry a too familiar frame of reference with you, like a snail carrying his home on his back. That is no way to journey. You must go with an open mind and be ready to sleep under the stars - ok, only literally perhaps in my twenties in Australia or the Sahara, but metaphorically speaking now and forever - accepting and welcoming what crosses your path.

Of course, mostly everyone has his or her limits of tolerance to the overload of new experience from which to retreat into the balm of the familiar. But open-mindedness is crucial to avoid the trap of lazy ignorance that is the precursor to the inability to process new experience. We are not good at this in Britain, perhaps a function of island status, and while there is plenty of evidence of prejudice from other cultures, we need to tackle our own before getting ready to point out such weakness in others. Empathy surely starts with questioning one's own standpoint before trying to understand the strengths and weaknesses in others.

Here's another example of getting out of one's comfort zone. Like most people, I know, I tend to read a particular newspaper because I recognise the journalists' writing and know my way round. But really, I should try to read newspapers with which I disagree, the ones that take me out of my comfort zone. Surely the purpose of developing a point of view is to measure it against another – usually with some dissent but all in the spirit of cognition and debate? Sadly, most people have read one newspaper - if they still read one at all - through most of their lives. You can tell, because they often become a conversational mirror of its contents. Comfort zones are not a good place for any length of time, to sustain an enquiring mind.

What of simpler measures which might demonstrate the common interests of Man? How do I measure myself against the universal endeavours of promoting love, life and the pursuit of happiness? To enable these, there are of course some basics - shelter, freedom from threat of violence or other crimes, health and well-being through clean water to drink and absence of threat to food supplies. Easier said than delivered of course, but throughout my career, I am proud to have played a small part in development projects that addressed some of these priorities from Abu Dhabi to Zululand and a lot of places in between.

On the whole, most things that stop war have got to be good. More subtly, anything that acts as a release to frustrations about the perceived inferiority or superiority of one group of people over another has got to be similarly beneficial. You can explore this at the highest statesmanlike or diplomatic level based on a scholarly grasp of history, but let me explain it in my own vernacular.

Wales is a small country within a larger one that has had little enough recognition in the world as the first definable linguistic conquest of the English language. I paid this little heed until I went to school just over the border in England, where 'being Welsh' was a label to be worn whether you wanted it or not. I like, but have no excessive pride in my fellow Welsh people, they seem as prone to human weakness as any other small group. But most of this is dealt with via humour, and a play on parochialism that is a national specialty. Most of it goes straight over the heads of our near neighbours, and that is precisely its point.

Maintenance of national pride, for most Welsh people is still better determined on the sports field than through the ballot box. If our selection of registered and nationally qualified rugby players can beat the equivalent selection comprising over ten times that number in England, we are more than satisfied. Since these encounters started in the 1880's, the win honours have been broadly equal despite the hugely disproportionate numbers of potential contestants on either side. That is just the way we like it. Not for nothing does the answer to, "what time is kick off?" include the reminder "bring your boots! Just in case you're needed, see." Rugby is one of the few occasions when the English take Wales seriously, given the former's sad disposition to ignore or take differences for granted and the latter's desperate desire to be noticed and counted as different.

I use a traditional sporting metaphor to show that for most people, self-respect comes from the respect of others. If that is openly offered and generously returned, we would all learn to live together more harmoniously. It was not always thus, as the waxing and waning of empires and their resultant wars demonstrate. However, if mutual respect could, for all top dog/underdog situations in the world, be determined on the sports field, then maybe sport could truly take the place of war!

Abuse of nature and the environment is another universal human weakness though slowly we are learning to deal with this better by applying more or less effective legislated good practice and common sense. But we should not forget that one man's meat is another's poison. Many people see Norway for example, as one of the most environmentally aware countries in the world, yet their culture supports whaling while most others do not, and their current sovereign wealth is dependent on oil and gas production, generating some of the highest of CO_2 footprints in the world. So, does Norway score high or low on an environmental scale of good practice? To me, they are no better or worse environmentalists than the rest of us, they merely work with what they have, as do we all. In this case, empathy is more a process of understanding and working with other people's perspectives than merely adopting a benign and non-judgmental disposition.

At the outset of this book, I listed many of the factors which make it such a challenge to gain empathy with people from far away – language, race, perceptions of history, physical environment, politics, poverty vs. riches and gender, all summed up by the generic term human culture. However, I have found in our time-poor world, that there is one common factor that trumps all others when seeking empathy in strangers. It is to find out and work with what is an individual's or a group's agenda for their encounter with you and over what timescale –

whether months, weeks, days, or even nowadays, the next ten minutes! The last of these options is a sad reflection on the attention span of people in the modern world, but it is more and more true as we encounter an increasing multitude of stimuli in our lives. Ten minutes is usually all one gets before judgments are formed, even if this is reduced, such as through the modern phenomena of speed dating. We need to compute such changes in society, if we are to connect. Miss the vital signs and signals and you will get nowhere; spot them early and empathy should be yours.

But consider the benefits of this connection! There are few feelings more empowering than finding common cause with strangers. It is easy enough to agree with people with whom you have grown up, live close to or with whom you have common experience and a mother tongue. But how much more satisfying it is to find that despite differences of politics, gender, language, history and wider aspects of culture, people can still connect and find common cause across these barriers. This can take the simplest form of agreeing on a single point, or reacting similarly to a given circumstance, or it can emerge out of complex objectives such as master planning and designing new towns and communities with which I have been engaged all through my career. Ultimately common cause between communities and even countries leads to alliances that are stronger precisely for the diversity of those who sign up to them. The ultimate connection is the most elusive of all, common cause between all of humanity's people. Its pursuit is the greatest challenge to us all.

Here then at the last, is one explanation for my long title. To find empathy with strangers is to anticipate what those you meet may be thinking and aspiring to, the better to act upon it to generate the optimum level of mutual benefit, understanding and harmony. Finding the means to create those conditions has motivated much of my lifetime of journeys, and while I am still in the foothills of understanding human nature, my eyes remain as wide open as when I started. It is as much a beautiful world as when I started journeys through it over sixty years ago. Empathy sought and empathy found!

'The author's close family, Mark, Sylvie and Shân.
Obviously, a red-letter day at Christmas 2013 in Cambrils Spain